Blindness and Insight

Blindness and Insight

Essays in the Rhetoric
of Contemporary Criticism

Second Edition, Revised

Paul de Man

Introduction by Wlad Godzich

Theory and History of Literature, Volume 7

University of Minnesota Press, Minneapolis

Published by the University of Minnesota Press,
2037 University Avenue Southeast, Minneapolis, MN 55414
Printed in the United States of America
Fifth printing, 1988

Library of Congress Cataloging in Publication Data

Man, Paul de.
  Blindness and Insight.

  (Theory and history of literature; v. 7)
  Includes bibliographical references and index.
  1. Criticism—Addresses, essays, lectures. I. Title.
II. Series.
PN85.M28 1983   801'.95   83-1379
ISBN 0-8166-1134-3
ISBN 0-8166-1135-1 (pbk.)

The original French versions of "Les exégèses de Hölderlin par Martin Heideg-
ger" and "Impasse de la critique formaliste" were published in *Critique* (Paris).
For permission to publish them in English the publisher is grateful to the editor
of *Critique*, Jean Piel. Permission to reprint "The Rhetoric of Temporality"
comes from the Johns Hopkins University Press; the essay originally appeared in
Charles Singleton, editor, *Interpretation* (Baltimore: Johns Hopkins University
Press, 1969). Thanks are due to Thomas R. Hart, editor of *Comparative
Literature*, for permission to reprint the review of Harold Bloom's *Anxiety of Influence*. Thanks are also due Ralph Cohen, editor of *New Literary History*, for
permission to reprint "Literature and Language: A Commentary." The first edition of *Blindness and Insight* was published by Oxford University Press, New
York.

The University of Minnesota
is an equal-opportunity
educator and employer.

Contents

Foreword

The group of essays brought together in this volume claims in no way to be a contribution to the history of criticism or to offer a survey, however sketchy, of the trends that make up present-day literary criticism in Europe. It is concerned with a different problem. Each essay deals with a question of literary understanding but none approaches this question in a systematic way. They were written for specific occasions—conferences, lectures, homages—and reflect interests that are bound to occur to someone whose teaching has been more or less evenly divided between the United States and Europe. The topics were chosen because of a spontaneous, sometimes personal, interest in a particular critic, without trying to present a comprehensive selection. Many essays are by-products of a more extensive study of romantic and post-romantic literature that does not deal with criticism. The recurrent pattern that emerges was established in retrospect and any resemblance to pre-established theories of literary interpretation is entirely coincidental or, in the terminology of the book, blind. I have made no attempt to bring the terminology of the

vii

earlier essays up to date and, except for minor changes, have left them as they were originally written.

I stress the somewhat unsystematic aspect of the volume in order to dispel a false impression that could be created by the emphasis on criticism at the expense of general literature. My interest in criticism is subordinate to my interest in primary literary texts. Just as I disclaim any attempt to contribute to a history of modern criticism, I feel equally remote from a science of criticism that would exist as an autonomous discipline. My tentative generalizations are not aimed toward a theory of criticism but toward literary language in general. The usual distinctions between expository writing *on* literature and the "purely" literary language *of* poetry or fiction have been deliberately blurred. The choice of critics who are also novelists or poets, the use of expository critical texts by such poets as Baudelaire or Yeats, the predilection for authors who combine discursive, essayistic writing with the writing of fiction, all tend in this same direction. I am concerned with the distinctive quality that all these modes of writing, as literary texts, have in common and it is toward the preliminary description of this distinctive quality that the essays are oriented.

Why then complicate matters further by choosing to write on critics when one could so easily find less ambivalent examples of literary texts among poets or novelists? The reason is that prior to theorizing about literary language, one has to become aware of the complexities of reading. And since critics are a particularly self-conscious and specialized kind of reader, these complexities are displayed with particular clarity in their work. They do not occur with the same clarity to a spontaneous, non-critical reader who is bound to forget the mediations separating the text from the particular meaning that now captivates his attention. Neither are the complexities of reading easily apparent in a poem or a novel, where they are so deeply embedded in the language that it takes extensive interpretation to bring them to light. Because critics deal more or less openly with the problem of reading, it is a little easier to read a critical text as *text*—i.e. with an awareness of the reading process involved—than to read other literary works in this manner. The study of critical texts, however, can never be an end in itself and has value only as a preliminary to the understanding of literature in general. The problems involved in critical reading reflect the distinctive characteristics of literary language.

The picture of reading that emerges from the examination of a few contemporary critics is not a simple one. In all of them a paradoxical discrepancy appears between the general statements they make about the nature of literature (statements on which they base their critical methods) and the actual results of their interpretations. Their findings about the structure of texts contradict the general conception that they use as their model. Not only do they remain unaware of this discrepancy, but they seem to thrive on it and owe their best insights to the assumptions these insights disprove.

I have tried to document this curious pattern in a number of specific instances. By choosing the critics among writers whose literary perceptiveness lies beyond dispute, I suggest that this pattern of discrepancy, far from being the consequence of individual or collective aberrations, is a constitutive characteristic of literary language in general. A somewhat more systematic formulation of the deluding interplay between text and reader is undertaken in the essay entitled "The Rhetoric of Blindness."

I have not extended the conclusions of the section on criticism to poetry or fiction but I have indicated, in the two concluding essays, how the insight derived from critical practice influences our conception of literary history. If we no longer take for granted that a literary text can be reduced to a finite meaning or set of meanings, but see the act of reading as an endless process in which truth and falsehood are inextricably intertwined, then the prevailing schemes used in literary history (generally derived from genetic models) are no longer applicable. The question of modernity, for example, can no longer be expressed by the usual metaphors of death and rebirth. These metaphors apply to natural objects and to conscious subjects but not to the elusive enigmas that literary texts turn out to be. The two concluding essays make the transition to the exegetic and historical questions raised by our own, post-romantic modernity.

My indebtednesses are too numerous to enumerate. They are particularly conspicuous with regard to the critics I write about, especially when I seem to dispute their assumptions. As a matter of fact, the ungracious relationship between the criticized text and the indebted critic of that text may well be what the book is really about.

P. de M.

Baltimore-Zürich
1970

Foreword
to Revised, Second Edition

This somewhat augmented new edition of *Blindness and Insight* was prepared at the initiative of the University of Minnesota Press. The essays that made up the original volume were all written during the sixties, while I was teaching at Cornell, at the University of Zürich, and at Johns Hopkins. Two of the additional papers (on the New Criticism and on Heidegger) go back almost ten years earlier, to 1954, and were written for the French journal *Critique*. Since they deal with questions of critical methodology, they fit naturally within the sequence that makes up the main part of *Blindness and Insight*. I have left all these texts exactly as they were first published and have made no attempt to update them or to make them more germane to present-day discussions about literary theory—also when, as is the case in the essay on Derrida, I am myself aware of inadequacies with which I have tried to cope elsewhere.

My concern with the work of literary or philosophical critics was not consciously guided by the desire to stake out a critical position of my own but occurred in response to theoretical questions about the possibility of literary interpretation. I wrote the essays on specific authors in conjunction with papers on more general matters; the essays on modernity and on the lyric in *Blindness and Insight* are instances of this pragmatically arrived at interaction between criticism and theory.

"The Rhetoric of Temporality," which I wrote around the same time as the papers collected in *Blindness and Insight*, is a slightly different case. With the deliberate emphasis on rhetorical terminology, it augurs what seemed to me to be a change, not only in terminology and in tone but in substance. This terminology is still uncomfortably intertwined with the thematic vocabulary of consciousness and of temporality that was current at the time, but it signals a turn that, at least for me, has proven to be productive.

I am not given to retrospective self-examination and mercifully forget what I have written with the same alacrity I forget bad movies—although, as with bad movies, certain scenes or phrases return at times to embarrass and haunt me like a guilty conscience. When one imagines to have felt the exhilaration of renewal, one is certainly the last to know whether such a change actually took place or whether one is just restating, in a slightly different mode, earlier and unresolved obsessions. Since, as Wlad Godzich's generous and searching preface makes clear, this question is itself of some theoretical interest, the possibility of confronting these pieces with later work may prove enlightening to some.

I am very grateful to Wlad Godzich and to Lindsay Waters, both at the University of Minnesota Press, for their interest in my work and for their competent and careful editing. Thus seeing a distant segment of one's past resurrected gives one a slightly uncanny feeling of repetition. But it is also a very personal experience and my gratitude is therefore more than merely intellectual.

New Haven
January 1983

Acknowledgments

The opening essay was originally delivered as a lecture at the University of Texas and appeared in *Arion* under the title "The Crisis of Contemporary Criticism" (Spring 1967). The essay on the New Criticism was first given as a lecture for the History of Ideas Club at the Johns Hopkins University. "Ludwig Binswanger et le moi poétique" was a contribution to a *Décade* on criticism at Cerisy-la-Salle in Normandy and was printed in the subsequent volume of the proceedings, Ricardou, ed., *Chemins actuels de la critique* (Paris: Plon, 1966). The short piece on Lukács was written for a conference on criticism held at Yale University and later published in *MLN* (December 1966). The study on Blanchot appeared in the special issue of *Critique* on Blanchot ("Circularité de l'interprétation dans la critique de Maurice Blanchot," *Critique*, June 1966). I wrote the next essay for my friend and colleague at the University of Zürich, Georges Poulet; a slightly shortened version appeared in *Critique* (July 1969). The seventh essay, centered on Jacques Derrida's reading of Rousseau, was written for this book. "Literary History and Literary Modernity" was a contribution to a conference on *The Use of Theory in Humanistic*

Studies sponsored by *Daedalus* and held at Bellagio in September 1969. "Lyric and Modernity" was delivered at the English Institute during the September 1969 session on the lyric chaired by Professor Reuben A. Brower. Permission to reprint from the various periodicals is gratefully acknowledged.

I have myself translated into English the four essays originally written in French as well as the quotations from various French and German authors.

Material for second edition, revised

The original French versions of "Les exégègeses de Hölderlin par Martin Heidegger" and "Impasse de la critique formaliste" were published in *Critique* (Paris). The translations are by Wlad Godzich. For permission to publish them in English the publisher is grateful to the editor of *Critique*, Jean Piel. Permission to reprint "The Rhetoric of Temporality" comes from the Johns Hopkins University Press; the essay originally appeared in Charles Singleton, editor, *Interpretation* (Baltimore: Johns Hopkins University Press, 1969). Thanks are due to Thomas R. Hart, editor of *Comparative Literature*, for permission to reprint the review of Harold Bloom's *Anxiety of Influence*. Thanks are also due Ralph Cohen, editor of *New Literary History*, for permission to reprint "Literature and Language: A Commentary." The first edition of *Blindness and Insight* was published by Oxford University Press, New York.

Introduction
Caution! Reader at Work!
Wlad Godzich

Some time ago, Michael Riffaterre proposed that the verbal existence of objects is best apprehended through the notion of "descriptive system": rather than merely having names, objects are, linguistically speaking, the nexus between a number of nouns, epithets, motifs, narrative plots and situations, images, metaphors, oppositions, etc., all of which can be summoned into print or consciousness directly or through each other's mediation.[1]

The notion is a rich one and deserving of widespread application: for example, there is little doubt that a descriptive system comes into play as soon as Paul de Man's name appears. His pre-eminence in the field of literary theory is generally acknowledged, and his lectures at professional meetings and conferences attract large audiences of scholars and students. He is found to be lucid, trenchant ("surgical" is much favored), uncompromisingly rigorous, austere, yet somehow affable, kind even. Although he deals with the leading critics and theoreticians of our day, his style is remarkably unpolemical. One listens to him as one witnesses a performance: one has the feeling beforehand that one knows what de Man will do, yet one still is awed by the elegance, precision,

1. Michael Riffaterre, "Le Poème comme représentation," *Poétique*, 4, 1970, pp. 417-18.

and economy of his performance; one has a reluctant but solid conviction that one could not duplicate it. De Man is thought to be highly
original, yet, in a sense, he does exactly what we expect him to do.
Therein lies the sense of our awe, but also of a certain malaise. If we
are willing to concede that a certain degree of physical endowment
enhanced by years of training does produce an exceptional athlete or
star performer, we are most reluctant to extend such a concession to
the realm of thought. Here feats must, indeed, be duplicated by others
before they gain assent (philosophers of science call it, verifiability)
and cannot remain the prerogative of their inventor, lest charlatanism
be suspected. Such is the critical temper of our times that lately a version of this charge has been leveled at Paul de Man: his is the criticism
of performance; he is arbitrary; he is not the slayer of the New Criticism
but its last faithful remnant, not a radical iconoclast but a pillar of
the establishment. Questions are raised: What is the status of a discourse
that questions the status of all discourses? Does de Man escape his
blindness? If so, by virtue of what dispensation? If not, where is it located
and why is it not fatal? Where does the authority of his discourse come
from? Is there more to it than a rhetoric of mastery?

In their contradiction, all of these assertions and questions do constitute a descriptive system, and it is one that presupposes that Paul
de Man has been read. And here we run into a problem—not that de
Man's books and articles have not been read, but rather because to
claim to have read de Man presupposes that we know how to read.
Yet if there is anything that de Man's work has been asserting with
a quiet but insistent resolve, it is that we do not know what reading
is. Thus, before making any determination on the accuracy of part or
the whole of the de Manian descriptive system, we must learn to read,
and learn to read the question of reading in de Man.

It is with this object in view that the editors of this series have decided
to reissue the text of Paul de Man's first collection of essays, *Blindness and Insight*, augmented with essays from his early years, newly
translated from the French, as well as the article that Jonathan Culler
once described as "the most photocopied essay in literary criticism"—
"The Rhetoric of Temporality."

I

Once upon a time, we all thought we knew how to read, and then
came de Man. . . . Even with its bathos alleviated by the fairytale motif

and the Boileau citation, such a statement remains misleading, for it is far from certain that *we*, as literary scholars, knew how to read. The institutionalization of literary studies in European and American universities in the nineteenth century took place under the aegis of philology and literary history, ignoring, for the most part, the tradition of classical poetics and rhetoric. The first sought to establish texts, to make them as reliable as possible, so that the second could weave them into a satisfactory narrative of emergent national cultural achievement. It is not clear that texts were read, or, if they were, how.[2] To the trained scholarly gaze, they were made to yield a certain documentary information about the state of language, their authorship, their sources, the influences they had been subject to,[3] and their place in a historical sequence or in some generic taxonomy. But alongside this function of information, they had nothing further to offer. It could in fact be suggested that, for the great age of literary history (roughly 1830-1939), literature had no cognitive value. The literary scholar in his or her capacity as historian certainly no longer felt authorized, let alone able, to state the truth, perhaps because truth no longer wore the same cloak or rose from the same old well; it was much easier to write glosses upon the texts of those who, in a naiveté becoming their olden times, had dared to utter it.

There arose then with respect to literature and other fields of inquiry, notably philosophy and history, a generic distinction between primary and secondary texts previously restricted to the relation of sacred text and commentary, the impact of which is still very much with us. It becomes clear in retrospect that it was constitutive of the disciplines themselves and, therefore, fundamental to the modern university. A division of labor results from this distinction: primary texts necessitated the development of techniques for the preservation and maintenance of their integrity and authenticity, while the writing of secondary texts posed problems of understanding and accuracy of account. Philology and textual criticism took care of the first (though

2. It is the specific merit of Hans Robert Jauss to have undertaken studies, theoretical and empirical, into past modes of readings. See, in this series, his *Toward an Aesthetic of Reception*, trans. Timothy Bahti, with an Introduction by Paul de Man (Minneapolis: University of Minnesota Press, 1982); and *Aesthetic Experience and Literary Hermeneutics*, trans. Michael Shaw, with an Introduction by Wlad Godzich (Minneapolis: University of Minnesota Press, 1982).
3. The astrological origin of the "concept" of influence is a telling index of the credibility of these claims, once endowed with "scientificity."

xviii BLINDNESS AND INSIGHT

not without encountering problems belonging to the realm of the second, as de Man rightly observes with reference to Hölderlin editions
[pp. 248ff.]), while the second took the form of an insistent preoccupation with methodology.

Divorced from inquiry into truth, the secondary discourse is always
in danger of falling into arbitrariness or divagation; only abeyance
by rigorous methodological principles and investigatory protocols can
ensure the verifiability and reproducibility of its assertions and results.
The rise of the biological and physical sciences, with their clear distinction between object of knowledge as given (*datum*) and procedures
of inquiry, served as a model for apprehending the relation of secondary discourse to primary text. Heidegger has been most persuasive
on this score, drawing attention to the widespread assumption of a
mode of thinking about things as the model for all forms of knowledge,
and the specific elaboration of that model in Kant.[4] It is not surprising then to find the preoccupation with methodology in the works
of the Neo-Kantians and in that of Dilthey who was most concerned
with endowing the *Geisteswissenschaften,* or the humanities as
we would call them, with what he saw as the rigor of scientific inquiry.

Modern literary studies, founded as they were upon the opposition
of primary text and secondary discourse, did not escape the effect of
this opposition; and the plethora of methodologies proposed in this
century attests to this fact. Formalism, phenomenological criticism, the
New Criticism, Structuralism, most forms of semiotics, to name but
a few of the more prominent, have in common a preoccupation with
the development of the right approach to the study of literary texts,
one that would provide the scholar, engaged in teaching as well as
research, with a degree of validation in his or her practice. Literary
critics, especially those of theoretical bent, rightly devote their energy
to the examination of these methodologies to assess their claims and
ascertain their validity. Such is the stuff of contemporary polemics in
literary studies, and quite proper it is.

Yet such is not the nature of de Man's own activity, although it bears
some resemblance to it. If it were, de Man would be but a methodologist

4. Martin Heidegger, *Die Frage nach dem Ding* (Tübingen: Max Niemayer Verlag, 1962);
trans. by W. B. Barton, Jr. and Vera Deutsch, with an analysis by Eugene T. Gendlin, *What
Is a Thing* (Chicago: Henry Regnery Co., 1967).

among others, for one can never mount a critique of an approach without, at least implicitly, holding some strong views on what the correct approach should be. Rather, his scrutiny of the critical practice of others—and that is what he does in the essays in this volume—seeks to go beyond an inquiry into the validity, or to speak rapidly, into the success or failure of a given methodology, to an elucidation of the relationship of that methodology to its own necessity. That is, while de Man does not neglect to consider the capacity of a methodology to abide by its own rules and to thus give us knowledge of the text it is applied to, such a consideration is, for him, secondary to the question of why the issue of methodology had to arise in the first place; and to the answer that the given methodology provides to that question, explicitly or not. For the practice of any methodological approach can be self-governing, whereas the question of the necessity of methodology raises the issue of what reading is.

II

It is a commonplace of undergraduate courses in literature to urge students to read a poem even though its opacity or denseness may initially rebuff them, for, it is held, there will suddenly occur a moment of illumination when everything will become clear, when they will understand; then, they will be able to re-read the poem and see how what was opaque or dense was necessary to build up the triggering mechanism of the illumination. Leaving aside the pedagogical implications of such injunctions and promises,[5] let us consider the underlying assumptions of this description of the process of reading.

To begin with, it opposes the immediately apprehensible darkness of the sensible to the eventuality of the great clarity of the intelligible, yet makes the first the condition and the means of access to the second. It relies upon a well-known yet complex notion of expression in which the immediately perceptible materiality of the poem—its verbal component—is a means of access, yet a barrier, to the central core of meaning of the poem. The verbal component needs to be overcome to reach that core, but the overcoming itself is not easily described, for its achievement may depend more upon the qualities and the skills

5. One of the more insidious ones has been the separation of students into two different groups on the basis of their success or failure in achieving illumination.

of the reader than, seemingly, upon any specific steps that can be taken to ensure its accomplishment. Moreover, it is not the case that the core of meaning is somehow held permanently imprisoned within that materiality, but rather that it becomes manifest in a flash of intuition that illuminates the whole and motivates its necessity.

There appear then to be two competing notions of expression at work here: the first is based upon the familiar model of the apparent and the hidden, where the hidden holds the key to the existential necessity of the apparent; whereas the second overcomes this model with an altogether different notion of expression whose matrix is lightning. In opposition to the inside/outside dialectic of the first theory of expression, the model of lightning proposes a perfect congruence between the expression and that which is expressed. Lightning cannot be said to be hidden before its manifestation, but rather it expresses itself (if the word still applies) fully in the instant of its illumination. In fact, it suspends the difference between the manifest and the manifesting, producing in its instantaneity a moment of perfect presence. However, the punctual brevity of its flash is such as to displace its significance away from itself onto the surrounding darkness whose internal composition it reveals. Even if the eye were to train itself on the flash, and were it able to predict the exact moment and place of its occurrence, it would remain unseeing, for it would be blinded by the force of the light, so that it is not lightning itself that we wish to see but what its flash reveals, the inner configuration of the surrounding landscape and the forces at play within it. The eye remains trained on the darkness knowing it to hold a secret that the flash will disclose. The flash is not the secret but the occasion of the moment when all is in the light; the reward for peering into the dark.

Although quite different in their characterization of the mode of being of that which we presumably read for, the two theories of expression are far from incompatible. Indeed, a dialectical necessity unites them, for the patience in the practice of perception enjoined by the first would be far too aleatory without the guarantee of revelation provided by the second, while the latter needs the ascetic practice of the first to avoid falling into the trap of understanding by predestination of the elect only. Both need each other as well as a discipline, in the sense of Ignatius of Loyola: the first to ensure that lightning does strike; the second, even more formidably, that it strike repeatedly, at will, in the same place and with the same intensity. Such a desideratum reveals at once the limitations of the model of lightning—it is well known that in nature lightning tends to be rather mobile—and the inordinate ambition of these theories of expression underlying the most common practice of reading. Yet this limitation and this ambition are the two parameters of the question of methodology, for what is a method but a procedure designed to produce at will a certain result through the adoption of specific steps, treating the text as a given that can be made to yield its inner configuration.

This description of reading, based upon the practice of undergraduate courses, is admittedly crude; yet it differs only in degree from that to be found in the writings of leading theoreticians of literature. It is Paul de Man's burden in the pages of this volume to describe these differences and to question the persistence of this model. He does so through the now familiar dialectic of blindness and insight that gives the volume its title, for it permits him to characterize various individuals' reading practices in terms of the necessary exclusion that their mode of reading implies, not simply as a form of neglect or ignorance but as the very originating locus of such insight as they achieve or illumination as they can provide.

Husserl states, or confirms, with great clarity that "philosophical knowledge can only come into being when it is turned back upon itself," but he does so only because he does not turn back upon his own statement that asserts as fundamental a crisis that is geographically and culturally localized. American New Criticism achieves its most productive insights when it describes the ironic play and the ambiguity of the texts that it began, and blindly continued, to consider as consisting of unitary form. Binswanger's inquiry into the ontology of the self and of art slides blindly, by its reliance upon spatial metaphors that are the vehicles of conceptions of temporality, into an empirical moment, and in the process is forced, against its initial assumptions—never abandoned—to see the actual work of art in terms of self-mystification instead of self-actualization, a process of which it is a good instance. The very power of Georg Lukács's *Theory of the Novel* lies in its break-up of the organicist conception of the genre by means of the elevation of irony to the role of structural category; yet this very achievement should not permit the wide historical sweep of the book since the latter is fully dependent upon a notion of temporality that is thoroughly organicist. Lukács is thus at once correct and wrong about the novel; correct insofar as he provides the ground for "a genuine hermeneutic of the novel," wrong in that he snatches this ground away just as it becomes manifest. He was able to reveal it, however, only because the very organicity he denounces in the structure of the novel is still at play in his own story of the novel. Blanchot's deconstruction of the self proceeds by similarly bracketing away from the critic's knowing self, the temporal dimension that allows him to also proceed in near narrative fashion to describe the circular process of depersonalization, to, ultimately, have to confront the problem of temporality and of the self that it continued to preserve. Poulet's quest for the originating self of the literary act is forced, in its rigor, to confer upon the language it seeks to ground, the status of origin that it continues to refuse it in order to maintain the self. Thus, thoroughly grounded in presence, it inevitably ends with the non-presence of literature that it must refuse to recognize. Heidegger's insight that poetry is the attempt to name Being requires, in the logic of his thought, that such an attempt should actually occur successfully somewhere; yet Heidegger will misread Hölderlin by holding him up as the justifying example of this instance, whereas the latter thematizes the impossibility of such a naming. The methodological project of I. A. Richards and William Empson was meant to reduce the dispersion produced by reading, yet, unbeknownst to itself and, most certainly against the very concept of form that is its starting ground, it winds up disclosing the ontological discontinuity of language just as it claims to have overcome its surface ruptures.[6]

The de Manian descriptive system is replete with laudatory characterizations of his readings of the critics and theoreticians just enumerated. It is rather laconic, though, on *how* de Man reads as opposed to *what* he reads. It may well be because this opposition of the *how* vs. the *what* is very much put into question in de Man's readings. Even in the course of a superficial perusal of these essays, one cannot fail to be struck by the relatively limited number of notions or concepts with which they deal: the self, temporality, the referential gap, ambiguity (as forerunner of undecidability), rhetoric, etc. This may explain why the suspicion has arisen that a rhetoric of mastery is deploy-

---

6. The case of Derrida in the important essay, "The Rhetoric of Blindness," is somewhat different. I discuss it at length in J. Arac, W. Godzich, and W. Martin, eds., *The Yale Critics: Deconstruction in America* (Minneapolis: University of Minnesota Press, 1983).

ing its own verbal armature over these texts and subjecting them to its domination. Such an assertion needs to be demonstrated though, rather than just made. Is it not rather the case that the return of the same analytic concepts is motivated by the persistence of the same problematic under different guises? Whether such a persistence is structural or historically circumscribable and even determined, we shall have occasion to examine below.

I have suggested that the writings of the critics discussed by de Man differ in degree only, insofar as their theory of reading is concerned, from the model I described earlier. De Man's readings confirm this, but why should this be the case? The complementarity of what I called the two theories of expression articulates far more than just a theory of reading, although that may be its most strategic location; it constitutes, to its very contradictions, the way we have been thinking about meaning since the late eighteenth century at least. The complementary opposition of primary text and secondary discourse, although it may ostensibly eschew the saying of truth, remains very much in its orbit. It suggests that in the primary text the truth remains somehow burdened by its mode of representation, and it acts upon the belief that the truth can be attained and that indeed it can be given a better representation, of which the secondary text would be the very instantiation. In other words, the primary vs. secondary opposition is predicated upon a prior opposition, which it locates in the primary text, between a truth or a meaning to be disclosed and the means of that disclosure. Although apparently granting the primary text the status of perfect presence that we saw in lightning, or, to speak the discourse of poetics, that of a symbol where the relation of sign to referent or signifier to signified, is fully motivated, the very practice of a secondary discourse is at least implicitly or unconsciously grounded in the belief that such a congruence has not been achieved, may not be achievable, or that it can be ruptured at will, since this practice proposes to substitute its own product—its text—as the vehicle for transporting the truth. Blindly, it sees itself as a better representation of the truth, whereas it is in fact engaged in an allegorical relation of mapping one sign with another, of sublating one sign by another.

The practice of a secondary discourse is thus founded on the premise that meaning, or the truth, is not "at home" in the language of represen-

xxiv BLINDNESS AND INSIGHT

tation of the primary text, and that, further, the secondary discourse can provide such a home. This claim is obviously tied to the ambition of methodology to have lightning strike at will, in the same place, and with the same intensity. In the dialectic of the two theories of expression, the role devolved upon the materiality of the text both before and after the bolt of lightning is that of the sensible appearance of that which can appear. The content of the apparent is therefore purified in the sense that it shows as superfluous its given trappings. Givenness, we have seen earlier, is the attribute of nature in the so-called natural sciences, and therefore, insofar as the epistemological structure of primary and secondary instances models itself upon the structure of knowledge of these sciences, the object of the secondary instance is to free the content of the first from its natural trappings. The content of the apparent is therefore the existent freed from its naturalness. It is represented figurally by the apparent but in such a way as to reduce the distance between its figuration and itself; meaning is congruent with its sign, hence the privileged status accorded to the primary text.

Yet, if this kind of free-standing appearance, to use Schiller's term,[7] does reduce its content to existence, or better, states the truth of the existent as a sort of nullity, it is not itself a truth or that truth. Rather, it states it, but in its own mode, which, paradoxically with respect to truth but appropriately to itself, does not require its undoing, its disappearance, just because it has revealed its nullity. In the primary text, the immediate is indeed canceled, but this cancellation is carried out through immediate means; in other words, the cancellation is not a final act but part of a strategy of continuous canceling; it is a denial that goes on forever, and, in that sense, the apparent, revealing itself as apparent and therefore as the immediate trapping of truth, nonetheless does not free up that truth, but keeps on stating its inadequacy to hold it while holding it. In Hegelian terms—and this is, after all, a very Hegelian story—the idealization achieved in the dialectic of the two theories of expression is necessarily incomplete. The im-

7. Johann Christoph Friedrich von Schiller, *Über die ästhetische Erziehung des Menschen* (1795), 26th letter. I shall use the words "the apparent" in this sense. This is meant to be the English equivalent of the German *Schein* or the French "le paraître" (in opposition to "l'être"). My later "simulacrity of the simulacrum" is thus "Schein des Scheinens" or "l'apparence de l'apparaître."

mediate is not reproduced, as some theories of mimesis would have it, but it is preserved; the materiality of the signs is essential to the aesthetic perspective. The superfluousness of the immediate can only be shown not as truth but mediately through more (superfluous) immediacy. If the immediate were truly susceptible to elimination, then art would indeed disappear.

In the meantime—and this form of temporal contingency would require a treatise unto itself[8]—the primary text is caught in a bind: it both announces the no longer mediate truth, yet blocks its advent through its own immediacy. It holds out the promise of the disappearance of the sensible and the manifestation of the perfect sign, yet it is powerless to achieve it, hence the awaiting of the bolt of lightning.

The bolt of lightning is, of course, meant to overcome the blocking action of the apparent, yet it is itself not wholly devoid of appearance; its mode of cancellation of the immediate, though, must be presumed to be more effective than the preserving cancellation of the apparent. In the latter, immediate being is negated; in fact it is there to be negated—idealized, in the Hegelian sense. But in the former, it is completely overcome, so that the truth can speak directly. The model of lightning implies this overcoming by suggesting that lightning is what it is in its very manifestation, that its manifestation is its Being, that its appearance is its essence; in other words, that it is truth's own voice. By opposition, the apparent is then seen to have been caught in the gap between appearance and saying, and the primary text must be seen as laboring to maintain the materiality of the figural. Again, in Hegelian terms, art attempts to salvage the materiality of signs, and, in this manner, makes them into indices of idealization, whereas in lightning we get idealization itself. Such a formulation permits then the elaboration of the Hegelian project of studying the various forms and periods of art as differences in degree of gap between appearance and saying— what de Man alludes to, in the essay on Richards and Empson, when he speaks of a genuine historical poetics. From after the lightning, meaning is shown to have been present in the apparent, but because the stress is on the showing of its presence, it cannot actually be claimed to *be* present. The structural gap of appearance and saying has thus a temporal dimension as well. For the theory of reading that we have

8. It receives some attention from W. Godzich and J. Kittay in *An Essay in Prosaics*, forthcoming.

been examining, a danger now arises, one that it has not fully exor-
cised though it attempts to bracket it away: namely, that truth is ineffable. The structural significance of the model of lightning in the dialectic of the two theories of expression lies in the exorcism of this possibility.

By positing a difference between aesthetic language and the language
of inquiry governed by reason—what we have been calling so far the
apparent and the order of manifestation of lightning—the oppositional
theory of primary vs. secondary status of text can describe the first
instance of language (aesthetic language) as superfluous, as reductive
of the presence of truth. A form of language trained upon reason—
logical in the strong sense of the term (derived from the *Logos*), as
well as in the technical one, that is a methodological use of language—
would no longer block access to meaning but manifest it, no longer
mediate it through figures but permit it to speak in its own voice. Such
a mode of discursive practice is superior to intuition even, for the latter may gain access to truth but leave it ineffable, whereas the object
of a methodological practice is to give truth or meaning a vehicle in
which it can make itself manifest unmediated. The methodological enterprise implies then that the language of representation is not only inadequate to the statement of the truth but that any language that is
not methodologically rigorous is going to be inadequate because it will
remain within the orbit of representation. By constraining one's
discourse to be answerable to the rules of reason—that is by constructing a methodology—one frees it from the constraints of representation and makes it into an adequate instrument for the conveyance of
truth.

Aesthetic appearance is thus disqualified for it gave us but false
presence; but is language, any form of language, up to playing the role
of representational vehicle that the methodological enterprise requires
of it? That is the question toward which de Man will find himself increasingly propelled as he reflects upon the reading practice of his subjects. By virtue of what dispensation is methodological discourse free
of the materiality that weighted aesthetic signs? Is this not an instance
of the eye being blinded by the lightning upon which it is trained and
claiming to have seen the truth? In methodological discourse, the
materiality of the signifier is not simply abrogated because the discourse
claims to be subjected to reason. Meaning continues to be mediate,
mediated by signs. To return to our earlier formulation: meaning may

not have been "at home" in aesthetic language but it was not because it was aesthetic but because it was language. We may have shed the notion of the ineffable and thus the concept of an occulted meaning or truth, but we do not have immediate truth; we are still within a structure of indicial signaling. In other words, we are back in the figural but in a specific mode, and it is Paul de Man's most important contribution to have drawn our attention to it, to have inquired into and described that mode.

The realm of the apparent holds the truth hidden away, so that its only means of access are the figures of the apparent; yet these figures are not known to be figures for they are the only mode of being that lends itself to knowledge, and, unless one wishes to invoke a Platonic theory of recollection, no conclusion concerning them is possible. During the brief reign of lightning, or in the (deluded) possibility of methodological absolutism, truth is meant to be visible in unmediated form, in and of itself, and especially free of figuration. In the realm that is ours, where we have shed any belief in the ineffable and know the impossibility of unmediated truth, we are indeed back in the figural; but, more specifically, in a relation to the figural where the figural is known as figural. In other words, we are in the rhetorical, as Paul de Man has been showing us all along.

Here we may aspire to the clarity of reason but all we may achieve is the elucidation of the understanding that, not knowing truth, nonetheless seeks to write its laws by reducing the numbing heterogeneity of the immediate to a set of apprehensible unities. The danger for this understanding is not so much the error of fact that methodologists are so concerned with, but the isolation of thoughts and ideas and their conversion into autonomous objects of knowledge independent of their productive ground; in other words, their reification. The understanding is prey to ideology and to the familiar dichotomies of our thinking: thought becomes abstract, knowledge partial, and theory opposed to practice.

Against this risk and this danger, de Man's theoretical practice consists in pushing the understanding by a relentless questioning into its last redoubts where, in the moment of undecidability—the place of aporia—it is forced to surrender its claim to being reason's lieutenant and to acknowledge that, unlike reason, it labors in the realm of representation and not that of the concept, and that it must come to terms with the materiality of its object as well as acknowledge its own continuity with that object.

In its ideological moment, understanding opposes the literary to the real, framing the former in its form and valorizing the latter as that which is outside the frame—the referent. At that moment, what is within the frame is thought of as the representation of that which is outside of it, the sign of a referent. But under de Man's questioning, the understanding must abandon its pretensions, and, as we have seen earlier, it turns out that there is no difference of being between what is within and what is without the frame: they are both of representation. The difference, for difference there is—and here one must be careful not to fall into Platonism—lies in the fact that what is within the frame is not the simulacrum of a simulacrum—which would, at best, lead back to the project of historical poetics—but the "simulacrity" of this simulacrum, and this constitutes a form of cognition of which the frame is probably the emblem.

In its determination of signifying value, reason can be presumed to be primarily semantic; the understanding relies upon syntax in its attempt to convert heterogeneity into unity, and de Man is well-known for his persistent interrogation of grammar. Rhetoric knows itself as rhetoric, hence its superiority to other textual practices. Their failure comes from their fall into objectivity: they are discourses upon an object—what I have called, following Hegel, the ideological position. Only rhetoric carries within its scope its for-itself and its in-itself. One could say, if the words still had meaning, that it comprises even its blindness.

Rhetoric, as a mode of language, accommodates itself to human finitude, for, unlike other modes, it need not locate anything beyond its boundaries: it operates on the materiality of the text and achieves effects. Since it is internally cleaved between a collection of tropes and a technique of persuasion, it is itself sufficiently mobile to avoid falling into positional ideology. In this manner the *how* and the *what* of reading converge. Against Descartes' injunction to examine an assertion for its hidden falsehood, or Kant's recommendation that a statement be projected against its horizon of illusion, de Man's rhetorical inquiry consists in recognizing the finiteness of the text and in bringing out its rhetorical machine. At first, this seems like an abandonment of the "higher" questions of truth and falsehood, self and experience, meaning and significance, that texts are ostensibly read for. That would be the case if the figural mechanism that de Man investigates were just a simulacrum of a simulacrum, but because it is much more than that, the inscription of the "simulacrity" of a simulacrum, it manages to achieve something that the "higher" pursuits do not. In their delusion, they believe that they have left the realm of representation and reside now in that of reason; de Man harbors no such illusion, but, having brought the understanding to a point of paralysis, and reached the point of the inscription of the "simulacrity" of the simulacrum, he stands at the very edge of human finitude, knowing such knowledge as there is within the compass of that finitude. To some, this may not seem enough; they may wish to take refuge in forms of utopian thought or seek to impose an ideal. De Man proposes a more modest form of activity. It is neither heroic because it is not transforming, nor fatalistic because it does not submit or follow blindly, but it seeks to collaborate in an explicitation that is already at work and whose movement it attempts to espouse.

De Man does not read then to constitute his identity or that of the text, nor to reach some beyond of the text, by whatever name it may be called. He seeks to locate the blind spot of the text as the organizer of the space of the vision contained in the text, and the vision's concomitant blindness. This spot of blindness is the solar position that blinds yet regulates the revolution of the spheres around itself. The sun itself has no "revolutionary" history; or, rather, its history lies elsewhere, in another dimension. That is why any critique of de Man that concludes somewhat hastily on the basis of the chronological span of his readings that the predicament he locates and describes can be explained as a general condition of, let us say, post-Enlightenment thought, is ultimately off the mark. De Man has no quarrel with history provided its finitude is recognized. In fact, if anything his inquiry is an attempt to ask the historical question at the very edge of that finitude, for how are we to consider the activity that does the inscribing of the "simulacrity" of the simulacrum? That question, which begins to emerge only now, poses the very problem of history since it forces us to confront the question of what that activity is.

De Man's characteristic stance can be described in terms of Hegel's notion of *Bildung*: to be cultivated is to practice a form of ascesis, for it requires not so much the acquisition of information or even knowledge but a progressive renunciation of the representational. For Hegel, who believed in the Absolute, it meant that we needed to die to the immediate in all of its forms. De Man's thought is resolutely secular, or more precisely, sufficiently freed of the transcendental to be called finite, and thus living in the realm of representation as we all do he simply "sees fewer and fewer new things; the substantial content of most new things seems to such a man rather well known" (*Enzyklopädie* § *454*). We may indeed know beforehand what de Man will do, but can we espouse his movement?

Blindness and Insight

I

Criticism and Crisis

When the French poet Stéphane Mallarmé visited Oxford in 1894 to deliver a lecture entitled *La Musique et les lettres* and dealing with the state of French poetry at the time, he exclaimed, with mock sensationalism:

"I am indeed bringing you news. The most surprising news ever. Nothing like it ever happened before. They have tampered with the rules of verse . . . *On a touché au vers*" (Pléiade ed., 643).

In 1970, one might well feel tempted to echo Mallarmé's words, this time with regard not to poetry, but to literary criticism. *On a touché à la critique*. . . . Well-established rules and conventions that governed the discipline of criticism and made it a cornerstone of the intellectual establishment have been so badly tampered with that the entire edifice threatens to collapse. One is tempted to speak of recent developments in Continental criticism in terms of *crisis*. To confine oneself for the moment to purely outward symptoms, the crisis-aspect of the situation is apparent, for instance, in the incredible swiftness with which often conflicting tendencies succeed each other, condemning to immediate obsolescence what

3

might have appeared as the extreme point of avant-gardisme briefly before. Rarely has the dangerous word "new" been used so freely; a few years ago, for very different reasons, there used to be in Paris a *Nouvelle Nouvelle Revue Française,* but today almost every new book that appears inaugurates a new kind of nouvelle nouvelle critique. It is hard to keep up with the names and the trends that succeed each other with bewildering rapidity. Not much more than ten years ago, names such as those of Bachelard, Sartre, Blanchot, or Poulet seemed to be those of daring pioneers, and younger men such as Jean-Pierre Richard or Jean Starobinski proudly considered themselves as continuators of the novel approaches that originated with their immediate predecessors. At that time, the main auxiliary discipline for literary criticism was undoubtedly philosophy. At the Sorbonne, which then as now saw its role primarily as one of conservation and even reaction, the theses considered too bold and experimental to be handled by the chairs of literature would quite naturally find their home among the philosophers. These philosophers were themselves engaged in working out a difficult synthesis between the vitalism of Bergson and the phenomenological method of Husserl; this tendency proved quite congenial to the combined use of the categories of sensation, consciousness and temporality that is prevalent among the literary critics of this group. Today, very little remains, at least on the surface, of this cooperation between phenomenology and literary criticism. Philosophy, in the classical form of which phenomenology was, in France, the most recent manifestation, is out of fashion and has been replaced by the social sciences.

But it is by no means clear which one of the social sciences has taken its place, and the hapless and impatient new new critic is hard put deciding in which discipline he should invest his reading time. For a while, after Lucien Goldman's theses on the sociology of Jansenism in the seventeenth century, it seemed as if sociology was in the lead, and the name of Lukács was being mentioned in Parisian intellectual circles with the same awe that used to surround the figures of Kierkegaard and Hegel a few years earlier. But then Lévi-Strauss' *Tristes tropiques* appeared, and anthropology definitely edged out sociology as the main concern of the literary critic. Hardly had he mastered the difficult terminology of tribal intersubjectivity when linguistics appeared over the horizon with an even more formidable technical jargon. And with the somewhat subterranean influence of Jacques Lacan, psychoanalysis has made a comeback, giving rise to a neo-Freudian rebirth that seems to be quite germane to the concerns of several critics.

This sudden expansion of literary studies outside their own province and into the realm of the social sciences was perhaps long overdue. What is nowadays labeled "structuralism" in France is, on a superficial level, nothing but an attempt to formulate a general methodology of the sciences of man. Literary studies and literary criticism naturally play a certain part in this inquiry. There is nothing particularly new or crisis-like about this. Such attempts to situate literary studies in relation to the social sciences are a commonplace of nineteenth-century thought, from Hegel to Taine and Dilthey. What seems crisis-like is, among outer signs, the sense of urgency, the impatient competitiveness with which the various disciplines vie for leadership.

What interest can this Gallic turbulence have for literary studies in America? The irony of Mallarmé's situation at his Oxford lecture was that his English listeners had little awareness of the emergency by which he claimed to be so disturbed. English prosody had not waited for some rather disreputable foreigners to start tampering with verse; free and blank verse were nothing very new in the country of Shakespeare and Milton, and English literary people thought of the alexandrine as the base supporting the column of the Spenserian stanza rather than as a way of life. They probably had difficulty understanding the rhetoric of crisis that Mallarmé was using, with an ironic slant that would not have been lost in Paris, but that certainly baffled his foreign audience. Similarly, speaking of a crisis in criticism in the United States today, one is likely to appear equally out of tone. Because American criticism is more eclectic, less plagued than its European counterpart by ideology, it is very open to impulses from abroad but less likely to experience them with the same crisis-like intensity. We have some difficulty taking seriously the polemical violence with which methodological issues are being debated in Paris. We can invoke the authority of the best historians to point out that what was considered a crisis in the past often turns out to be a mere ripple, that changes first experienced as upheavals tend to become absorbed in the continuity of much slower movements as soon as the temporal perspective broadens.

This kind of pragmatic common sense is admirable, up to the point where it lures the mind into self-satisfied complacency and puts it irrevocably to sleep. It can always be shown, on all levels of experience, that what other people experience as a crisis is perhaps not even a change; such observations depend to a very large extent on the standpoint of the observer. Historical "changes" are not like changes in nature, and the vocabulary of change and movement as it applies to historical process is a mere metaphor, not devoid of meaning, but without an objective correlative that can unambiguously be pointed to in empirical reality, as when we speak of a change in the weather or a change in a biological organism. No set of arguments, no enumeration of symptoms will ever prove that the present effervescence surrounding literary criticism is in fact a crisis that, for better or worse, is reshaping the critical consciousness of a generation. It remains relevant, however, that these people are experiencing it as a crisis and that they are constantly using the language of crisis in referring to what is taking place. We must take this into account when reflecting on the predicament of others as a preliminary before returning to ourselves.

Again, Mallarmé's text of his Oxford lecture, very closely linked to another prose text of his that was written a little later on the same subject and is entitled *Crise de vers,* can give us a useful hint. Apparently, in these texts, Mallarmé is speaking about the experiments in prosody undertaken by a group of younger poets who call themselves (often without his direct encouragement) his disciples, and whom he designates by name: Henri de Régnier, Moréas, Vielé-Griffin, Gustave Kahn, Charles Morice, Émile Verhaeren, Dujardin, Albert Mockel, and so on. And he pretends to believe that their partial rejection of traditional verse, in favor of free verse forms that he calls "polymorphic," represents a major crisis, the kind of apocalyptic tempest that often reappears as a central symbol in much of his own later poetry. It is obvious, for any historian of French literature, that Mallarmé exaggerates the importance of what is happening around him, to the point of appearing completely misled, not only in the eyes of his more phlegmatic British audience, but in the eyes of future historians as well. The poets he mentions are hardly remembered today, and certainly not praised for the explosive renovation with which Mallarmé seems to credit them. Moreover, one can rightly point out that Mallarmé not only overstates their importance, but that he seems to be blind to the forces within his own time that were indeed to have a lasting effect: he makes only a passing reference to Laforgue, who is somewhat incongruously linked with Henri de Régnier, but fails to mention Rimbaud. In short, Mallarmé seems to be entirely mystified into over-evaluating his own private circle of friends, and his use of the term "crisis" seems to be inspired by propaganda rather than by insight.

It does not take too attentive a reading of the text, however, to show that Mallarmé is in fact well aware of the relative triviality of what his disciples are taking so seriously. He is using them as a screen, a pretext to talk about something that concerns him much more; namely, his own experiments with poetic language. That is what he is referring to when he describes the contemporary condition of poetry as follows: "Orage, lustral; et dans des bouleversements, tout à l'acquit de la génération, récente, l'acte d'écrire se scruta jusqu'en l'origine. Très avant, au moins, quant au point, je le formule;—à savoir s'il y a lieu d'écrire." Freely translated and considerably flattened by filling in the elliptic syntax this becomes: "A tempest cleared the air: the new generation deserves credit for bringing this about. The act of writing scrutinized itself to the point of reflecting on its own origin, or, at any rate, far enough to reach the point where it could ask whether it is necessary for this act to take place." It matters little whether the "recent" generation to which Mallarmé refers indicates his younger disciples or his own contemporaries such as Verlaine, Villiers or even potentially Rimbaud. We know with certainty that something crisis-like was taking place at that moment, making practices and assumptions problematic that had been taken for granted.

We have, to a large extent, lost interest in the actual event that Mallarmé was describing as a crisis, but we have not at all lost interest in a text that pretends to designate a crisis when it is, in fact, itself the crisis to which it refers. For here, as in all of

Mallarmé's later prose and poetic works, the act of writing reflects indeed upon its own origin and opens up a cycle of questions that none of his real successors have been allowed to forget. We can speak of crisis when a "separation" takes place, by self-reflection, between what, in literature, is in conformity with the original intent and what has irrevocably fallen away from this source. Our question in relation to contemporary criticism then becomes: Is criticism indeed engaged in scrutinizing itself to the point of reflecting on its own origin? Is it asking whether it is necessary for the act of criticism to take place?

The matter is still further complicated by the fact that such scrutiny defines, in effect, the act of criticism itself. Even in its most naïve form, that of evaluation, the critical act is concerned with conformity to origin or specificity: when we say of art that it is good or bad, we are in fact judging a certain degree of conformity to an original intent called artistic. We imply that bad art is barely art at all; good art, on the contrary, comes close to our preconceived and implicit notion of what art ought to be. For that reason, the notion of crisis and that of criticism are very closely linked, so much so that one could state that all true criticism occurs in the mode of crisis. To speak of a crisis of criticism is then, to some degree, redundant. In periods that are not periods of crisis, or in individuals bent on avoiding crisis at all cost, there can be all kinds of approaches to literature: historical, philological, psychological, etc., but there can be no criticism. For such periods or individuals will never put the act of writing into question by relating it to its specific intent. The Continental criticism of today is doing just that, and it therefore deserves to be called genuine literary criticism. It will become clear, I hope, that this is not to be considered as an evaluative but as a purely descriptive statement. Whether authentic criticism is a liability or an asset to literary studies as a whole remains an open question. One thing, however, is certain; namely, that literary studies cannot possibly refuse to take cognizance of its existence. It would be as if historians refused to acknowledge the existence of wars because they threaten to interfere with the serenity that is indispensable to an orderly pursuit of their discipline.

The trend in Continental criticism, whether it derives its language from sociology, psychoanalysis, ethnology, linguistics, or even from certain forms of philosophy, can be quickly summarized: it represents a methodologically motivated attack on the notion that a literary or poetic consciousness is in any way a privileged consciousness, whose use of language can pretend to escape, to some degree, from the duplicity, the confusion, the untruth that we take for granted in the everyday use of language. We know that our entire social language is an intricate system of rhetorical devices designed to escape from the direct expression of desires that are, in the fullest sense of the term, unnameable— not because they are ethically shameful (for this would make the problem a very simple one), but because unmediated expression is a philosophical impossibility. And we know that the individual who chose to ignore this fundamental convention would be slated either for crucifixion, if he were aware, or, if he were naïve, destined to the total ridicule accorded such heroes as Candide and all other fools in fiction or in life. The contemporary contribution to this age-old problem comes by way of a rephrasing of the problem that develops when a consciousness gets involved in interpreting another consciousness, the basic pattern from which there can be no escape in the social sciences (if there is to be such a thing). Lévi-Strauss, for instance, starts out from the need to protect anthropologists engaged in the study of a so-called "primitive" society from the error made by earlier positivistic anthropologists when they projected upon this society assumptions that remained nonconsciously determined by the inhibitions and shortcomings of their own social situation. Prior to making any valid statement about a distant society, the observing subject must be as clear as possible about his attitude towards his own. He will soon discover, however, that the only way in which he can accomplish this self-demystification is by a (comparative) study of his own social self as it engages in the observation of others, and by becoming aware of the pattern of distortions that this situation necessarily implies. The observation and interpretation of others is always also a means of leading to the observation of the self; true anthropological knowledge (in the ethnological as well as in the philosophical, Kantian sense of the term) can only become worthy of being called knowledge when this alternating process of mutual interpretation between the two subjects has run its course. Numerous complications arise, because the observing subject is no more constant than the observed, and each time the observer actually succeeds in interpreting his subject he changes it, and changes it all the more as his interpretation comes closer to the truth. But every change of the observed subject requires a subsequent change in the observer, and the oscillating process seems to be endless. Worse, as the oscillation gains in intensity and in truth, it becomes less and less clear who is in fact doing the observing and who is being observed. Both parties tend to fuse into a single subject as the original distance between them disappears. The gravity of this development will at once be clear if I allow myself to shift, for a brief moment, from the anthropological to the psychoanalytical or political model. In the case of a genuine analysis of the psyche, it means that it would no longer be clear who is analyzing and who is being analyzed; consequently the highly embarrassing question arises, who should be paying whom. And on a political level, the equally distressing question as to who should be exploiting whom, is bound to arise.

The need to safeguard reason from what might become a dangerous *vertige*, a dizziness of the mind caught in an infinite regression, prompts a return to a more rational methodology. The fallacy of a finite and single interpretation derives from the postulate of a privileged observer; this leads, in turn, to the endless oscillation of an intersubjective demystification. As an escape from this predicament, one can propose a radical relativism that operates from the most empirically specific to the most loftily general level of human behavior. There are no longer any standpoints that can a priori be considered privileged, no structure that functions validly as a model for other structures, no postulate of ontological hierarchy that can serve as an organizing principle from which particular structures derive in the manner in which a deity can be said to engender man and the world. All structures are, in a sense, equally fallacious and are therefore called myths. But no myth ever has sufficient coherence not to flow back into neighboring myths or even has an identity strong enough to stand out by itself without an arbitrary act of interpretation that defines it. The relative unity of traditional myths always depends on the existence of a privileged point of view to which the method itself denies any status of authenticity. "Contrary to philosophical reflection, which claims to return to the source," writes Claude Lévi-Strauss in *Le Cru et le cuit,* "the reflective activities involved in the structural study of myths deal with light rays that issue from a virtual focal point. . . ." The method aims at preventing this virtual focus from being made into a *real* source of light. The analogy with optics is perhaps misleading, for in literature everything hinges on the existential status of the focal point; and the problem is more complex when it involves the disappearance of the self as a constitutive subject.

These remarks have made the transition from anthropology to the field of language and, finally, of literature. In the act of anthropological intersubjective interpretation, a fundamental discrepancy always prevents the observer from coinciding fully with the consciousness he is observing. The same discrepancy exists in everyday language, in the impossibility of making the actual expression coincide with what has to be expressed, of making the actual sign coincide with what it signifies. It is the distinctive privilege of language to be able to hide meaning behind a misleading sign, as when we hide rage or hatred behind a smile. But it is the distinctive curse of all language, as soon as any kind of interpersonal relation is involved, that it is forced to act this way. The simplest of wishes cannot express itself without hiding behind a screen of language that constitutes a world of intricate intersubjective relationships, all of them potentially inauthentic. In the everyday language of communication, there is no a priori privileged position of sign over meaning or of meaning over sign; the act of interpretation will always again have to establish this relation for the particular case at hand. The interpretation of everyday language is a Sisyphean task, a task without end and without progress, for the other is always free to make what he wants differ from what he says he wants. The methodology of structural anthropology and that of post-Saussurian linguistics thus share the common problem of a built-in discrepancy within the intersubjective relationship. As Lévi-Strauss, in order to protect the rationality of his science, had to come to the conclusion of a myth without an author, so the linguists have to conceive of a meta-language without speaker in order to remain rational.

Literature, presumably, is a form of language, and one can argue that all other art forms, including music, are in fact proto-literary languages. This, indeed, was Mallarmé's thesis in his Oxford lecture, as it is Lévi-Strauss' when he states that the language of music, as a language without speaker, comes closest to being the kind of meta-language of which the linguists are dreaming. If the radical position suggested by Lévi-Strauss is to stand, if the question of structure can only be asked from a point of view that is not that of a privileged subject, then it becomes imperative to show that literature constitutes no exception, that its language is in no sense privileged in terms of unity and truth over everyday forms of language. The task of structuralist literary critics then becomes quite clear: in order to eliminate the constitutive subject, they have to show that the discrepancy between sign and meaning (*signifiant* and *signifié*) prevails in literature in the same manner as in everyday language.

Some contemporary critics have more or less consciously been doing this. Practical criticism, in France and in the United States, functions more and more as a demystification of the belief that literature is a privileged language. The dominant strategy consists of showing that certain claims to authenticity attributed to literature are in fact expressions of a desire that, like all desires, falls prey to the duplicities of expression. The so-called "idealism" of literature is then shown to be an idolatry, a fascination with a false image that mimics the presumed attributes of authenticity when it is in fact just the hollow mask with which a frustrated, defeated consciousness tries to cover up its own negativity.

Perhaps the most specific example of this strategy is the use made by structuralist critics of the historical term "romantic"; the example also has the virtue of revealing the historical scheme within which they are operating, and which is not always openly stated. The fallacy of the belief that, in the language of poetry, sign and meaning can coincide, or at least be related to each other in the free and harmonious balance that we call beauty, is said to be a specifically romantic delusion. The unity of appearance (sign) and idea (meaning)—to use the terminology that one finds indeed among the theoreticians of romanticism when they speak of *Schein* and *Idee*—is said to be a romantic myth embodied in the recurrent topos of the "Beautiful Soul." The *schöne Seele,* a predominant theme of pietistic origin in eighteenth- and nine-teenth-century literature, functions indeed as the *figura* of a privileged kind of language. Its outward apparance receives its beauty from an inner glow (or *feu sacré*) to which it is so finely attuned that, far from hiding it from sight, it gives it just the right balance of opacity and transparency, thus allowing the holy fire to shine without burning. The romantic imagination embodies this figure at times in the shape of a person, feminine, masculine or hermaph-rodite, and seems to suggest that it exists as an actual, empirical subject: one thinks, for instance, of Rousseau's Julie, of Hölderlin's Diotima, or of the beautiful soul that appears in Hegel's *Phenomenology of the Spirit* and in Goethe's *Wilhelm Meister.*

At this point, it is an irresistible temptation for the demystifying critic, from Voltaire down to the present, to demonstrate that this person, this actual subject, becomes ludicrous when it is trans-planted in the fallen world of our facticity. The beautiful soul can be shown to spring from fantasies by means of which the writer sublimates his own shortcomings; it suffices to remove the entity for a moment from the fictional world in which it exists to make it appear even more ridiculous than Candide. Some authors, writing in the wake of the romantic myth, have been well aware of this. One can see how certain developments in nineteenth-cen-tury realism, the ironic treatment of the Rousseauistic figure by Stendhal, of the quixotic figure by Flaubert, or of the "poetic" figure by Proust, can be interpreted as a gradual demystification of romantic idealism. This leads to a historical scheme in which ro-manticism represents, so to speak, the point of maximum delusion in our recent past, whereas the nineteenth and twentieth centuries represent a gradual emerging from this aberration, culminating in the breakthrough of the last decades that inaugurates a new form of insight and lucidity, a cure from the agony of the romantic disease. Refining on what may appear too crude in such a historical scheme, some modern critics transpose this movement within the consciousness of a single writer and show how the development of a novelist can best be understood as a successive process of mystifications and partial demystifications. The process does not necessarily move in one single direction, from delusion to insight; there can be an intricate play of relapses and momentary recoveries. All the same, the fundamental movement of the literary mind espouses the pattern of a demystifying consciousness; literature finally comes into its own, and becomes authentic, when it discovers that the exalted status it claimed for its language was a myth. The function of the critic then naturally becomes coextensive with the intent at demystification that is more or less consciously present in the mind of the author.

This scheme is powerful and cogent, powerful enough, in fact, to go to the root of the matter and consequently to cause a crisis. To reject it convincingly would require elaborate argument. My remarks are meant to indicate some reasons, however, for considering the conception of literature (or literary criticism) as demystification the most dangerous myth of all, while granting that it forces us, in Mallarmé's terms, to scrutinize the act of writing "jusqu'en l'origine."

For reasons of economy, my starting point will have to be oblique, for in the language of polemics the crooked path often travels faster than the straight one. We must ask ourselves if there is not a recurrent epistemological structure that characterizes all statements made in the mood and the rhetoric of crisis. Let me take an example from philosophy. On May 7 and May 10 of 1935, Edmund Husserl, the founder of phenomenology, delivered in Vienna two lectures entitled "Philosophy and the Crisis of European Humanity"; the title was later changed to "The Crisis of European Humanity and Philosophy," to stress the priority of the concept of crisis as Husserl's main concern. The lectures are the first version of what was to become Husserl's most important later work, the treatise entitled *The Crisis of the European Sciences and Transcendental Phenomenology,* now the sixth volume of the complete works edited by Walter Biemel. In these various titles, two words remain constant: the word "crisis" and the word "European"; it is in the interaction of these two concepts that the epistemological structure of the crisis-statement is fully revealed.

Reading this text with the hindsight that stems from more than thirty years of turbulent history, it strikes one as both prophetic and tragic. Much of what is being stated seems relevant today. It is not by a mere freak of language that the key word "demythification" (*Entmythisierung*), that was destined to have such an important career, appears in the text (VI.340.4), although the context in which the term is used, designating what takes place when the superior theoretical man observes the inferior natural man, is highly revealing. There is a very modern note in Husserl's description of philosophy as a process by means of which naïve assumptions are made accessible to consciousness by an act of critical self-understanding. Husserl conceived of philosophy primarily as a self-interpretation by means of which we eliminate what he calls *Selbstverhülltheit,* the tendency of the self to hide from the light it can cast on itself. The universality of philosophical knowledge stems from a persistently reflective attitude that can take philosophy itself for its theme. He describes philosophy as a prolegomenon to a new kind of praxis, a "universal critique of all life and all the goals of life, of all the man-created cultural systems and achievements" and, consequently, "a criticism of man himself (*Kritik der Menschheit selbst*) and of the values by which he is consciously or pre-consciously being governed."

Alerted by this convincing appeal to self-critical vigilance, Husserl's listeners and his present-day readers may well be tempted to turn this philosophical criticism on Husserl's own text, especially on the numerous sections in which philosophy is said to be the historical privilege of European man. Husserl speaks repeatedly of non-European cultures as primitive, prescientific and pre-philosophical, myth-dominated and congenitally incapable of the disinterested distance without which there can be no philosophical meditation. This, although by his own definition philosophy, as unrestricted reflection upon the self, necessarily tends toward a universality that finds its concrete, geographical correlative in the formation of supratribal, supernational communities such as, for instance, Europe. Why this geographical expansion should have chosen to stop, once and forever, at the Atlantic Ocean and at the Caucasus, Husserl does not say. No one could be more open to Lévi-Strauss' criticism of the mystified anthropologist than Husserl when he warns us, with the noblest of intentions, that we should not assume a potential for philosophical attitudes in non-

European cultures. The privileged viewpoint of the post-Hellenic, European consciousness is never for a moment put into question; the crucial, determining examination on which depends Husserl's right to call himself, by his own terms, a philosopher, is in fact never undertaken. As a European, it seems that Husserl escapes from the necessary self-criticism that is prior to all philosophical truth about the self. He is committing precisely the mistake that Rousseau did not commit when he carefully avoided giving his concept of natural man, the basis of his anthropology, any empirical status whatever. Husserl's claim to European supremacy hardly stands in need of criticism today. Since we are speaking of a man of superior good will, it suffices to point to the pathos of such a claim at a moment when Europe was about to destroy itself as center in the name of its unwarranted claim to be the center.

The point, however, transcends the personal situation. Speaking in what was in fact a state of urgent personal and political crisis about a more general form of crisis, Husserl's text reveals with striking clarity the structure of all crisis-determined statements. It establishes an important truth: the fact that philosophical knowledge can only come into being when it is turned back upon itself. But it immediately proceeds, in the very same text, to do the opposite. The rhetoric of crisis states its own truth in the mode of error. It is itself radically blind to the light it emits. It could be shown that the same is true of Mallarmé's *Crise de vers*, which served as our original starting point—although it would be a great deal more complex to demonstrate the self-mystification of as ironical a man as Mallarmé than of as admirably honest a man as Husserl.

Our question, rather, is the following: How does this pattern of self-mystification that accompanies the experience of crisis apply to literary criticism? Husserl was demonstrating the urgent philosophical necessity of putting the privileged European standpoint into question, but remained himself entirely blind to this necessity, behaving in the most unphilosophical way possible at the very moment when he rightly understood the primacy of philosophical over empirical knowledge. He was, in fact, stating the privileged status of philosophy as an authentic language, but withdrawing at once from the demands of this authenticity as it applied to him-self. Similarly, demystifying critics are in fact asserting the privi-leged status of literature as an authentic language, but withdraw-ing from the implications by cutting themselves off from the source from which they receive their insight.

For the statement about language, that sign and meaning can never coincide, is what is precisely taken for granted in the kind of language we call literary. Literature, unlike everyday language, begins on the far side of this knowledge; it is the only form of language free from the fallacy of unmediated expression. All of us know this, although we know it in the misleading way of a wishful assertion of the opposite. Yet the truth emerges in the fore-knowledge we possess of the true nature of literature when we refer to it as *fiction*. All literatures, including the literature of Greece, have always designated themselves as existing in the mode of fiction; in the *Iliad,* when we first encounter Helen, it is as the emblem of the narrator weaving the actual war into the tapestry of a fictional object. Her beauty prefigures the beauty of all future narratives as entities that point to their own fictional nature. The self-reflecting mirror-effect by means of which a work of fiction asserts, by its very existence, its separation from empirical reality, its divergence, as a sign, from a meaning that depends for its exist-ence on the constitutive activity of this sign, characterizes the work of literature in its essence. It is always against the explicit assertion of the writer that readers degrade the fiction by confusing it with a reality from which it has forever taken leave. "Le pays des chimères est en ce monde le seul digne d'être habité," Rousseau has Julie write, "et tel est le néant des choses humaines qu'hors l'Etre existant par lui-même, il n'y a rien de beau que ce qui n'est pas" (*La Nouvelle Heloïse,* Pléiade ed. II, 693). One entirely misunderstands this assertion of the priority of fiction over reality, of imagination over perception, if one considers it as the compen-satory expression of a shortcoming, of a deficient sense of reality. It is attributed to a fictional character who knows all there is to know of human happiness and who is about to face death with Socratic equanimity. It transcends the notion of a nostalgia or a desire, since it discovers desire as a fundamental pattern of being that discards any possibility of satisfaction. Elsewhere, Rousseau speaks in similar terms of the nothingness of fiction (*le néant de mes chimères*): "If all my dreams had turned into reality, I would still remain unsatisfied: I would have kept on dreaming, imagining, desiring. In myself, I found an unexplainable void that nothing could have filled; a longing of the heart towards another kind of fulfillment of which I could not conceive but of which I nevertheless felt the attraction" (Letter to Malesherbes, Pléiade ed. I, 1140).

These texts can be called romantic, and I have purposely chosen them within the period and the author that many consider the most deluded of all. But one hesitates to use terms such as nostalgia or desire to designate this kind of consciousness, for all nostalgia or desire is desire of something or for someone; here, the consciousness does not result from the absence of something, but consists of the presence of a nothingness. Poetic language names this void with ever-renewed understanding and, like Rousseau's longing, it never tires of naming it again. This persistent naming is what we call literature. In the same manner that the poetic lyric originates in moments of tranquility, in the absence of actual emotions, and then proceeds to invent fictional emotions to create the illusion of recollection, the work of fiction invents fictional subjects to create the illusion of the reality of others. But the fiction is not myth, for it knows and names itself as fiction. It is not a demystification, it is demystified from the start. When modern critics think they are demystifying literature, they are in fact being demystified by it; but since this necessarily occurs in the form of a crisis, they are blind to what takes place within themselves. At the moment that they claim to do away with literature, literature is everywhere; what they call anthropology, linguistics, psychoanalysis is nothing but literature reappearing, like the Hydra's head, in the very spot where it had supposedly been suppressed. The human mind will go through amazing feats of distortion to avoid facing "the nothingness of human matters." In order not to see that the failure lies in the nature of things, one chooses to locate it in the individual, "romantic" subject, and thus retreats behind a historical scheme which, apocalyptic as it may sound, is basically reassuring and bland.

Lévi-Strauss had to give up the notion of subject to safeguard reason. The subject, he said, in fact, is a "foyer virtuel," a mere hypothesis posited by the scientists to give consistency to the behavior of entities. The metaphor in his statement that "the reflective activities [of the structuralists] deal with light that issues from a virtual focal point . . ." stems from the elementary laws of optical refraction. The image is all the more striking since it plays on the confusion between the imaginary loci of the physicist and the *fictional* entities that occur in literary language. The virtual focus is a quasi-objective structure posited to give rational integrity to a process that exists independently of the self. The subject merely fills in, with the dotted line of geometrical construction, what natural reason had not bothered to make explicit; it has a passive and unproblematic role. The "virtual focus" is, strictly speaking, a nothing, but its nothingness concerns us very little, since a mere act of reason suffices to give it a mode of being that leaves the rational order unchallenged. The same is not true of the imaginary source of fiction. Here the human self has experienced the void within itself and the invented fiction, far from filling the void, asserts itself as pure nothingness, *our* nothingness stated and restated by a subject that is the agent of its own instability. Lévi-Strauss' suppression of the subject is perfectly legitimate as an attempt to protect the scientific status of ethnology; by the same token, however, it leads directly into the larger question of the ontological status of the self. From this point on, a philosophical anthropology would be inconceivable without the consideration of literature as a primary source of knowledge.

II

Form and Intent in the
American New Criticism

Not longer than ten years ago, a comparison of American and European criticism would in all likelihood have had to focus on the differences between a stylistic and a historical approach to literature. In evaluating what American criticism stood to gain from a closer contact with Europe, one would have stressed the balance achieved in some of the best European works between historical knowledge and a genuine feeling for literary form. For reasons that are themselves part of history, the same synthesis was rarely achieved in America; the intellectual history that originated with Lovejoy and that could have combined a European sense of history with an American sense of form was the exception rather than the norm. The predominant influence, that of the New Criticism, was never able to overcome the anti-historical bias that presided over its beginnings. This inability certainly was one of the reasons that prevented it from making major contributions, in spite of considerable methodological originality and refinement. One can think of several ways in which a closer contact with European methods could have contributed to a broadening of the New Critical approach. Opportunities for such contacts were never lacking. After all, some of the most representative European historians, as well as some of the best practitioners of contemporary stylistics, spent much time in America: one thinks of Erich Auerbach, Leo Spitzer, Georges Poulet, Damaso Alonso, Roman Jakobson, and several others. That their influence remained by and large confined to their national field of specialization indicates how difficult it is to break down the barriers that, in our universities, keep the various departments separated from each other. Perhaps American formalism needed this isolation to come fully into its own. Whatever the case may be, even when the influence of the New Criticism reached its height, it remained confined within its original boundaries and was allowed to do so without being seriously challenged.

Such a challenge could have come from various sources, without really having to upset the traditional patterns of literary studies. But today, it is too late to bring about this kind of encounter. One can regret this, yet an analysis of the causes that prevented the confrontation is purely academic. Over the last five years, a far-reaching change has taken place here and abroad, putting the entire question of literary studies in a different perspective. Whether American or European, whether oriented toward form or toward history, the main critical approaches of the last decades were all founded on the implicit assumption that literature is an autonomous activity of the mind, a distinctive way of being in the world to be understood in terms of its own purposes and intentions. This autonomy is now again being successfully challenged. Contemporary French structuralism applies methodological patterns derived from the social sciences (especially anthropology and linguistics) to the study of literature; similar tendencies can be observed in the renewed interest of American critics in sociological, political, and psychological considerations that had never ceased to be present, but had been kept in the background. Ironically enough, the long-awaited unification of European and American criticism seems to be coming about, albeit in the form of a radical questioning of the autonomy of literature as an aesthetic activity.

The trend can be welcomed, though not uncritically. It forces a long overdue re-examination of the assumptions on which the position of autonomy was founded, for it is not at all certain that this position had been well understood by the American formalists; their conviction may very well have been founded on preconceptions that were themselves derived from non-literary models. The kind of autonomy to be found in literary works is certainly far from self-evident; it has to be redefined before we can ask whether it is being challenged in the name of regressive trends, methods that apply to less rigorous modes of consciousness than those at work in literary language. As one of the questions that can give insight into this matter, the nature of the relationship between form and intent provides a possible way of approach.

We can take as a point of departure a remark of the English semanticist Stephen Ullmann in a work on the stylistics of French fiction. Ullmann is led to a discussion of the method of Leo Spitzer and speaks of the rebuke that is frequently addressed to Spitzer; namely, that his apparently objective philological analyses are, in fact, *a posteriori* rationalizations of emotional convictions that he held long beforehand. Ullmann writes:

> Professor Spitzer has strongly repudiated this allegation; but even if it is true, it does not really affect the value of the method. As long as the demonstration is conclusive, it surely does not matter in what order the various steps were taken; the main point is that a link has been established between a stylistic peculiarity, its root in the author's psyche, and other manifestations of the same mental factor. The great merit of Spitzer's procedure is indeed that it has lifted stylistic facts out of their isolation and has related them to other aspects of the writer's experience and activity.[1]

Interpreted in a certain way—which is not necessarily how Mr. Ullmann intends it—this affirmation postulates a continuity between the initial subjective experience of the writer and characteristics that belong to the surface dimensions of language—such as properties of sound, of meter, or even of imagery, all of which belong to the domain of sensory experience. This continuity im-

1. Stephen Ullmann, *Style in the French Novel* (Cambridge, Eng., 1957), pp. 28–29.

plies a debatable presupposition about the nature of literary language. The formula is tempting for it seems to dispense with adventurous inquiries that reach into the darker areas of human subjectivity and to leave us instead in a clear and precise zone in which properties can be observed and even measured. But can we take this continuity between depth and surface, between style and theme, for granted? Is it not rather the most problematic issue with which the theory of poetry will have to deal?

In another work—historical and thematic in scope rather than purely stylistic—Erich Auerbach's *Mimesis*, the author, in speaking of the tension that exists in Western literature between the Biblical and the Hellenic traditions, characterizes Western literature as a "struggle between sensory appearance and meaning (Kampf zwischen sinnlicher Erscheinung und Bedeutung) which pervades the Christian sense of reality from the beginning and, in truth, in its totality." [2] And, as is clear from the context, the "meaning" to which Auerbach alludes here is not just the immediate semantic *donnée* of a text but the deeper inward experience that determines the choice and articulation of the themes. However, if this is indeed the case, the study of the "sensory appearances" that is the field of stylistics can never lead to the real meaning of the themes since both, at least in Western literature, are separated by a radical discontinuity that no dialectic is able to bridge. It would be of the utmost importance, in that case, to know whether Leo Spitzer has taken a subjective or a sensory element for his point of departure since we would end up, in each case, in the opposite camp.

It is easy to see to what species of entities Ullmann's description does apply. Certain entities exist the full meaning of which can be said to be equal to the totality of their sensory appearances. For an ideal perception, entirely devoid of complications resulting from the interference of the imagination, the "meaning" of "stone" could only refer to a totality of sensory appearances. The same applies to all natural objects. But even the most purely intuitive consciousness could never conceive of the significance of an object such as, for instance, a chair, without including in the description

2. Erich Auerbach, *Mimesis* (Bern, 1946), Chapter II, p. 55.

an allusion to the *use* to which it is put; the most rigorous description of the perceptions of the object "chair" would remain meaningless if one does not organize them in function of the potential
act that defines the object; namely, that it is destined to be sat on.
The potential act of sitting down is a constitutive part of the
object. If it were absent, the object could not be conceived in
its totality. The difference between the stone and the chair
distinguishes a natural object from an intentional object. The
intentional object requires a reference to a specific act as constitutive of its mode of being. By asserting *a priori,* as in Ullmann's
text, that, in literary language, the meaning is equal to the totality
of the sensory appearances, one postulates in fact that the language
of literature is of the same order, ontologically speaking, as a
natural object. The intentional factor has been bypassed.

A clarification of the notion of "intent" is of great importance
for an evaluation of American criticism, for at the rare moments
when the New Critics consented to express themselves theoretically, the notion of intent always played a prominent part, although it was mostly a negative one. Wimsatt and Beardsley
coined the expression "intentional fallacy" as far back as 1942 and
this formula, better than any other, delimits the horizon within
which this criticism has operated. The expression was developed
later on by Wimsatt in his book *The Verbal Icon,* where it is used
to assert the autonomy and the unity of the poetic consciousness.
Wimsatt wants to defend the province of poetry against the intrusion of crude deterministic systems, historical or psychological, that
oversimplify the complex relationship between theme and style.
And he focuses on the concept of intention as the breach through
which these foreign bodies reach into the poetic domain. But, in
so doing, he allows us to observe the very moment at which his
concern with autonomy, most legitimate in itself, leads him into
contradictory assumptions about the ontological status of the work
of literature. Too sensitive an aesthetician to distort things altogether, Wimsatt writes at first: "the poem conceived as a thing
in between the poet and the audience is, of course, an abstraction.
The poem is an act"—a statement to which an intentional theory
of poetry would gladly subscribe. Then Wimsatt continues: "But
if we are to lay hold of the poetic act to comprehend and evaluate

it, and if it has to pass current as critical object, it must be hypostatized." [3]

If such a hypostasis, which changes the literary act into a literary object by the suppression of its intentional character, is not only possible but necessary in order to allow for a critical description, then we have not left the world in which the status of literary language is similar to that of a natural object. This assumption rests on a misunderstanding of the nature of intentionality. "Intent" is seen, by analogy with a physical model, as a transfer of a psychic or mental content that exists in the mind of the poet to the mind of a reader, somewhat as one would pour wine from a jar into a glass. A certain content has to be transferred elsewhere, and the energy necessary to effect the transfer has to come from an outside source called intention. This is to ignore that the concept of intentionality is neither physcial nor psychological in its nature, but structural, involving the activity of a subject regardless of its empirical concerns, except as far as they relate to the intentionality of the structure. The structural intentionality determines the relationship between the components of the resulting object in all its parts, but the relationship of the particular state of mind of the person engaged in the act of structurization to the structured object is altogether contingent. The structure of the chair is determined in all its components by the fact that it is destined to be sat on, but this structure in no way depends on the state of mind of the carpenter who is in the process of assembling its parts. The case of the work of literature is of course more complex, yet here also, the intentionality of the act, far from threatening the unity of the poetic entity, more definitely establishes this unity.

The rejection of intentionality, by which Wimsatt formulated theoretically what other New Critics were practicing, has proven to be remarkably tenacious. In *The Anatomy of Criticism,* Northrop Frye still refers to the "intentional fallacy" as one of the methodological cornerstones of his system of archetypal rhetorical categories. His formulation seems to be closer to Wimsatt's "act" than to his hypostatized "thing." Frye sees the structure of an inten-

3. William Wimsatt, *The Verbal Icon* (Lexington, Ky., 1954), Chapter I, p. xvii.

tional act as analogous to that of taking aim, as when an object is taken for a target by a weapon directed toward it.[4] He concludes that this type of structure belongs to discursive language which "aims" for the exact relationship and not to poetic language which does not "aim" at anything, being tautologically itself; that is to say, entirely autonomous and without exterior referent. This part of Frye's theory—which hardly detracts from the suggestive value of his further classifications—is founded on a misunderstanding of intentional language and, be it said in passing, of discursive language as well. Up to a point, the act of taking aim provides a correct model for an intentional act, provided an important distinction is made. When a hunter takes aim at a rabbit, we may presume his intention is to eat or to sell the rabbit and, in that case the act of taking aim is subordinated to another intention that exists beyond the act itself. But when he takes aim at an artificial target, his act has no other intention than aim-taking for its own sake and constitutes a perfectly closed and autonomous structure. The act reflects back upon itself and remains circumscribed within the range of its own intent. This is indeed a proper way of distinguishing between different intentional objects such as the tool (the gun that takes aim at the rabbit) and the toy (the gun that takes aim at a clay pipe). The aesthetic entity definitely belongs to the same class as the toy, as Kant and Schiller knew well before Huizinga. In failing to make this distinction, Northrop Frye falls into exactly the same error as Wimsatt and reifies the literary entity into a natural object: with the added danger, moreover, that put in less ironic hands than his own, his theory could cause much more extensive damage. A formalist such as Wimsatt hypostatizes only the particular text on which he is working, but a literal minded disciple of a mythologist like Frye could go a lot further. He is given license to order and classify the whole of literature into one single thing which, even though circular, would nevertheless be a gigantic cadaver. Frye's formula defining all literary creation as "an activity whose intention it is to abolish intention"[5] is only sound if it is allowed to remain forever suspended as an eternal intent.

A truly systematic study of the main formalist critics in the

4. Northrop Frye, *The Anatomy of Criticism* (Princeton, 1957), p. 86.
5. *Ibid.* p. 89.

English language during the last thirty years would always reveal the more or less deliberate rejection of the principle of intentionality. The result would be a hardening of the text into a sheer surface that prevents the stylistic analysis from penetrating beyond the sensory appearances to perceive this "struggle with meaning" of which all criticism, including the criticism of forms, should give an account. For surfaces also remain concealed when they are being artificially separated from the depth that supports them. The partial failure of American formalism, which has not produced works of major magnitude, is due to its lack of awareness of the intentional structure of literary form.

Yet this criticism has merits that prevail despite the weakness of its theoretical foundations. The French critic, Jean-Pierre Richard, alludes to these merits when he writes defensively in the introduction to his study of Mallarmé that "the reproach [of destroying the formal structure of the work] will especially be made by English and American critics for whom, as is well known, the objective and architectural reality of particular works is of the utmost importance." [6] It is true that American textual interpretation and "close reading" have perfected techniques that allow for considerable refinement in catching the details and nuances of literary expression. They study texts as "forms," as groupings from which the constitutive parts cannot be isolated or separated. This gives a sense of context that is often lacking in French or in German interpretations.

But are we not confronted here with a flagrant contradiction? On the one hand, we blame American criticism for considering literary texts as if they were natural objects but, on the other hand, we praise it for possessing a sense of formal unity that belongs precisely to a living and natural organism. Is not this sense of the unity of forms being supported by the large metaphor of the analogy between language and a living organism, a metaphor that shapes a great deal of nineteenth-century poetry and thought? One could even find historical confirmation of this filiation in the line that links, especially by way of I. A. Richards and Whitehead, the structural formalism of the New Critics to the "organic" im-

6. Jean-Pierre Richard, *L'Univers imaginaire de Mallarmé* (Paris, 1961), p. 31.

agination so dear to Coleridge. The introduction of the principle of intentionality would imperil the organic analogy and lead to a loss of the sense of form; hence the understandable need of the New Critics to protect their greatest source of strength.

It should be remembered that, going back to Coleridge himself, what he called the "esemplastic" power of the imagination was not unambiguously founded on a participation of consciousness in the natural energy of the cosmos. M. H. Abrams, in *The Mirror and the Lamp*, rightly insists on the importance of free will in Coleridge. "Coleridge," he writes, "though admitting an unconscious component in invention, was determined to demonstrate that a poet like Shakespeare 'never wrote anything without design.' What the plant is by an act not its own and unconsciously, Coleridge exhorts us 'that must thou *make* thyself to become' " [7] And, in *La Métamorphose du cercle*, Georges Poulet, speaking of Coleridge's sense of form, insists that it results from "the explicit action of·our will" which "imposes its law and unique form upon the poetic universe." [8] This is to say that the structural power of the poetic imagination is not founded on an analogy with nature, but that it is intentional. Abrams perceives this very well when he comments that Coleridge's notion of free will "runs counter, it would appear, to an inherent tendency of his elected analogue." [9]

The ambivalence reappears among modern disciples of Coleridge, in a curious discrepancy between their theoretical assumptions and their practical results. As it refines its interpretations more and more, American criticism does not discover a single meaning, but a plurality of significations that can be radically opposed to each other. Instead of revealing a continuity affiliated with the coherence of the natural world, it takes us into a discontinuous world of reflective irony and ambiguity. Almost in spite of itself, it pushes the interpretative process so far that the analogy between the organic world and the language of poetry finally explodes. This unitarian criticism finally becomes a criticism of ambiguity, an ironic reflection on the absence of the unity it had postulated.

But from where then does the contextual unity, which the

7. M. H. Abrams, *The Mirror and the Lamp* (New York, 1953), pp. 173–74.
8. Georges Poulet, *La Métamorphose du cercle* (Paris, 1961), p. 154.
9. Abrams, *op. cit.* p. 174.

study of texts reconfirms over and over again and to which American criticism owes its effectiveness, stem? Is it not rather that this unity—which is in fact a semi-circularity—resides not in the poetic text as such, but in the act of interpreting this text? The circle we find here and which is called "form" does not stem from an analogy between the text and natural things, but constitutes the hermeneutic circle mentioned by Spitzer[10] of which the history has been traced by Gadamer in *Wahrheit und Methode*[11] and whose ontological significance is at the basis of Heidegger's treatise *Sein und Zeit*.

What happened in American criticism could then be explained as follows: because such patient and delicate attention was paid to the reading of forms, the critics pragmatically entered into the hermeneutic circle of interpretation, mistaking it for the organic circularity of natural processes. This happened quite spontaneously, for Spitzer's influence at the time of the New Criticism was confined to a small area, and Heidegger's influence was non-existent.

Only some aspects of Heidegger's theory of hermeneutic circularity have to be stressed here. It combines in fact two equally important ideas. The first has to do with the epistemological nature of all interpretation. Contrary to what happens in the physical sciences, the interpretation of an intentional act or an intentional object always implies an *understanding* of the intent. Like scientific laws, interpretation is in fact a generalization that expands the range of applicability of a statement to a wider area. But the nature of the generalization is altogether different from what is most frequently encountered in the natural sciences. There we are concerned with the predictability, the measurement, or the mode of determination of a given phenomenon, but we do not claim in any way to understand it. To interpret an intent, however, can only mean to understand it. No new set of relationships is added to an existing reality, but relationships *that were already there* are being disclosed, not only in themselves (like the events of nature) but as they exist *for us*. We can only understand that which is in

10. Leo Spitzer, *A Method of Interpreting Literature* (Northampton, Mass., 1949).
11. Hans Georg Gadamer, *Wahrheit und Methode* (Tübingen, 1960).

a sense already given to us and already known, albeit in a fragmentary, inauthentic way that cannot be called unconscious. Heidegger
calls this the *Forhabe,* the forestructure of all understanding.

> This is a fact [he writes], that has always been remarked,
> even if only in the area of derivative ways of understanding
> and interpretation, such as philological interpretation. . . .
>   Scientific knowledge demands the rigors of demonstration
> for its justification. In a scientific proof, we may not pre-
> suppose what it is our task to demonstrate. But if interpre-
> tation must in any case operate in the area of what is already
> understood, and if it must feed on this understanding, how
> can it achieve any scientific results without moving in a
> circle? . . . Yet, according to the most elementary rules of
> logic, this circle is a *circulus vitiosus.* But if we think this
> to be a vicious circle and try to avoid it, even if we merely
> suspect it of being an imperfection, then the act of understand-
> ing has been entirely misunderstood. . . . If the basic con-
> ditions that make interpretation possible are to be fulfilled,
> we must recognize from the start the circumstances under
> which it can be performed. What is decisive is not to get out
> of the circle but to come into it in the right way. The circle
> of understanding is not an orbit in which any random kind
> of knowledge is allowed to move; it is the expression of the
> existential forestructure of *Dasein* itself. . . . In the circle
> is hidden a positive possibility of the most primordial kind of
> knowledge.[12]

For the interpreter of a poetic text, this foreknowledge is the
text itself. Once he understands the text, the implicit knowledge
becomes explicit and discloses what was already there in full light.
Far from being something added to the text, the elucidating commentary simply tries to reach the text itself, whose full richness
is there at the start. Ultimately, the ideal commentary would indeed become superfluous and merely allow the text to stand fully
revealed. But it goes without saying that this ideal commentary
can never exist as such. When Heidegger, in his foreword to his
commentaries on the poetry of Hölderlin, claims to write from
the standpoint of the ideal commentator, his claim is disquieting

12. Martin Heidegger, *Sein und Zeit* (1927), I, Chapter V.

because it goes against the temporal structure of the hermeneutic process. The implicit foreknowledge is always temporally ahead of the explicit interpretative statement that tries to catch up with it.

The notion of the hermeneutic circle is not introduced by Heidegger in connection with poetry or the interpretation of poetry, but applied to language in general. All language is, to some extent, involved in interpretation, though all language certainly does not achieve understanding. Here the second element of the hermeneutic process comes into play: the notion of circularity or totality. Only when understanding has been achieved does the circle seem to close and only then is the foreknowing structure of the act of interpretation fully revealed. True understanding always implies a certain degree of totality; without it, no contact could be established with a foreknowledge that it can never reach, but of which it can be more or less lucidly aware. The fact that poetic language, unlike ordinary language, possesses what we call "form" indicates that it has reached this point. In interpreting poetic language, and especially in revealing its "form," the critic is therefore dealing with a privileged language: a language engaged in its highest intent and tending toward the fullest possible self-understanding. The critical interpretation is oriented toward a consciousness which is itself engaged in an act of total interpretation. The relationship between author and critic does not designate a difference in the type of activity involved, since no fundamental discontinuity exists between two acts that both aim at full understanding; the difference is primarily temporal in kind. Poetry is the foreknowledge of criticism. Far from changing or distorting it, criticism merely discloses poetry for what it is.

Literary "form" is the result of the dialectic interplay between the prefigurative structure of the foreknowledge and the intent at totality of the interpretative process. This dialectic is difficult to grasp. The idea of totality suggests closed forms that strive for ordered and consistent systems and have an almost irresistible tendency to transform themselves into objective structures. Yet, the temporal factor, so persistently forgotten, should remind us that the form is never anything but a process on the way to its completion. The completed form never exists as a concrete aspect of the work that could coincide with a sensorial or semantic dimen-

sion of the language. It is constituted in the mind of the interpreter as the work discloses itself in response to his questioning.
But this dialogue between work and interpreter is endless. The
hermeneutic understanding is always, by its very nature, lagging
behind: to understand something is to realize that one had always
known it, but, at the same time, to face the mystery of this hidden
knowledge. Understanding can be called complete only when it
becomes aware of its own temporal predicament and realizes that
the horizon within which the totalization can take place is time
itself. The act of understanding is a temporal act that has its own
history, but this history forever eludes totalization. Whenever the
circle seems to close, one has merely ascended or descended one
more step on Mallarmé's "spirale vertigineuse conséquente."

The lesson to be derived from the evolution of American formalist criticism is twofold. It reaffirms first of all the necessary presence
of a totalizing principle as the guiding impulse of the critical
process. In the New Criticism, this principle consisted of a purely
empirical notion of the integrity of literary form, yet the mere
presence of such a principle could lead to the disclosure of distinctive structures of literary language (such as ambiguity and irony)
although these structures contradict the very premises on which
the New Criticism was founded. Second, the rejection of the
principle of intentionality, dismissed as fallacious, prevented the
integration of these discoveries within a truly coherent theory of
literary form. The ambivalence of American formalism is such
that it was bound to lead to a state of paralysis. The problem remains how to formulate the mode of totalization that applies to
literary language and that allows for a description of its distinctive
aspects.

Some similarities can be pointed out between the successes and
the shortcomings of the American New Criticism and corresponding developments in present-day French criticism. The danger of
a reification of the form also seems to threaten the declared ob-
jectivism of several structuralist interpreters of literature. Yet the
theoretical foundations of the two trends have by now moved in
very different directions. In structuralism the loss of the intentional
factor does not result from a debatable identification of language

with the organic world but is due to the suppression of the constitutive subject. The consequences of this suppression reach much
further than in the relatively harmless case of an organicist formalism. A material analogism, as one finds it in the criticism of
Bachelard or of Jean-Pierre Richard, can leave the play of the
poetic imagination quite free. As long as the theoretical assumptions remain weak and loose, the hermeneutic process can take
place more or less unhampered. But the theoretical assumptions
that underlie the methods of structuralism are a great deal more
powerful and consistent. They cannot be dealt with in the course
of a single brief essay.

The critical examination of the structuralist premises will have
to focus on the same set of problems that appeared in the discussion
of formalism: the existence and the nature of the constitutive subject, the temporal structure of the act of interpretation, the necessity for a distinctively literary mode of totalization. It could be
that, in a legitimate desire to react against reductive ways of
thought, the structuralists have bypassed or oversimplified some of
these questions.[13]

In the first critical reactions to arise in response to the structuralist challenge, it is primarily the question of the subject that has
been stressed. Thus Serge Doubrovsky, in the first volume of a
general study on modern French criticism, re-establishes the link
between literary totality and the intent of the writer or subject.
This intent is conceived in Sartrian terms, with a definite awareness of the temporal complexities involved in the process of interpretation. It is doubtful, however, if Doubrovsky remains faithful
to the demands of literary language when he defines its intentionality as the act of an individual "projecting the original relations
between man and reality, the total sense of the human condition,
on the level of the imagination (le plan de l'imaginaire)."[14]
What is this "plan de l'imaginaire" that seems to exist by itself,
independently of language, and why would we need to "project"
ourselves upon it? Doubrovsky answers these questions by referring
to the theories of perception contained in the work of Merleau-
Ponty. He describes all expression as being at the same time dis-

13. The question is discussed in more detail in Chapter VII of this study.
14. Serge Doubrovsky, *Pourquoi la nouvelle critique?* (Paris, 1966), p. 193.

closure as well as dissimulation; the function of art and of literature would be to reveal the reality that is hidden as well as that which is visible. The world of the imagination then becomes a more complete, more totalized reality than that of everyday experience, a three-dimensional reality that would add a factor of depth to the flat surface with which we are usually confronted. Art would be the expression of a completed reality, a kind of over-perception which, as in the famous Rilke poem on the "Archaic Torso of Apollo" would allow us to see things in their completeness and so "change our lives."

The reference to Merleau-Ponty reveals that Doubrovsky has chosen perception as a model for his description of the literary act. And what characterizes perception for Merleau-Ponty is that the intent and the content of the act can be co-extensive.[15] Not only does Doubrovsky accept this essentially positive concept of perception with much less dialectical anxiety than his master, but he extends it at once to include all facets of our relationships toward the world. From being a model for the act of literary invention, perception is extended to coincide in its structure with the entirety of the existential project. It makes our entire existence benefit from the plenitude of an original act, the cogito "I perceive, therefore, I am" experienced as an unquestionable assertion of being. Consequently, the real and the imaginary, the life and the work, history and transcendence, literature and criticism, are all harmoniously integrated in an infinite extension of the perfect unity that stands at the beginning of things.

In so doing, Doubrovsky pushes Merleau-Ponty's thought far beyond its prudent limits. The author of *The Phenomenology of Perception* had sketched the outline of a theory of plastic form in the late essay, *Eye and Mind,* but he refrained from extending his theory to include literary language. It would have been difficult for him to do so, for literature bears little resemblance to perception, and less still to this over-perception of which Doubrovsky is dreaming. It does not fulfill a plenitude but originates in the void that separates intent from reality. The imagination takes its flight only after the void, the inauthenticity of the existential

15. Maurice Merleau-Ponty, *Phénoménologie de la perception* (Paris, 1952), III, Chapter I, "Le cogito."

project has been revealed; literature begins where the existential demystification ends and the critic has no need to linger over this preliminary stage. Considerations of the actual and historical existence of writers are a waste of time from a critical viewpoint. These regressive stages can only reveal an emptiness of which the writer himself is well aware when he begins to write. Many great writers have described the loss of reality that marks the beginning of poetic states of mind, as when, in a famous poem by Baudelaire,

> . . . palais neufs, échafaudages, blocs,
> Vieux faubourgs, tout pour moi devient allégorie. . . .

This "allegorical" dimension, which appears in the work of all genuine writers and constitutes the real depth of literary insight could never be reached by a method like that of Serge Doubrovsky, for it originates on the far side of the existential project. The critic who has written some of the most perceptive pages on Baudelaire, the German essayist Walter Benjamin, knew this very well when he defined allegory as a void "that signifies precisely the non-being of what it represents." We are far removed from the plenitude of perception that Doubrovsky attributes to Merleau-Ponty. But we are much closer to the process of negative totalization that American criticism discovered when it penetrated more or less unwittingly into the temporal labyrinth of interpretation.

III

Ludwig Binswanger and the Sublimation of the Self

The methodological questions that are being debated in some sectors of modern German criticism are often centered on the same problems as in France or in America, although the terminology and the historical background are different enough to make direct contact very difficult. It would be impossible moreover to sketch a clear and concise summary that would do justice to the complexity of the various critical trends that have emerged in the German academic and literary world of the last decades. These trends are less centralized than in France, and their diversity reflects a set of historical and sociological conditions that requires detailed analysis. We prefer to use one specific writer as an example of the problem that concerns us: the relationship, in the critical act, between the consciousness of the author and that of the interpreter. This will also allow us to introduce the name of Ludwig Binswanger—a figure well known in the world of psychiatry and of existential philosophy, but whose contribution to literary theory has received too little attention. The work of this Swiss psychiatrist has several ramifications of interest to contemporary criticism. We are referring in particular to an essay entitled *Hendrik Ibsen und das Problem der Selbstrealisation in der Kunst,* which appeared in 1949 and which we are using, in this essay, as our basic text.

We can take for our point of departure a remark of the French philosopher Michel Foucault in a recent and ambitious book entitled *Les Mots et les choses.* Foucault speaks of the changes that introduce radical discontinuities in the history of consciousness, such as the articulation he sees appear at the end of the eighteenth century when the idea of consciousness as representation begins to be challenged. Reflecting on the nature of the event and on the law that governs such mutations, he writes:

> For a study of the origins and the history of knowledge (une archéologie du savoir) that wants to proceed by rigorous analysis, this deep breach in the existing continuities could not be "explained" or even designated in the vocabulary of a single intellectual discipline. It is a radical event that spreads over the entire visible surface of our knowledge and of which the symptoms, the shocks and the consequences can be traced in great detail. Only thought understanding itself at the root of its own history could safely establish what the singular truth of this event may have been. But an "archaeology" of knowledge must be satisfied with describing the observable manifestations of the event. . . . (L'archéologie doit parcourir l'évènement selon sa disposition manifeste.)[1]

Two possible attitudes are being suggested here in dealing with the problem of the constitutive power of consciousness—for this is indeed what we are dealing with in speaking of consciousness as having a history, as being capable of changing its own mode of action. Advocated by Foucault, the first will describe the outward signs of the transformations when they occur within manifest forms of existence; hence Foucault's orientation toward disciplines such as economics, politics, sociology, or, in general, any structure that operates on the level of the empirical and the concrete. The other attitude would be precisely that of "thought understanding itself at the root of its own history." It seems that, for Foucault

1. Michel Foucault, *Les Mots et les choses* (Paris, 1966), p. 230.

this second road is no longer accessible and that the past can only be studied as a network of surface-structures, without any attempt to understand the movements of consciousness from the inside in an act of self-reflection. What Foucault calls an *archaeology* of ideas (in deliberate contrast to a *history* of ideas) takes for its object the ruins of the edifice erected in the course of the nineteenth century by the humanistic philosophical anthropology on which our historical and interpretative methods are founded.

Certain aspects of contemporary German thought may appear closely related to such an attitude, especially in its attempt to move beyond the classical "science of man" derived from Kant. This certainly was the case with Nietzsche; closer to our own time and to our concern with literary problems, it is also the case with the criticism that Heidegger and others have addressed to the anthropological historicism of Dilthey, whose influence on German literary studies still persists today. But the similarity stops there, for phenomenological and Heideggerian trends, especially in their application to literature, lead into altogether different directions than Foucault's archaeology of intellectual structures. They tend instead toward a deepening investigation of the question of the self which remains the starting-point of the attempt at a philosophical understanding of existence. But this does not mean that these trends persist in taking a preconceived notion of "man" for granted. Heidegger especially, ever since *Sein und Zeit,* has consistently denied that his undertaking leads toward a philosophical anthropology in the Kantian sense of the term. His purpose is directed toward a fundamental ontology, not toward a science of empirical man. The question of the self is not asked in terms of a more or less elaborated conception of consciousness, whether this conception be empirical, psychological, or even, as for Dilthey, historical. It is asked only in terms of its relationship to the constitutive categories of being. This reductive rigor, which wants to see the self only as it stands out against the background of more fundamental categories, requires a difficult and constant effort of interpretative vigilance. We fall prey to an almost irresistible tendency to relapse unwittingly into the concerns of the self as they exist in the empirical world. Binswanger's own work, despite the strong influence of Heidegger, provides a good instance of pre-

cisely this kind of relapse. Part of its interest stems from the insight
it gives into the very process of falling-back. It is often in connection with literature, where the problem of the self is particularly delicate, that this onto-ontological confusion occurs in the
most revealing manner. However, such confusions are in the long
run more instructive than the peremptory dismissal of the question of the subject on historical grounds, leading to the *a priori*
rejection of all attempts to elaborate a phenomenology of consciousness as a constitutive act.

In the study of literature, the question of the self appears in a
bewildering network of often contradictory relationships among
a plurality of subjects. It appears first of all, as in the Third
Critique of Kant, in the act of judgment that takes place in the
mind of the reader; it appears next in the apparently intersubjective relationships that are established between the author and the
reader; it governs the intentional relationship that exists, within
the work, between the constitutive subject and the constituted
language; it can be sought, finally, in the relationship that the subject establishes, through the mediation of the work, with itself.
From the start, we have at least four possible and distinct types of
self: the self that judges, the self that reads, the self that writes,
and the self that reads itself. The question of finding the common
level on which all these selves meet and thus of establishing the
unity of a literary consciousness stands at the beginning of the
main methodological difficulties that plague literary studies.

The title of the essay by Ludwig Binswanger that we have
chosen for our text clearly indicates that we are dealing with the
fourth type of self, that of the author as he is changed and interpreted by his own work. The essay is entitled, "Hendrik Ibsen and
the Problem of the Development of the Self *in art*" (Das Problem
der Selbstrealisation *in der Kunst*). The self under development
is that of Ibsen as it was shaped by his deliberate choice to carry
out the work to its final end. For that purpose, Ibsen had to relinquish the self that he had inherited, so to speak, at birth; he had
to leave behind the set of particular circumstances that defined his
initial situation in the world: family, place of birth, psychological
and sociological conditions, all had to fade before the project of a
future literary work. The original Ibsen had to undergo a funda-

mental change in order to grow and to find his genuine dimension. For Binswanger the literary enterprise can nowhere be distinguished from the project of self-realization. Both are so intimately bound up with each other that the critic can move back and forth between the realm of the self and that of the work without any apparent tension. The expansion of the self seems to occur in and probably by means of the work. The authenticating function of the work that "elevates" the writer above his original identity is so fundamentally implicit in Binswanger's thought that he takes it entirely for granted, without feeling called upon to state it as a distinctive theme or thesis.

He would hold little interest for us if this positive conception of the relationship between the work and the author were entirely unproblematic, the mere strength of an example that, simply by being stated, could at once become effective. The poetic happiness that Binswanger considers to be the fulfillment of the self in art is for him (as for Bachelard with whom he has much in common), the most fragile form of happiness imaginable. For we were certainly misrepresenting his thought when we referred, a while ago, to this self-realization as an *expansion*. The sacrifices and renunciations that are demanded from the writer are not to be understood as a kind of bargain in which false values are being traded for safe ones. To the contrary, in the process the self is stripped of eminently concrete and legitimate attributes and is exposed at once to much more insidious forms of inauthenticity. Instead of speaking of *expansion* or fulfillment, Binswanger forces us to consider first of all the contraction, the reduction, that takes place in the subject as it engages in literary activity.

This reduction is paradoxical, for if we consider the question no longer from the point of view of the writer, but from that of the work he produces, we find nothing that resembles a reduction. The world created by the author and which can be called a "form" possesses attributes of fullness and totality. "Artistic productivity," writes Binswanger, "is the highest form of human productivity . . . because the form itself and only the form makes up the content of the productive action. The form constitutes the entity in its totality (die ganze Seinsphäre) and, as a result, it totally fulfills the modality of the aesthetic intention." "The work of art represents the total revelation of all entities in an artistic form that is necessarily liberating." [2]

In this context, the term "form" is not to be understood in a narrowly aesthetic sense, but as a project of fundamental totalization; in all these passages, the emphasis falls on the complete, fulfilled aspect of the work. But this totality of the form by no means implies a corresponding totality of the constitutive self. Neither in its origin, nor in its later development does the completeness of the form proceed from a fulfillment of the person who constitutes this form. The distinction between the personal self of the author and the self that reaches a measure of totality in the work becomes concretely manifest in these divergent destinies. The divergence is not a contingent accident but is constitutive of the work of art as such. Art originates in and by means of this divergence.

Binswanger finds a theoretical justification for the paradox that the plenitude of the work stems from a reduction of the self in an important, but perhaps not sufficiently known, article by Georg Lukács that dates back to 1917. The essay appeared in the journal *Logos* and is entitled "The Subject-Object Relationship in Aesthetics." Written in terminology that is primarily neo-Kantian and influenced by Rickert (the same Rickert who was one of Heidegger's teachers), the essay sets out to characterize the distinctive qualities of the aesthetic activity by distinguishing it from the structure of the logical and the ethical activities of the mind; the division corresponds to that of the three Kantian critiques. Without entering into the details of the analysis, we can limit ourselves to Lukács's conclusions about the relationship between the structure of the work and the subjectivity of the author. The structure is summarized in the description of the work as a "windowless monad" (eine fensterlose Monade), a concept that unites a notion of isolation with a notion of totality. On the one hand, the work is an entity that exists for and by itself, without any inherent possibility of entering into a relationship with other entities, even when these other entities are themselves aesthetic in kind. On the other hand, it is a cosmos; that is to say, perfectly self-sufficient within this isolation, since it can find within its own confines all

2. Ludwig Binswanger, *Hendrik Ibsen und das Problem der Selbstrealisation in der Kunst* (Heidelberg, 1949), pp. 21–22.

it needs for its existence and is in no way dependent on anything
that would exist outside its boundaries. These boundaries, says
Lukács, "are genuinely immanent, the kind of boundaries that
only a cosmos can possess." [3] Even more important than the
monadic structure of the work is the reason for its apparent immanence. It is not due to the objective nature of the aesthetic
entity but, on the contrary, to the subjective intent that stands at
the onset of its elaboration. The transcendental principle that determines the specificity of the work of art resides in the intent of
the constitutive self to reduce itself to its own immanence, to eliminate everything that is not accessible to the immediate experience
(Erlebbarkeit) of the self as self. The generality of the work of art
is not a generality based on an act of reason—as in the case of a
logical judgment—but based on the decision of a consciousness
to clear itself of whatever, in consciousness, is not entirely immanent to it. "Contrary to the theoretical subject of logic," writes
Lukács, "and contrary to the hypothetical subject of ethics, the
stylized subject of aesthetics is a living unity that contains within
itself the fullness of experience that makes up the totality of the
human species." [4] But the only way in which this subject can
succeed in remaining fully and exclusively consistent in its subjective nature is by concentrating on the elaboration of a fictional
entity, by projecting itself into a form which although appearing
to be autonomous and complete is actually determined by the subject itself. This fulfillment of the form clearly does not correspond
to what one would consider, on the ethical or the practical level,
as the harmonious development of a personality, the well-balanced
development of faculties. Such a development would necessarily
have to include objective factors of a physical, biological, social,
and intersubjective nature that play no part in the autonomous
world of aesthetics. The totalization is not a totalization in width
but in depth, by means of which the subject resists any temptation
of being distracted from its own self. Whereas the empirical self
strives to take in as much as it can encompass and opens itself up
to the presence of the world, the aesthetic self strives for a mode of

3. Georg Lukács, "Die Subjekt-Objekt Beziehung in der Ästhetik," *Logos*
1917–18, p. 19.
4. *Ibid.* p. 19.

totalization that is reductive but, in Lukács's term, "homogeneous" with its original intent at self-immanence.

For theoretical reasons, Lukács is led to consider what the monadic structure of the work implies for the self of the artist who produced it. His purpose in asking this question is not psychological, but appears in a discussion of the plurality inherent in any attempt to define the aesthetic entity. The work changes entirely with the point of view from which it is being examined, depending on whether one considers it as a finished form (*forma formata*) or, with the artist, as a form in the process of coming into being (*forma formans*). The problematic relationship between subject and object that prevails in the sphere of aesthetics is better understood when one considers it from the point of view of the author rather than from the point of view of the reader (or beholder). For the author is directly engaged in the ambiguities of aesthetic invention. As a free agent, his natural tendency would be to expand and to satisfy himself in the world-at-large, but he is constantly frustrated and curtailed by the restrictions that the form imposes upon him. Hence, in Lukács's words, "his isolation from all kinds and types of objective entities, from all forms . . . of human and collective relationships, as well as his isolation, as a subject, from all experiences not intended exclusively as the accomplishment of the work . . . his isolation, in short, from the entirety of his own personality." But, on the other hand, the artist knows that it is only by achieving the form that he can discover the objective correlative of the need for pure subjectivity that he carries within himself. Only in this way "can he reach the true and authentic subject-object relationship"—true and authentic as compared with the contrived relationship that exists in the field of logic or of ethics. He is therefore caught within a dilemma from which he can only escape by means of a Kierkegaardian leap: the work must become a project aimed toward an unreachable goal, and its partial success takes on the form of "a renunciation at the very moment when it comes into being." The work is a hyperbole in the Mallarméan sense, demanding that the subject forget itself in a projective act that can never coincide with its own desire. Expressing in a philosophical language a relationship between artist and work that resembles statements of Maurice Blanchot,

Lukács writes: "As the fulfillment of an artistic activity, the work is fully transcendental in relation to the constitutive subject. But the fact that it is . . . more than an object, although it is the only adequate objective expression of a subjectivity, is reflected in the infinite process of artistic activity and in the leap in which this activity culminates." [5]

This "solitary leap" of the poet—Mallarmé speaks, in a different but revealing context of death as a "solitaire bond"—reappears in the work of Binswanger in a more openly psychological form. Between Lukács's and Binswanger's text, however, intervenes a study by the phenomenologist Oskar Becker published in 1929 under the elaborate title: "Of the Fragility of the Beautiful and the Adventurous Nature of the Artist" ("Von der Hinfälligkeit des Schönen [the expression stems from Friedrich Solger's philosophical dialogue *Erwin*] und der Abenteuerlichkeit des Künstlers"). [6] In the time interval between the Lukács and the Becker essay, the publication of Heidegger's *Sein und Zeit* had taken place and Becker indeed interprets Lukács's conclusions in Heideggerian terms. The new self that results from Lukács's "homogeneous reduction" is now understood as a self capable of revealing the truth of its own destiny and of interpreting correctly its own mode of being. From the point of view of this "authentic" self, the distinction between author and reader—a distinction that was still momentarily maintained by Lukács—disappears. On the ontological level, reader and author are engaged in the same fundamental project and share an identical intent. The authentic reader —or critic—as well as the author now participate in the same perilous enterprise. This peril is described by Becker in terms of a new experience of temporality, as an attempt to exist in a time that would no longer be the fallen temporality of everyday existence. The artist projects himself into the future of his work as if it were possible to maintain an authentic temporality, but at the same time he knows this to be impossible, a pure *gageure*. He acts like an adventurer in entering upon a domain that he knows to lie beyond his reach. Becker characterizes the ambivalent status

5. *Ibid.* p. 35.
6. Oskar Becker, "Von der Hinfälligkeit des Schönen und der Abenteuerlichkeit des Künstlers" in *Festschrift für Edmund Husserl zum 70. Geburtstag* (1929).

of the aesthetic consciousness by the manner in which it fluctuates between two experiences of time: the temporality of everyday
existence, that always falls back into estrangement and falsification,
and another temporality that would remain clearly aware of its
true mode of being. Becker's term for this mixed temporality is
Getragenheit, "being carried." The artist is suspended as in the
"rhythmique suspens du sinistre" that Mallarmé evokes by a succession of "suspended" sentences in *Un Coup de Dés,* carried aloft
in the ambiguous time-structure of the monadic work.

Binswanger's own contribution consists in an interpretation of
the "suspended" state of the artistic consciousness. He understands
the urge to leap out of historical and everyday time first in negative
terms, as it appears in the mood of harassment and oppression that
torments a self imprisoned within its own facticity. A 1943 article
has for its theme a quotation from Hugo von Hofmannsthal:
"Was Geist ist, erfaszt nur der Bedrängte."[7] The term "der Bedrängte" is difficult to translate. It combines an idea of being locked
up in too narrow a space, with the temporal ordeal of being steadily urged on, of being unable to remain at rest. One thinks of
Pascal, of course, but also of man in Baudelaire, driven and
harassed, "imitant la toupie et la boule":

> Singulière fortune où le but se déplace,
> Et, n'étant nulle part, peut être n'importe où!
> Où l'homme, dont jamais l'espérance n'est lasse
> Pour trouver le repos court toujours comme un fou!

Only the man who knows this feeling of harassed confinement,
says Hofmansthal, can find access to the spirit, can aspire to the
kind of tranquillity that exists nowhere but in the realm of the
mind. Caught in this predicament, his first reaction will be the
Baudelairian voyage into space, what Binswanger calls the "march
into the distance," a search for new experiences to which one can
find access without having to leave the horizontal expanse of the
world. However, since the confinement is due not only to a lack
of space, but is primarily caused by the excessive presence of time,
these movements of horizontal expansion can never free the artist

7. Now in Ludwig Binswanger, *Ausgewählte Vorträge und Aufsätze,* Band II
(Bern, 1955), pp. 243–52.

from his initial predicament. The failure of his quest for expansion
—which is indeed the theme of the Baudelaire poem "Le Voyage,"
as it is the theme of several essays by Binswanger—becomes clearly
apparent when it turns out that these horizontal displacements
are, in fact, devoid of danger. It is possible to lose one's way in the
distance, to be waylaid in the world of action to the point of
criminal transgression, but the kind of peril associated with the
fragility of the artist's mind can only occur when the *level* of existence undergoes a radical change. The transformation that allows
the artist to move from self-expansion and self-development to the
conquest of an altogether different kind of self is described by
Binswanger in terms of the metaphor of climbing and descending.
The phenomenology of distances, which befits the behavior of
the man of action, is replaced by a phenomenology of heights and
depths; the horizontal landscape of plain and sea becomes the
vertical landscape of the mountains.

The fragility of poetic transcendence, as compared with the relative safety of direct action, is represented by the anxieties associated with the feelings of height. The comings and goings of the
wanderer or the seafarer are voluntary and controlled actions but
the possibility of falling, which is forced upon the mountain
climber by an outside force, exists only in vertical space. The same
is true of experiences that are closely related to falling, such as
dizziness or relapses. This is another way of saying that, in the
experience of verticality, death is present in a more radical way
than in the experiences of the active life.

To the eventuality of the fall corresponds the possibility of an
equally involuntary ascent. It would seem at first sight that the
fall can only be oriented downwards, but Binswanger derives from
his own dream-theories the imaginative possibility of what could
be called an upward fall, and he finds a confirmation of his insight
in Gaston Bachelard's book *L'Air et les songes*. Bachelard and
Binswanger are referring to the feeling of being "carried away" by
an act of pure imagination, a feeling of levitation that is familiar
to readers of Keats and Wordsworth, for example. Poetic transcendence is closely akin to this act of spontaneous ascent, which
resembles an act of grace although it is only the manifestation of a
desire. As a result the subsequent "let-down," the possibility of

falling and of despondency that follows such moments of flight, is much more tragic and definitive than the mere fatigue of someone who climbs down, by his own devices, into the lower world of everyday cares.

There is still another danger that threatens the man willing to let himself be carried into the heights by the power of his own imagination: the danger of ascending beyond his own limits into a place from which he can no longer descend. Binswanger calls this condition a state of *Verstiegenheit,* a term that can be used in reference to a mountain-climber as well as to a symptom of mental pathology. The term plays an important part in Binswanger's psychiatric observations among the different types of false consciousness likely to lead to neuroses of the self. The man who, by his own vision, climbed above the limits of his own self and who is unable to return to earth without the assistance of others may well end up falling to his own destruction. According to Binswanger, artists are particularly susceptible to *Verstiegenheit* which, rather than hysteria or melancholy, appears as the pathological aspect of the poetic personality.

In trying to follow Binswanger's thought, we have been forced to introduce a terminology that derives from experimental psychology. Starting out from an ontological problem (the experience of the spatial structures of being) we have returned to problems of personality; in the last analysis Binswanger's concern seems to be aimed at the problems of the poetic personality rather than at the impersonal truth of the works. The reductive study of the self has led to the description of a specific type of false consciousness that is associated with the poetic temper; as a psychiatrist, Binswanger may feel called upon to reveal or even to cure this potential neurosis. This is not the intent of his more theoretical writings, however; for there can be no doubt that he consistently asserts the priority of literary over psychological concerns. Nevertheless, the organization of his essay on Ibsen suggests that, for him, the thematic content of a work of art must reveal the state of false consciousness to which the author has been brought by the very act of inventing the work. As a result, he chooses as an object for his inquiry a dramatist rather than a poet because the dramatist, Ibsen, has to stage more or less objectified states of false consciousness in

conflict with each other, thus showing that he is able to understand and eventually to overcome these conflicts. And this is why,
of all the plays by Ibsen, Binswanger prefers *The Master Builder,*
which is precisely the story of a man who destroys himself because he has, in a very literal way, built too tall a house on too
shallow a foundation. The play is the perfect symbolical representation of *Verstiegenheit.* It therefore represents, for Binswanger,
the clearest illustration of the self-mystification to which all artists,
as artists, are bound to fall prey. This suffices for him to consider
it Ibsen's masterpiece. He does not imply that Ibsen would have
represented himself in the play in order to take shelter from
dangers that threatened him while he was writing it. Binswanger
is well aware of the mediations that separate the person from the
work, and he never confuses poetic invention with therapy. But he
sees the writer as necessarily reflecting the psychological dangers
and satisfactions open to the transcendental self that is constituted
both by and in the work of art.

This conclusion calls for some comment. It seems true enough
that the destiny of a poetic consciousness is irrevocably bound up
with the ontological "fall" that plays such a prominent part in
Binswanger's thought and images. One could go so far as to say
that the kind of knowledge contained in art is specifically the
knowledge of this fall, the transformation of the experience of falling into an act of knowledge. A certain degree of confusion arises
when this knowledge is interpreted as a *means* to act upon the
destiny that the knowledge reveals. This is the very moment at
which the ontological inquiry is abandoned for empirical concerns that are bound to lead it astray. Binswanger's depth is best
in evidence when he speaks of the initial anxiety of the poet as a
harassed confinement, revealing his awareness of existence as a
temporal predicament. Even as his description of the "fall," captive of the pseudo-analogy implicit in his favorite spatial metaphor,
gives a deceptive impression of concreteness, it remains less substantial than in his predecessors: Lukács, Heidegger, and Becker.
The upward fall is a highly suggestive way of designating the
ambivalence that makes artistic invention into a paradoxical combination of free will and grace: he sees the imagination as an act
of the individual will that remains determined, in its deepest in-

tent, by a transcendental moment that lies beyond our own vo-
lition; in this, he stays within the main tradition of the leading
theories of the imagination. But he fails to pursue the philosophical consequences of his insight and falls back upon a normative
precept favoring a harmonious relationship between extension and
depth as a necessary condition for a well-balanced personality. In
the last analysis, as a good psychiatrist, what interests Binswanger
most is the achievement of balance, not the truth of the fall.

Before we construe this as a criticism, we should remember how
difficult it is to remain rigorously confined to the disinterestedness
of non-empirical thought. Michel Foucault shows his awareness of
this difficulty when he criticizes phenomenology in the following
terms:

> Phenomenology, although it originated first of all in a climate
> of anti-psychologism . . . has never been able to free itself
> entirely from this insidious parenthood, from its tempting and
> threatening proximity to the empirical study of man. There-
> fore, although it starts out as a reduction to the *cogito*, it has
> always been led to ask questions, to ask the ontological ques-
> tion. We can see the phenomenological project dissolve under
> our very eyes into a description of actual experience that is
> empirical in spite of itself, and into an ontology of what lies
> beyond thought and thus bypasses the assumed primacy of
> the *cogito*.[8]

This could very well have been written with Binswanger in mind,
but it does not apply to either Husserl or Heidegger, both of whom
include this very danger among the constituents of their philosophical insight. Foucault himself owes his awareness of the problem to his grounding in phenomenology.

Some of the difficulties of contemporary criticism can be traced
back to a tendency to forsake the barren world of ontological reduction for the wealth of lived experience. Because it implies a
forgetting of the personal self for a transcendental type of self
that speaks in the work, the act of criticism can acquire exemplary
value. Although it is an asceticism of the mind rather than a
plenitude or a harmony, it is an asceticism that can lead to onto-

8. Michel Foucault, *op. cit.* p. 337.

logical insight. Contrary to Foucault's assertion, such an ontology can only bypass the primacy of the cogito if the "I" in the "I think" is conceived in too narrow a way. Literary criticism, in our century, has contributed to establishing this crucial distinction between an empirical and an ontological self; in that respect, it participates in some of the most audacious and advanced forms of contemporary thought.

IV

Georg Lukács's *Theory of the Novel*

The rather belated discovery of the work of Georg Lukács in the West and, most recently, in this country, has tended to solidify the notion of a very deep split between the early, non-Marxist and the later Marxist Lukács. It is certainly true that a sharp distinction in tone and purpose sets off such early essays as *Die Seele und die Formen* (1911) and *Die Theorie des Romans* (1914–15) from recently translated essays on literary subjects such as the *Studies in European Realism* (1953) or the political pamphlet *Wieder den mißverstandenen Realismus* (1957) published here under the title *Realism*. But the distinction can be overstated and misunderstood. It would be unsound, for instance, to hold on to the reassuring assumption that all the evil in the later Lukács came in as a result of his Marxist conversion; a considerable degree of continuity exists between a pre-Marxist work such as *Die Theorie des Romans* and the Marxist *Geschichte und Klassenbewußtsein*; it would be impossible for an admirer of the former to dismiss the latter entirely. There is a similar danger in an oversimplified view of a *good* early and a *bad* late Lukács. The works on realism have been treated very harshly on their American publication by such diverse critics as Harold Rosenberg (in *Dissent*) and Peter Demetz (in the *Yale Review*); on the other hand, *The Theory of the Novel* is being called by Harry Levin (*JHI*, January–March 1965, p. 150) "possibly the most penetrating essay that ever addressed itself to the elusive subject of the novel." If the blanket condemnation of the books on realism is clearly unjustified, especially if one bears in mind the considerable amount of debatable but interesting theoretical justification offered in Lukács's late *Ästhetik* (1963), the almost unqualified endorsement of *The Theory of the Novel* seems equally unwarranted. Whatever one may think of Lukács, he is certainly an important enough mind to be studied as a whole, and the critical interpretation of his thought has not been helped by the oversimplified division that has been established. The weaknesses of the later work are already present from the beginning, and some of the early strength remains operative throughout. Both weakness and strength, however, exist on a meaningful philosophical level and can only be understood in the larger perspective of nineteenth and twentieth-century intellectual history: they are part of the heritage of romantic and idealist thought. This stresses again the historical importance of Georg Lukács and rejects the frequent reproach made against him that he remains overconcerned with nineteenth-century modes of thought (a reproach that appears in both the Demetz and the Rosenberg reviews). Such criticism is inspired by an ill-conceived modernism or is made for propagandistic reasons.

I do not intend to address myself to the complex task of defining the unifying elements in Lukács's thought. By a brief critical examination of *The Theory of the Novel*, I hope to make some preliminary distinctions between what seems to remain valid and what has become problematic in this very concentrated and difficult essay. Written in a language that uses a pre-Hegelian terminology but a post-Nietzschean rhetoric, with a deliberate tendency to substitute general and abstract systems for concrete examples, *The Theory of the Novel* is by no means easy reading. One is particularly put off by the strange point of view that prevails throughout the essay: the book is written from the point of view of a mind that claims to have reached such an advanced degree of

generality that it can speak, as it were, for the novelistic consciousness itself; it is the Novel itself that tells us the history of its own
development, very much as, in Hegel's *Phenomenology*, it is the
Spirit who narrates its own voyage. With this crucial difference,
however, that since Hegel's Spirit has reached a full understanding
of its own being, it can claim unchallengeable authority, a point
which Lukács's novelistic consciousness, by its own avowal, is
never allowed to reach. Being caught in its own contingency, and
being indeed an expression of this contingency, it remains a mere
phenomenon without regulative power; one would be led to expect
a reductive, tentative and cautiously phenomenological approach
rather than a sweeping history asserting its own laws. By translating the work in a less exalted language, one loses its moving and
impressive philosophical pathos, but some of the preconceptions
become more apparent.

Compared to a formalistic work such as, for instance, Wayne
Booth's *Rhetoric of Fiction,* or to a work grounded in a more traditional view of history such as Auerbach's *Mimesis, The Theory
of the Novel* makes much more radical claims. The emergence of
the novel as the major modern genre is seen as the result of a
change in the structure of human consciousness; the development
of the novel reflects modifications in man's way of defining himself
in relation to all categories of existence. Lukács is not offering us,
in this essay, a sociological theory that would explore relationships
between the structure and development of the novel and those of
society, nor is he proposing a psychological theory explaining the
novel in terms of human relationships. Least of all do we find
him conferring an autonomy on formal categories that would give
them a life of their own, independently of the more general intent
that produces them. He goes instead to the most general possible
level of experience, a level on which the use of terms such as Destiny, the Gods, Being, etc. seems altogether natural. The vocabulary and the historical scheme is that of later eighteenth-century
aesthetic speculation; one is indeed constantly reminded of Schiller's philosophical writings on reading Lukács's formulation of the
distinctions between the main literary genres.

The distinction between the epic and the novel is founded on a
distinction between the Hellenic and the Western mind. As in

Schiller, this distinction is stated in terms of the category of alienation, seen as an intrinsic characteristic of the reflective consciousness. Lukács's description of alienation is eloquent, but not strikingly original; the same could be said of his corresponding description at the beginning of the essay of a harmonious unity in the
ideal Greece. The original unified nature that surrounds us in
"the blessed times . . . when the fire that burns in our souls is
of the same substance as the fire of the stars" [1] has now been split
in fragments that are "nothing but the historical form of the alienation (Entfremdung) between man and his works (seine Gebil-
den)." And the following text could take its place among the great
elegiac quotations of the early nineteenth century: "The epic individual, the hero of the novel, originates in the alienation from
the outside world. As long as the world is inwardly one, no real
qualitative distinctions occur among its inhabitants; they may well
be heroes and scoundrels, worthy men and criminals, but the greatest hero only rises by a head's length above his fellow-men, and
the noble words of the wise can be understood even by the fools.
The autonomy of inwardness becomes possible and necessary only
when the differences between men have grown to be an unbreachable gap; when the gods have grown silent and no sacrifice or prayer
is capable of loosening their tongues; when the world of action
loses contact with that of the self, leaving man empty and powerless, unable to grasp the real meaning of his deeds . . . : when
inwardness and adventure are forever distinct." We are much
closer here to Schiller than to Marx.

A definitely post-Hegelian element is introduced with Lukács's
insistence on the need for totality as the inner necessity that shapes
all works of art. The unity of the Hellenic experience of the world
has a formal correlative in the creation of closed, *total* forms, and
this desire for totality is an inherent need of the human mind. It
persists in modern, alienated man, but instead of fulfilling itself in
the mere expression of his given unity with the world, it becomes
instead the statement of an intent to retrieve the unity it no
longer possesses. Clearly, Lukács's idealized fiction of Greece is a
device to state a theory of consciousness that has the structure of

1. All quotations from *Die Theorie des Romans*, Zweite Auflage, Berlin, 1963.
The first edition is from 1920.

an intentional movement. This implies, in turn, a presupposition about the nature of historical time, to which we will have to return later.

Lukács's theory of the novel emerges in a cogent and coherent way out of the dialectic between the urge for totality and man's alienated situation. The novel becomes "the epic of a world from which God has departed" (p. 87). As a result of the separation between our actual experience and our desire, any attempt at a total understanding of our being will stand in contrast to actual experience, which is bound to remain fragmentary, particular and unfulfilled. This separation between life (Leben) and being (Wesen) is reflected historically in the decline of the drama and the parallel rise of the novel. For Lukács, the drama is the medium in which, as in Greek tragedy, the most universal predicament of man is to be represented. At a moment in history in which such universality is absent from all actual experiences, the drama has to separate itself entirely from life, to become ideal and otherworldly; the German classical theater after Lessing serves Lukács as an example for this retreat. The novel, to the contrary, wishing to avoid this most destructive type of fragmentation remains rooted instead in the particularlity of experience; as an epical genre, it can never give up its contact with empirical reality, which is an inherent part of its own form. But, in a time of alienation, it is forced to represent this reality as imperfect, as steadily striving to move beyond the boundaries that restrict it, as constantly experiencing and resenting the inadequacy of its own size and shape. "In the novel, what is constituted is not the totality of life but rather the relationship, the valid or mistaken position of the writer who enters the scene as an empirical subject in his full stature, but also in his full limitation as a mere creature, towards this totality." The theme of the novel is thus necessarily limited to the individual, and to this individual's frustrating experience of his own inability to acquire universal dimensions. The novel originates in the Quixotic tension between the world of romance and that of reality. The roots of Lukács's later dogmatic commitment to realism are certainly to be found in this aspect of his theory. However, at the time of *The Theory of the Novel*, the insistence on the necessary presence of an empirical element in the novel is altogether convincing, all the more so since it is counterbalanced by the attempt to overcome the limitations of reality.

This thematic duality, the tension between an earth-bound destiny and a consciousness that tries to transcend this condition, leads to structural discontinuities in the form of the novel. Totality strives for a continuity that can be compared with the unity of an organic entity, but the estranged reality intrudes upon this continuity and disrupts it. Next to a "homogeneous and organic stability" the novel also displays a "heterogeneous and contingent discontinuity" (p. 74). This discontinuity is defined by Lukács as irony. The ironic structure acts disruptively, yet it reveals the truth of the paradoxical predicament that the novel represents. For this reason, Lukács can state that irony actually provides the means by which the novelist transcends, within the form of the work, the avowed contingency of his condition. "In the novel, irony is the freedom of the poet in relation to the divine . . . for it is by means of irony that, in an intuitively ambiguous vision, we can perceive divine presence in a world forsaken by the gods." This concept of irony as the positive power of an absence also stems directly from Lukács's idealist and romantic ancestors; it reveals the influence of Friedrich Schlegel, of Hegel and most of all of Hegel's contemporary Solger. Lukács's originality resides in his use of irony as a structural category.

For if irony is indeed the determining and organizing principle of the novel's form, then Lukács is indeed freeing himself from preconceived notions about the novel as an imitation of reality. Irony steadily undermines this claim at imitation and substitutes for it a conscious, interpreted awareness of the distance that separates an actual experience from the understanding of this experience. The ironic language of the novel mediates between experience and desire, and unites ideal and real within the complex paradox of the form. This form can have nothing in common with the homogeneous, organic form of nature: it is founded on an act of consciousness, not on the imitation of a natural object. In the novel ". . . the relationship of the parts to the whole, although it tries to come as close as possible to being an organic relationship, is in fact an ever-suspended *conceptual* relationship, not a truly organic one" (p. 74). Lukács comes very close, in statements of this kind, to reaching a point from which a genuine hermeneutic of the novel could start.

His own analysis, however, seems to move in a different direction; the second part of the essay contains a sharp critical rejection of the kind of inwardness that is associated with a hermeneutic theory of language. In the 1961 preface which Lukács added to the recent reissue of his essay, he scornfully refers to the phenomenological approach as a "right-wing epistemology," that runs counter to the left-wing ethics. This criticism was already implicit in the original text. When he comes closest to dealing with contemporary developments in the novel and with moments in which the novel itself seems to become conscious of its real intent, a revealing shift in the argument takes place. He shows us, convincingly enough, how inwardness for its own sake can lead to an evasion of the novel into a falsely Utopian realm "a Utopia which, from the start, has a bad conscience and a knowledge of its own defeat" (p. 119). The romantic novel of disillusion (Desillusionsromantik) is the example of this distortion of the genre, in which the novel loses contact with empirical reality; Lukács is thinking of Novalis, who was attacked in similar terms in an essay from the earlier book *Die Seele und die Formen,* but he also gives examples from Jacobsen's *Niels Lyhne* and Gontcharov's *Oblomov.* He fully realizes, however, that these examples do not account for other developments in European fiction in which the same theme of disillusion is obviously present and which he neither can nor wishes to dismiss. Flaubert's *Sentimental Education,* of course, is the most striking instance, a truly modern novel shaped by the overpowering negativity of an almost obsessive inwardness but which nevertheless, in Lukács's own judgment, represents the highest achievement of the genre in the nineteenth century. What is present in Flaubert's *Sentimental Education* that saves it from being condemned together with other post-romantic novels of inwardness?

At this moment in the argument, Lukács introduces an element that had not been explicitly mentioned up till now: temporality. In the 1961 Preface, he points with pride to the original use of the category of time, at a moment when Proust's novel was not yet known to the public. For the decadent and belated romantic, time is experienced as pure negativity; the inward action of the novel is a hopeless "battle against the erosive power of time." But in Flaubert, according to Lukács, this is precisely not the case. In spite of the hero's continuous defeats and disappointments, time triumphs as a positive principle in the *Sentimental Education,* because Flaubert succeeds in recapturing the irresistible feeling of flow that characterizes Bergsonian *durée.* "It is time which makes possible this victory. The uninterrupted and irrepressible flow of time is the unifying principle that gives homogeneity to the disjointed parts, by putting them in a relationship that, although irrational and ineffable, is nevertheless one of unity. Time gives order to the random agitation of men and confers upon it the appearance of organic growth . . ." (p. 128). On the level of true temporal experience, the ironic discontinuities vanish and the treatment of time itself, in Flaubert, is no longer ironic.

Can we admit Lukács's interpretation of the temporal structure of the *Sentimental Education?* When Proust, in a polemical exchange with Thibaudet, discussed Flaubert's style in terms of temporality, what he emphasized was not homogeneity but precisely the opposite: the manner in which Flaubert's use of tenses allowed him to create discontinuities, periods of dead and negative time alternating with moments of pure origination, complexities in memory structures comparable to those achieved by Gérard de Nerval in *Sylvie.* The single-directed flow of mere *durée* is replaced by a complex juxtaposition of reversible movements that reveal the discontinuous and polyrhythmic nature of temporality. But such a disclosure of non-linear temporality demands reductive moments of inwardness in which a consciousness confronts its own true self; and this moment is precisely the one at which the organic analogy between subject and object reveals itself as false.

It seems that the organicism which Lukács had eliminated from the novel when he made irony its guiding structural principle, has reentered the picture in the guise of time. Time in this essay acts as a substitute for the organic continuity which Lukács seems unable to do without. Such a linear conception of time had in fact been present throughout the essay. Hence the necessity of narrating the development of the novel as a continuous event, as the fallen form of the archetypal Greek epic which is treated as an ideal concept but given actual historical existence. The later development of Lukács's theories on the novel, the retreat from Flaubert back to Balzac, from Dostoevsky to a rather simplified view of Tolstoi, from a theory of art as interpretation to a theory of art as reflected imitation (Wiederspiegelung) should be traced back to the reified idea of temporality that is so clearly in evidence at the end of *Theory of the Novel*.

V

Impersonality in the Criticism of Maurice Blanchot

Since the end of the war, French literature has been dominated by a succession of quickly alternating intellectual fashions that have kept alive the illusion of a fecund and productive modernity. First came the vogue of Sartre, Camus, and the humanistic existentialism that followed immediately in the wake of the war, soon to be succeeded by the experimentalism of the new theater, bypassed in turn by the advent of the *nouveau roman* and its epigones. These movements are, to a large extent, superficial and ephemeral; the traces they will leave on the history of French literature is bound to be slighter than it appears within the necessarily limited perspective of our own contemporaneity. Not all the more significant literary figures necessarily remained aloof from these trends; several took part in them and were influenced by them. But the true quality of their literary vocation can be tested by the persistence with which they kept intact a more essential part of themselves, a part that remained untouched by the vicissitudes of a literary production oriented toward public recognition—arcane and esoteric as this "public" may have been.

For some, like Sartre, this self-assertion took the form of a frantic attempt to maintain a firm inner commitment in open and po-lemical contact with the changing trends. But others kept them-selves more consciously out of the reach of the surface-currents and were carried by a slower and deeper wave, closer to the con-tinuities that link French writing of today to its past. When we will be able to observe the period with more detachment, the main proponents of contemporary French literature may well turn out to be figures that now seem shadowy in comparison with the celebrities of the hour. And none is more likely to achieve future prominence than the little-publicized and difficult writer, Maurice Blanchot.

Even the fashionable trends to which we alluded are charac-terized by a constant intermingling of literary practice and critical theory. Sartre and his group were the theoretical exponents of their own stylistic devices, and the affinities between structuralist criticism and the *nouveau roman* are obvious. In Blanchot, the same interplay occurs, in a more complex and problematic way, between his work as a writer of narrative prose and his critical essays. An intensely private figure, who has kept his personal affairs strictly to himself and whose pronouncements on public issues, literary or political, have been very scarce, Blanchot is primarily known as a critic. A sizable group of readers have followed his essays, often appearing in the form of topical book-reviews in various journals none of which is particularly esoteric or avant-garde: *Journal des débats, Critique,* and more recently in *La Nouvelle revue française* to which Blanchot used to contribute a monthly article. These essays have been gathered in volumes (*Faux-pas,* 1943, *La Part du feu,* 1949, *L'Espace littéraire,* 1955, *Le Livre à venir,* 1959) that bring out Blanchot's almost ob-sessive preoccupation with a few fundamental concerns, thus reducing their apparent diversity to an implacably repetitive uniformity. The influence of the critical work has been far-reach ing. More philosophical and abstract than Charles du Bos and less conducive to practical application than Bachelard's theories of material imagery, Blanchot's criticism has remained aloof from recent methodological debates and polemics. Yet his already con siderable impact is bound to increase; rather than directly affecting existing critical methods, his work puts into question the very conditions prior to the elaboration of all critical discourse and in that way reaches a level of awareness no other contemporary critic has reached.

It is clear that Blanchot derives much of his insight into the work of others from his own experience as a writer of narrative prose.[1] Until now, his novels and *récits* have remained nearly inaccessible in their labyrinthine obscurity. All that has to be said about them, in an article dealing with the critical work, is that it is fortunately a great deal easier to gain access to the fiction of Blanchot through his criticism than the other way round. The crux of the interpretation of this writer, one of the most important of the century, lies no doubt in a clarification of the relationship between the critical and the narrative part of his work. A description of the movement of his critical mind is a valid preliminary to such an inquiry.

Reading Maurice Blanchot differs from all other reading experiences. One begins by being seduced by the limpidity of a language that allows for no discontinuities or inconsistencies. Blanchot is, in a way, the clearest, the most lucid of writers: he steadily borders on the inexpressible and approaches the extreme of ambiguity, but always recognizes them for what they are; consequently, as in Kant, the horizon of our understanding remains clearly circumscribed. When we read him on one of the poets or novelists he happens to choose for a theme, we readily forget all we assumed to know up till then about this writer. This does not happen because Blanchot's insight necessarily compels us to modify our own perspective; this is by no means always the case. Returning afterwards to the author in question, we will find ourselves back at the same point, our understanding barely enriched by the comments of the critic. Blanchot, in fact, never intended to perform a task of exegesis that would combine earlier acquired knowledge with new elucidations. The clarity of his

1. Some of these fictions are called novels, such as, among others, *Thomas l'obscur* (1941), *Aminadab* (1942), *Le Très-haut* (1948); while others are called *récits*: *Thomas l'obscur*, new version (1950), *Au Moment voulu* (1951), *Celui qui ne m'accompagnait pas* (1953).

critical writings is not due to exegetic power; they seem clear, not because they penetrate further into a dark and inaccessible domain but because they suspend the very act of comprehension. The light they cast on texts is of a different nature. Nothing, in fact, could be more obscure than the nature of this light.

For how are we to understand a reading-process which, in Blanchot's words, is located "au delà ou en deçà de la compréhension" before or beyond the act of understanding? (*L'Espace littéraire*, p. 205.) The difficulty of defining this conception indicates how much it differs from our ordinary assumptions about criticism. Blanchot's critical reflections offer us no personal confessions or intimate experiences, nothing that would give immediate access to another person's consciousness and allow the reader to espouse its movements. A certain degree of inwardness prevails in his work and makes it into the very opposite of an objective narrative. But this intimacy does not seem to belong to a particularized self, for his prose reveals nothing about his private experience. The language is as little a language of self-confession as it is a language of exegesis. And, even in the articles that are obviously inspired by topical literary considerations, it is least of all a language of evaluation or of opinion. In reading Blanchot, we are not participating in an act of judgment, of sympathy, or of understanding. As a result, the fascination we experience is accompanied by a feeling of resistance, by a refusal to be led to a confrontation with something opaque on which our consciousness can find no hold. The ambivalence of this experience can be somewhat clarified by Blanchot's own statements.

> The act of reading does not change anything, nor does it add anything to what was already there; it lets things be the way they were; it is a form of freedom, not the freedom that gives or takes away, but a freedom that accepts and consents, that says yes. It can only say yes, and, in the space opened up by this affirmation, it allows the work to assert itself as the unsettling decision of its will to be—and nothing more.[2]

At first sight this passive and silent encounter with the work seems to be the very opposite of what we usually call interpretation. It

2. *L'Espace littéraire* (Paris, 1955), p. 202.

differs entirely from the subject-object polarities involved in objective observation. The literary work is given no objective status whatever; it has no existence apart from that constituted by the inward act of reading. Neither are we dealing with a so-called intersubjective or interpersonal act, in which two subjects engage in a self-clarifying dialogue. It would be more accurate to say that the two subjectivities involved, that of the author and that of the reader, co-operate in making each other forget their distinctive identity and destroy each other as subjects. Both move beyond their respective particularity toward a common ground that contains both of them, united by the impulse that makes them turn away from their particular selves. It is by means of the act of reading that this turning away takes place; for the author, the possibility of being read transforms his language from a mere project into a work (and thus forever detaches it from him). In turn, it brings the reader back, for a moment, to what he might have been before he shaped himself into a particular self.

This conception of reading seems to differ altogether from interpretation. "It adds nothing to what was already there," says Blanchot; whereas it seems to be of the essence of interpretation to generate a language at the contact of another language, to be a kind of over-language added to that of the work. But we must not be misled by concepts of interpretation that derive from objective and intersubjective models. Blanchot expects us to understand the act of reading in terms of the work and not in terms of the constitutive subject, although he carefully avoids giving the work an objective status. He wants us "to take the work for what it is and thus to rid it of the presence of the author . . ." (*L'Espace littéraire*, p. 202). What we are reading is located closer to its origin than we are and it is our purpose to be attracted by it to the place whence it issued. The work has an undeniable ontological priority over the reader. It follows that it would be absurd to claim that in reading we "add" something, for any addition, be it in the form of an explication, a judgment, or an opinion, will only remove us further from the real center. We can only come under the true spell of the work by allowing it to remain what it is. This apparently passive act, this "nothing" that, in reading, we should *not* add to the work, is the very definition of a truly interpretative language. It designates a positive way of addressing the text, noticeable in the positive emphasis that characterizes the description of the act of reading, a rare example of affirmation in an author not prone to positive statement. The urge to let a work be exactly what it is requires an active and unrelenting vigilance, which can only be exercised by means of language. In this manner, an interpretative language originates in contact with the work. To the extent that reading merely "listens" to the work, it becomes itself an act of interpretative understanding.[3] Blanchot's description of the act of reading defines authentic interpretation. In depth, it transcends descriptions of interpretation that derive from the study of things or from the analysis of individual subjects.

Yet, Blanchot feels the need to qualify his definition by an all-important reservation. The act of reading, by means of which the authentic dimensions of a work can be revealed, can never be performed by the author on his own writings. Blanchot frequently states this impossibility perhaps most clearly at the beginning of *L'Espace littéraire*:

> . . . the writer can never read his own work. It is, for him, strictly inaccessible, a secret which he does not wish to confront. . . . The impossibility of self-reading coincides with the discovery that, from now on, there is no longer room for any added creation in the space opened up by the work and that, consequently, the only possibility is that of forever writing the same work over again. . . . The particular loneliness of the writer . . . stems from the fact that, in the work, he belongs to what always precedes the work.[4]

The statement is of central importance for an understanding of Blanchot. At first sight, it seems convincing enough: we can find many examples, in the course of literary history, of the estrangement experienced by writers who handle their language seriously, when they face the expression of their own thought, and Blanchot links this estrangement with the difficulty of renouncing the belief that all literature is a new beginning, that a work is a sequence of beginnings. We may believe that the greater proximity to origin

3. Cf. Martin Heidegger, "Logos" in *Vorträge und Aufsätze* (Neske: Pfullingen, 1954), pp. 215 ff.
4. *L'Espace littéraire*, p. 14; see also p. 209.

confers upon the work some of the "firmness of beginnings" that Blanchot is willing to grant to the work of others. But this strength is only an illusion. The poet can only start his work because he is willing to forget that this presumed beginning is, in fact, the repetition of a previous failure, resulting precisely from an inability to begin anew. When we think that we are perceiving the assertion of a new origin, we are in fact witnessing the reassertion of a failure to originate. Acceding to the work in its positivity, the reader can very well ignore what the author was forced to forget: that the work asserted in fact the impossibility of its own existence. However, if the writer were really reading himself, in the full interpretative sense of the term, he would necessarily remember the duplicity of his self-induced forgetfulness, and this discovery would paralyze all further attempts at creation. In that sense, Blanchot's *noli me legere*, the rejection of self-interpretation, is an expression of caution, advocating a prudence without which literature might be threatened with extinction.

The impossibility of a writer's reading his own work sharply distinguishes the relationship between work and reader from that between work and author. Reading, as well as criticism (conceived as the actualization in language of the potential language involved in reading), can grow into a genuine interpretation, in the deepest sense of the term, whereas the relationship between author and work would be one of total estrangement, refusal, and forgetting. This radical distinction raises several questions. It seems primarily motivated by caution, a virtue that is not typical of the almost ruthless audacity of Blanchot's thought. Moreover, the study of Blanchot's later work reveals that the process of forgetting, itself deeply linked with the impossibility of the author's reading his own work, is, in fact, a much more ambiguous matter than may have appeared at first sight. The positive assertion of the work is not merely the result of a complicity between reader and author that enables the one to ignore what the other is willing to forget. The will to forget enables the work to exist and becomes a positive notion leading to the invention of an authentic language. Blanchot's recent work compels us to become aware of the full ambivalence of the power contained in the act of forgetting. It reveals the paradoxical presence of a kind of anti-memory at the very source of literary creation. If this is so, can we still believe that Blanchot refuses to read his work and dodges confrontation with his literary self? The remembrance of a forgetting can occur only while reading the work, not in the course of its composition. The reading that allows Blanchot to move from the first to the second version of his early novel *Thomas l'obscur* could still be explained as an attempt "to repeat what was said earlier . . . with the power of an increased talent." But the dialogue of the late text entitled, *L'Attente l'oubli* could only be the result of a relationship between the completed work and its author. The impossibility of self-reading has itself become the main theme, demanding in its turn to be read and interpreted. A circular movement seems to take the writer, at first alienated in the work, back to himself, by means of an act of self-interpretation. In Blanchot, this process first takes the form of his critical reading of others as preparatory to the reading of himself. It can be shown that Blanchot's criticism pre-figures the self-reading toward which he is ultimately oriented. The relationship between his critical work and his narrative prose has to be understood in these terms, the former being the prepara-tory version of the latter. A complete study of Blanchot should illustrate this by means of several examples; we have space for one instance only, the sequence of articles he wrote on Mallarmé. This may suffice to indicate that the movement of Blanchot's critical mind reflects the circular pattern that can be found in all acts of literary invention.

Mallarmé is one of the writers who have constantly engaged Blanchot's attention; the poet of *Un Coup de Dés* reappears as one of his main topics at all stages of his development. Since Blanchot writes in the traditional French format of the periodical review, his choice of subject-matter is not always dictated by a deeper affinity with the book he criticizes; it may be inspired by current fashion or by the pressure of literary events. In accordance with his conception of criticism, he is not interested in the dis-covery of new talent or in the revaluation of established names. In his selection of topics, he is generally content to follow a cosmopoli-tan current of opinion that is well informed but lays no claim to originality. There are, however, a few figures that recur as the true centers of his concern. Mallarmé is undoubtedly one of them; the identity of the other writers that influenced Blanchot may often remain hidden, but Mallarmé is explicitly discussed on various occasions.

Above all, Mallarmé fascinates Blanchot by his claim to absolute impersonality. The other main themes of Mallarmé's work, the large negative themes of death, ennui, and sterility, or even the self-reflection by which literature "scrutinizes its very essence," all take second place to the *gageure* of letting the work exist only by and for itself. Blanchot frequently quotes the statement of Mallarmé which he considers of central importance: "Impersonifié, le volume, autant qu'on s'en sépare comme auteur, ne réclame approche de lecteur. Tel, sache, entre les accessoires humains, il a lieu tout seul: fait, étant." [5] Impersonality means, in the first place, the absence of all personal anecdotes, of all confessional intimacies, and of all psychological concerns. Mallarmé eschews such forms of experience, not because he considers them as devoid of importance, but because the generality of poetic language has moved far beyond them. Hence the naïveté of reductive critical methods that try to gain access to Mallarmé's poetry by tracing it back to actual private experiences. One is never so far removed from the center as when one assumes to have recaptured the origin of the self in an empirical experience that is taken to be the cause. Blanchot is not likely to be misled in this direction: his negative comments on Charles Mauron's first psychoanalytical study of Mallarmé, dating as far back as 1943, are still altogether valid and topical.

Mallarmé's impersonality cannot be described as the antithesis, or the compensatory idealization, of a regressive obsession, as a strategy by means of which the poet tries to free himself from haunting emotional or sexual trauma. We do not find in him a dialectic of the empirical and the ideal self, as Freud describes it in the Narcissus essay. More than all other critics who have written on Mallarmé, Blanchot stressed most emphatically, from the start, that the impersonality of Mallarmé does not result from a conflict

5. "The book when we, as authors, separate ourselves from it, exists impersonally, without requiring the presence of a reader. Know that, among all human accessories, it is the one that comes into being by itself; it is made, and exists, by itself." (*L'Action restreinte, Oeuvres complètes* [Paris, 1945], p. 372.)

within his own person. It stems instead from a confrontation with an entity as different from himself as non-being differs from being. Mallarmé's alienation is neither social nor psychological, but ontological; to be impersonal does not mean, for him, that one shares a consciousness or a destiny with a number of others, but that one is reduced to no longer being a person, to being no one, because one defines onself in relation to being and not in relation to some particular entity.

In an article that dates back to 1949, Blanchot stresses that, for Mallarmé, the only medium by means of which such impersonality can be achieved is language. "Many striking points [about Mallarmé's conception of language] are to be remembered. The most remarkable, however, is the impersonality of language, the autonomous and absolute existence Mallarmé is willing to grant it. . . . Language supposes for him neither a speaker, nor a listener: it speaks and writes by itself. It is a kind of consciousness without a subject." [6] The poet thus encounters language as an alien and self-sufficient entity, not at all as if it were the expression of a subjective intent with which he could grow familiar, still less a tool that could be made to fit his needs. Yet it is well known that Mallarmé always used language in the manner of the Parnassian poets, the way a craftsman uses the material in which he is working. Well aware of this, Blanchot adds: "But language is also an incarnate consciousness that has been seduced into taking on the material form of words, their life and their sound, and leading one to believe that this reality can somehow open up a road that takes one to the dark center of things." [7] This important qualification leads us at once to the heart of the Mallarméan dialectic. For it is true that Mallarmé always conceived of language as a separate entity radically different from himself, and which he was incessantly trying to reach; the model for this entity, however, was mostly for him the mode of being of a natural substance, accessible to sensation. Language, with its sensory attributes of sound and texture, partakes of the world of natural objects and introduces a positive element in the sheer void that would surround a consciousness left entirely to itself. The double aspect of language, capable

6. *La Part du feu* (Paris, 1949), p. 48.
7. *La Part du feu*, p. 48.

of being at the same time a concrete, natural thing and the product of an activity of consciousness, serves Mallarmé as the starting point of a dialectical development that runs through his entire work. Nature, far from representing the satisfaction of a happy, unproblematic sensation, evokes instead separation and distance; nature is for him the substance from which we are forever separated. But it is also "La première en date, la nature" and, as such, it precedes all other entities and occupies a privileged position of priority. This assumption is of determining importance for the genesis and the structure of Mallarmé's work. The symbols of failure and of negativity that play such an important role in his poetry must be understood in terms of the underlying polarity between the world of nature and the activity of consciousness. Reacting against the natural world in an attempt to assert his autonomy, the poet discovers that he can never free himself from its impact. The final image of Mallarmé's work shows the protagonist of *Un Coup de Dés* sinking into the "ocean" of the natural world. Nevertheless, in a gesture that is both heroic and absurd, the will to consciousness keeps asserting itself, even from beyond the catastrophic event in which it was destroyed. The persistence of this effort keeps carrying the work forward and engenders a trajectory that seems to escape, to some extent, from the chaos of indetermination. This trajectory is reflected in the very structure of Mallarmé's development and constitutes the positive element that allows him to pursue his task. The work consists of a sequence of new beginnings that are not, however, as for Blanchot, identical repetitions. The eternal repetition, the *ressassement* of Blanchot is replaced, in Mallarmé, by a dialectical movement of becoming. Each successive failure knows and remembers the failure that went before, and this knowledge establishes a progression. Mallarmé's self-reflection is rooted in experiences that are not altogether negative, but that nevertheless maintain a certain measure of self-awareness, "la clarté reconue, qui seule demeure. . . ." [8] Subsequent work can start on a higher level of consciousness than their predecessors. There is room in Mallarmé's world for some form of memory; from work to work, one is not allowed to forget

8. ". . . a recognized clarity, the only thing to remain" (*Igitur, Oeuvres complètes,* p. 435).

what went before. A link is maintained, despite the discontinuities, and a movement of growth takes place. The impersonality is the result of a dialectical progression, leading from the particular to the universal, from personal to historical recollection. The work depends for its existence on this dialectical substructure, which is itself rooted in an obscure assertion of the priority of material substances over consciousness. Mallarmé's poetics remain founded on the attempt to make the semantic dimensions of language coincide with its material, formal attributes.[9]

Such an attempt should not be confused with Blanchot's experiments. When Blanchot speaks, in the passage previously quoted, of language as an "incarnate consciousness" (adding at once that this may well be a delusion), he is describing a conception of language that differs altogether from his own. Blanchot's writing very seldom lingers over the material qualities of things; without being abstract, his language is rarely a language of sensation. His preferred literary form is not, as for René Char with whom he is often compared, that of a poetry oriented toward material things, but rather the *récit*, a purely temporal type of narrative. It should not surprise us, therefore, that his presentation of Mallarmé at times misses the mark. This is particularly true of the sections of *L'Espace littéraire* in which Blanchot deals with the theme of death as it appears in Mallarmé's prose text *Igitur*. However, when Blanchot returns to Mallarmé later, in the articles now included in *Le Livre à venir*, his observations lead to a general view that is a genuine interpretation.

What is missing, perhaps deliberately, in Blanchot's commentaries on *Igitur*, is precisely this sense of dialectical growth by

9. Recent interpreters of Mallarmé, such as Jacques Derrida and Philippe Sollers, anticipated in some respects by the American critic Robert Greer Cohn, find in Mallarmé a movement that takes place within the textual aspect of language as mere signifier, regardless of a natural or subjective referent. As is clear from the spatial, representational interpretation of the ideograms of *Un Coup de Dés* (as in the passages quoted below and identified by footnotes 11 and 12), Blanchot's reading of Mallarmé never reaches this point. He remains within a negative subject/object dialectic in which an impersonal non-subject confronts an abolished non-object ("rien" or "l'absente"). This layer of meaning is undoubtedly present in Mallarmé and we can remain within the orbit of this understanding for an argument that deals with Blanchot (or, more restrictively, with Blanchot's critical assumptions) and not with Mallarmé.

means of which the particular death of the protagonist becomes a universal movement, corresponding to the historical development of human consciousness in time. Blanchot translates the experience at once in ontological terms and sees it as a direct confrontation of a consciousness with the most general category of being. Igitur's death then becomes for him a version of one of his own main obsessions, what he calls "la mort impossible," a theme more closely affiliated with Rilke and one that does not fully coincide with Mallarmé's chief concern at the time of *Igitur*. The distortion is in keeping with Blanchot's deeper commitments: Mallarmé's theme of the universal historical consciousness, with its Hegelian overtones, is of slight interest to him. He considers the dialectic of subject and object, the progressive temporality of a historical growth, as inauthentic experiences, misleading reflections of a more fundamental movement that resides in the realm of being. Later, when Mallarmé will have pursued his own thought to its most extreme point, he will at last convey the oscillatory movement within being that Blanchot prematurely claims to find stated in *Igitur*. It is at this point that a real encounter between Blanchot and Mallarmé can take place.

Blanchot's final interpretation of Mallarmé occurs in the essays from *Le Livre à venir* that deal with *Un Coup de Dés* and with the preparatory notes which Jacques Scherer edited in 1957 under the title *Le "Livre" de Mallarmé*. In *Hérodiade*. *Igitur*, and the poems that follow these texts, Mallarmé's main theme had been the destruction of the object under the impact of a reflective consciousness, the near dissolution ("la presque disparition vibratoire") of natural entities and of the self, raised to an advanced level of impersonality when, in the mirror of self-reflection, it becomes the object of its own thought. But in the process of depersonalization, the self could, to some degree, maintain its power; enriched by the repeated experience of defeat, it remained as the center of work, the point of departure of the spiral that grows out of it. Later on, in *Un Coup de Dés*, the dissolution of the object occurs on such a large scale that the entire cosmos is reduced to total indetermination; "la neutralité identique du gouffre," an abyss in which all things are equal in their utter indifference to the human mind and will. This time, however, the conscious self participates in the process to the point of annihilation: "The poet," writes Blanchot, "disappears under the pressure of the work, caught in the same movement that prompted the disappearance of the reality of nature." [10] Pushed to this extreme point, the impersonality of the self is such that it seems to lose touch with its initial center and to dissolve into nothingness. It now becomes clear that dialectical growth toward a universal consciousness was a delusion and that the notion of a progressive temporality is a reassuring but misleading myth. In truth, consciousness was caught unawares within a movement that transcends its own power. The various forms of negation that had been "surmounted" as the work progressed—death of the natural object, death of the individual consciousness in *Igitur*, or the destruction of a universal, historical consciousness destroyed in the "storm" of *Un Coup de Dés* —turn out to be particular expressions of a persistent negative movement that resides in being. We try to protect ourselves against this negative power by inventing stratagems, ruses of language and of thought that hide an irrevocable fall. The existence of these strategies reveals the supremacy of the negative power they are trying to circumvent. For all his apparent lucidity, Mallarmé was mystified by this philosophical blindness until he recognized the illusory character of the dialectic on which he had founded his poetic strategy. In his last work, consciousness as well as natural objects are threatened by a power that exists on a more fundamental level than either of them.

And yet, even beyond this destruction of the self, the work can remain in existence. In Mallarmé's final poem, survival is symbolized in the image of a constellation that seems to escape from the destruction to which everything else has succumbed. Interpreting the image of the constellation, Blanchot states that in the poem, "the dispersion takes on the form and appearance of unity." [11] The unity is first stated in spatial terms: Mallarmé literally depicts the typographical, spatial disposition of the words on the page. Creating a highly complex network of relationships between the words, he gives the illusion of a three-dimensional reading analogous to the experience of space itself. The poem

10. *Le Livre à venir* (Paris, 1959), p. 277.
11. *Ibid.* p. 286.

becomes "the material, sensory affirmation of the new space. It is this space become poem." [12] We have a late, extreme version of the attempt to make the semantic and the sensory properties of language coincide. As the words in the poem that designate a ship are grouped in the shape of a sinking sailboat, the meaning of language is represented in a material form. In *Un Coup de Dés*, however, such experimentations come very close to being a deliberate hoax. If we have actually moved beyond the antithesis between subject and object, then such pseudo-objective games can no longer be taken seriously. In a typically Mallarméan form of irony, the spatial resources of language are exploited to the full at the very moment that they are known to be completely ineffective. It is no longer valid to speak, with Blanchot, of the earth as a spatial abyss that, reversing itself, becomes the corresponding abyss of the sky in which "words, reduced to their own space, make this space shine with a purely stellar light." [13] The idea of a reversal, however, is essential, provided one understands the reversal no longer in a spatial sense but in a temporal sense, as an axis around which the metaphor of space revolves to disclose the reality of time.

Blanchot participates in the reversal as he gradually discovers the temporal structure of *Un Coup de Dés*. The central articulation of this poem is very clearly marked: near the middle of the text, Mallarmé shifts from Roman type to italics and inserts an extended episode beginning with the words "comme si." At that moment, we change from a temporality that follows the course of an event presented as if it were actually taking place, to another, prospective temporality that exists only as fiction, strictly in the mode of "comme si." The fictional time is included in the historical time, like the play within the play of the Elizabethan theater. This enveloping structure corresponds to the relationship between history and fiction. The fiction in no way changes the outcome, the destiny of the historical event. In the terms of Mallarmé's poem, it will not abolish the random power of chance; the course of events remains unchanged by this long grammatical *apposition* that continues over six pages. The outcome is determined from the start by the single word "jamais," pointing to a past that

12. *Ibid.* p. 287.
13. *Ibid.* p. 288.

precedes the beginning of the fiction and to a future that will follow it. The purpose of the fiction is not to intervene directly: it is a cognitive effort by means of which the mind tries to escape from the total indetermination that threatens it. The fiction influences the mode of abolition of consciousness, not by opposing it, but by mediating the experience of destruction; it interposes a language that accurately describes it. "History," says Blanchot, "is replaced by hypothesis." [14] Yet this hypothesis can derive its statement only from a knowledge that was already previously given, and that asserts precisely the impossibility of overcoming the arbitrary nature of this knowledge. The verification of the hypothesis confirms the impossibility of its elaboration. Fiction and the history of actual events converge toward the same nothingness; the knowledge revealed by the hypothesis of fiction turns out to be a knowledge that already existed, in all the strength of its negativity, before the hypothesis was construed. Knowledge of the impossibility of knowing precedes the act of consciousness that tries to reach it. This structure is a circular one. The prospective hypothesis, which determines a future, coincides with a historical, concrete reality that precedes it and that belong to the past. The future is changed into a past, in the infinite regression that Blanchot calls a *ressassement*, and that Mallarmé describes as the endless and meaningless noise of the sea after the storm has destroyed all sign of life, "l'inférieur clapotis quelconque."

But does this knowledge of the circular structure of fictional language not have, in its turn, a temporal destiny? Philosophy is well acquainted with the circularity of a consciousness that puts its own mode of being into question. This knowledge complicates the philosopher's task a great deal, but it does not spell the end of philosophical understanding. The same is true of literature. Many specifically literary hopes and illusions have to be given up: Mallarmé's faith in the progressive development of self-consciousness, for example, must be abandoned, since every new step in this progression turns out to be a regression toward a more and more remote past. Yet it remains possible to speak of a certain development, of a movement of becoming that persists in the

14. *Ibid.* pp. 291–92.

fictional world of literary invention. In a purely temporal world, there can be no perfect repetition, as when two points coincide in space. As soon as the reversal described by Blanchot has taken place, the fiction is revealed as a temporal movement, and the question of its direction and intent must again be asked. "Mallarmé's ideal Book is thus obliquely asserted in terms of the movement of change and development that expressed perhaps its real meaning. This meaning will be the very movement of the circle." [15] And elsewhere: "We necessarily always write the same thing over again, but the development of what remains the same has infinite richness in its very repetition." [16] Blanchot is very close here to a philosophical trend which tries to rethink the notion of growth and development no longer in organic but in hermeneutic terms by reflecting on the temporality of the act of understanding.[17]

Blanchot's criticism, starting out as an ontological meditation, leads back into the question of the temporal self. For him, as for Heidegger, Being is disclosed in the act of its self-hiding and, as conscious subjects, we are necessarily caught up in this movement of dissolution and forgetting. A critical act of interpretation enables us to see how poetic language always reproduces this negative movement, though it is often not aware of it. Criticism thus becomes a form of demystification on the ontological level that confirms the existence of a fundamental distance at the heart of all human experience. Unlike the recent Heidegger, however, Blanchot does not seem to believe that the movement of a poetic consciousness could ever lead us to assert our ontological insight in a positive way. The center always remains hidden and out of reach;

15. *Le Livre à venir,* p. 296.
16. *Ibid.* p. 276.
17. See, for example, Hans-Georg Gadamer, *Wahrheit und Methode* (Tübingen, 1960), second edition, pp. 250 ff. In *Sein und Zeit,* Heidegger is certainly one of those who have laid the groundwork for this form of thought in our century. The affinity between Blanchot and Heidegger, despite the divergence in their subsequent development, should be studied more systematically than has been done up till now. The French philosopher Levinas, in his opposition to Heidegger and in his influence on Blanchot, would have to play a prominent part in such a study. There exists a brief article by Levinas on Blanchot and Heidegger published in March 1956 in *Monde nouveau,* a now defunct review.

we are separated from it by the very substance of time, and we never cease to know that this is the case. The circularity is not, therefore, a perfect form with which we try to coincide, but a directive that maintains and measures the distance that separates us from the center of things. We can by no means take this circularity for granted: the circle is a path that we have to construct ourselves and on which we must try to remain. At most, the circularity proves the authenticity of our intent. The search toward circularity governs the development of consciousness and is also the guiding principle that shapes the poetic form.

This conclusion has brought us back to the question of the subject. In his interpretative quest, the writer frees himself from empirical concerns, but he remains a self that must reflect on its own situation. As the act of reading "had to leave things exactly as they were," he tries to see himself the way he really is. He can only do this by "reading" himself, by turning his conscious attention toward himself, and not toward a forever unreachable form of being. Blanchot finally reaches this same conclusion with reference to Mallarmé.

> How can [the Book] assert itself in conformity with the rhythm of its own constitution, if it does not get outside itself? To correspond with the intimate movement that determines its structure, it must find the outside that will allow it to make contact with this very distance. The Book needs a mediator. The act of reading performs the mediation. But not just any reader will do . . . Mallarmé himself will have to be the voice of this essential reading. He has been abolished and has vanished as the dramatic center of his work, but this very annihilation has put him into contact with the reappearing and disappearing essence of the Book, with the ceaseless oscillation which is the main statement of the work.[18]

The necessity for self-reading, for self-interpretation, reappears at the moment when Mallarmé rises to the level of insight that allows him to name the general structure of all literary consciousness. The suppression of the subjective moment in Blanchot, asserted in the form of the categorical impossiblity of self-reading, is only a

18. *Ibid.* p. 294.

preparatory step in his hermeneutic of the self. In this way, he frees his consciousness of the insidious presence of inauthentic concerns. In the askesis of depersonalization, he tries to conceive of the literary work, not as if it were a thing, but as an autonomous entity, a "consciousness without a subject." This is not an easy undertaking. Blanchot must eliminate from his work all elements derived from everyday experience, from involvements with others, all reifying tendencies that tend to equate the work with natural objects. Only when this extreme purification has been achieved, can he turn toward the truly temporal dimensions of the text. This reversal implies a return toward a subject that, in fact, never ceased to be present. It is significant that Blanchot reaches this conclusion only with reference to an author like Mallarmé, who came upon it obliquely and whose actual itinerary needs to be revealed by interpretation, the way a watermark becomes visible only when held to the light. When he is dealing with writers who have given a more explicit version of the same process, Blanchot refuses them his full understanding. He tends to rate explicit forms of insight with other inessential matters that serve to make everyday life bearable—such as society, or what he calls history. He prefers hidden truth to revealed insight. In his critical work, this theoretician of interpretation prefers to describe the act of interpretation rather than the interpreted insight. He wanted, in all likelihood, to keep the latter in reserve for his narrative prose.

VI

The Literary Self as Origin:
The Work of Georges Poulet

A few years hence, the discussions that give to the literary studies of today such a controversial and didactic tone, will have faded before the intrinsic value of works that, in spite of being works of criticism, are nevertheless literary achievements in the fullest sense of the term. The case of poets or novelists that would occasionally write criticism is far from unusual; in modern French literature alone one can think of a long line that goes from Baudelaire to Butor and that includes Mallarmé, Valéry, and Blanchot. The nature of this double activity has often been wrongly understood. One assumes that these writers, out of dilettantism or out of necessity, have from time to time deserted the more important part of their work to express their opinion on the writings of their predecessors or contemporaries—a little in the manner of retired champions evaluating the performance of younger athletes. But the reasons that prompted these writers to take up criticism have only a limited interest. What matters a great deal is that Baudelaire's *Essay on Laughter*, Mallarmé's *La Musique et les Lettres*, or Blanchot's *Le Chant des Sirènes* are more than equal in verbal and thematic complexity to a prose poem of the *Spleen de Paris*, a page of *Un Coup de Dés* or a chapter of *Thomas l'obscur*. We are not suggesting that the poetic or novelistic parts of these works exist on the same level as the critical prose, and that both are simply interchangeable without making essential distinctions. The line that separates them marks out two worlds that are by no means identical or even complementary. The precise itinerary of such a line, however, would in most cases reveal a more subterranean path than one might originally have suspected and would indicate that the critical and the poetic components are so closely intertwined that it is impossible to touch the one without coming into contact with the other. It can be said of these works that they carry a constitutive critical element within themselves, exactly as Friedrich Schlegel, at the onset of the nineteenth century, characterized all "modern" literature by the ineluctable presence of a critical dimension.[1] If this is true, then the opposite is just as likely, and critics can be granted the full authority of literary authorship. Some contemporary critics can already lay claim to such a distinction.

More than any other, the criticism of Georges Poulet conveys the impression of possessing the complexity and the scope of a genuine work of literature, the intricacy of a city which has its avenues, its dead-ends, its underground labyrinths and panoramic lookouts. For the last forty years, he has pursued a meditation that takes the whole of Western literature for its theme; the orientation of his thought has remained remarkably stable throughout, directed toward a totalization that constantly seemed about to be achieved. On the other hand, he has shown considerable mobility, constantly putting his thought into question, returning to its original premises and starting afresh, even in his most recent texts. The combination of dynamicism with stability may explain apparent contradictions between the public and the private side of Poulet's criticism. From its beginnings, in the early 1920's, until the five consecutive volumes of the *Studies on Human Time*, the progression of the work has been incessant, almost monumental. It seems

1. Athenäum Fragment, no. 238, p. 204 in Friedrich Schlegel, *Kritische Ausgabe*, Band II, *Charakteristiken und Kritiken* I (1796–1801), Hans Eichner, ed., 1967.

to be carried by a methodological self-assurance that readily accounts for its considerable influence and authority. This self-
assurance is by no means merely apparent; any study will have to
account for the positive strength of the method. But, especially in
the polemical mood that prevails for the moment, when every
critical attitude has to become at once a critical position, the outward rigidity may well mask the other side, the more intimate
aspect that keeps Poulet's work open-ended, problematic, irre-
ducibly personal, and incapable of being transmitted, affiliated as
it is with a historical tradition that bears only the most distant
relation to the quarrels of the hour. In the numerous conferences
and public debates on criticism that have taken place of late, the
position of Poulet has been a prominent one. It was possible to
achieve this, however, only by hardening and schematizing categories that are a great deal more flexible when applied to texts
than when used against other critical methods. For this reason,
we prefer not to begin our reading of Georges Poulet with the
systematic parts, but rather with the ambivalences, the depths and
uncertainties that make up his more hidden side. The relative
serenity of the method can be better understood in terms of the
difficult experience of truth that stands behind it. The reverse
road, starting out from the established assurances, runs the risk of
missing the essential point.

Georges Poulet himself invites us to search, in the study of a
writer, for his "point of departure," an experience that is both
initial and central and around which the entire work can be
organized. The "points of departure" differ in kind for each
author and define him in his individuality; the test of their relevance consists in their ability to serve effectively as organizing
principle for all his writings, whatever their period or genre may
be (finished work, fragment, journal, letter, etc.). On the other
hand, it seems that only a body of writing that can be so grasped
and organized fully deserves to be called a "work." The point of
departure serves as a unifying principle within a single corpus
while also serving to differentiate between writers, or even between
periods of literary history.
   It is tempting to consider Poulet's own itinerary in this manner,

but it soon becomes clear that, in his case, the notion is not simple; the fact that it serves at the same time as a principle that unifies and as a principle that differentiates indicates a certain degree of complexity. This complexity, however, is not more problematic than the simultaneous unity and differentiation that one encounters in any action committed by a conscious subject. Greater difficulties arise from the need to define the point of departure as center as well as origin. As its name indicates, it can function as a temporal origin, as the point before which no previous moment exists that, with regard to the work, has to be taken into account. In temporal terms therefore, the point of departure is a moment entirely oriented toward the future and separated from the past. On the other hand, when it acts as a center, it no longer functions as a genetic but as a structural and organizing principle. Since the center organizes a substance that can have a temporal dimension (and this seems, at first sight, to be the case for literature as Poulet conceives it), it serves as a co-ordinating point of reference for events that do not coincide in time. This can only mean that the center permits a link between past and future, thereby implying the active and constitutive intervention of a past. In temporal terms, a center cannot at the same time also be an origin, a source. The problem does not exist in the same manner in space, where one can conceive of a center that could also, as in the case of the Cartesian axes of analytical geometry, be an origin. But then the origin is a purely formal concept devoid of generative power, a mere point of reference rather than a point of departure. "Source" and "center" are by no means a priori identical. A very productive tension can develop between them. The work of Georges Poulet grows under the impact of this tension and reaches, for this reason, into the hidden foundations of literature.

We encounter the problem of the center and the origin from Poulet's earliest writings on; it will never cease to haunt him, regardless of the later knowledge and mastery. He meets it first of all, not in an abstract and theoretical way, but as a young novelist confronted with the practical question of constructing a convincing narrative. In a very interesting article that dates back to 1924, the expression "point of departure" is frequently used, although often with a negative accent.[2] Poulet tries to define the *nouveau roman* of his era in opposition to his elders, Gide and Proust, and seems convinced that in narrative fiction there can be no true origin, since one is always dependent on previous events. The novelists engaged in "creating" a character by the description of acts and feelings that seem spontaneous must in fact already be in the possession of a preconceived scheme that more or less consciously serves as a principle of selection. The fluid, dynamic, and continuous world of the fictional narration must be preceded by a static and determined world that serves as its "point of departure"; between these two worlds, there can be no actual contact.

> The figure [of the acts that narrate a story] exists at all times. Before acting it is already formed. Its only movement is a gradual unfolding. It moves in order to breathe, to exist. Only after this preparatory labor can it begin to grow. One may be surprised in thus hearing a truth conceived simultaneously in two modes, that of *being* and that of *becoming,* without any effort on the part of the author to establish a link between them, to discover a factor that they could have in common. . . . We behold a hero who has been consciously selected, his acts precalculated and his behavior adapted to an adventure that was foreseen even before it came into being. We witness a point of departure, a birth, then a movement. The writer concentrates on a sudden, startling development to which he may come back later, or he gives us a slow and static preparation that proceeds by minute detail, an analysis, visible or hidden, involuntary at times, in which the idea of the action is contained, albeit in an amended, distorted way, integrated within an exposition but incommensurable with it.

Further, in the course of the same article, the so-called "classical" novel (the reference is to *Adolphe* and *Dominique*) is defined in

2. "A propos du Bergsonisme" in *Sélection,* April 1924, pp. 65–75. The essay purports to be a study on a volume edited by Albert Thibaudet entitled *Le Bergsonisme* (*Trente Ans de pensée française,* vol. III). The five quotations that follow are from this article.

terms of a similar discontinuity between the appearance of a unified action and a static, earlier *donnée:*

> A common action of which the successive phases are chosen in such a way as to suggest reciprocal coherence, demands the creation of a point of departure, a kind of postulate located in the character of the protagonist as well as in the setting of the future action. Prior to the novel itself, one has to invent another novel, entirely devoid of action, but that nevertheless contains the development of the plot in all its irrevocable logic; two different fictional constructions preside over the same subject. These constructions, however, are not only different but opposed, utterly irreconcilable within the usual movement of life. The first contains a point of departure, fully shaped characters, a stable past, a moral overtone; the other consists only of the actions that mark the development of characters, but it contains neither the characters themselves, nor their ultimate destiny.

These texts combine a clear knowledge of the requirements that govern the narrative techniques of fiction with a nostalgic desire to share in the generative strength of sources and origins. The need for composition, for articulation of discontinuous elements, is constantly asserted: "Every artist is in fact a *Homo faber* who can deliberately, by an act of his intelligence, achieve a 'willed, reasoned and systematic detachment' that, as well as a natural detachment, allows him to combine heterogeneous elements. We openly admit that composition and ornamentation depend on 'devices' and on 'tricks.'"[3] But, next to the need for composition, an entirely different need is finally asserted as being the writer's true project: rebelling against the artifice of a pseudo-continuous narrative, knowing that the story is in fact the result of a radical break between a present and an earlier world, he may choose instead to remain entirely passive. He gives himself up to the intuitive presence of the moment and, carried along by a deeper current that fuses past and present, object and subject, presence and distance, the writer hopes to reach a more funda-

3. A book review by Edmond Jaloux published around that time characterizes Georges Poulet as "concerned with the study of composition" (voué à l'étude de la composition), *Nouvelles littéraires,* November 26, 1927.

mental continuity, which is the continuity of the source, of the
creative impulse itself.

> By an act of forgetting, like Proust forgetting the numberless
> ideas and memories that get in the way of his sensations, as
> well as by an act of trust in our sense-perceptions, akin to
> what Bergson calls sympathy, we can come to consider what
> takes place in ourselves as existing on the same plane as
> what takes place in the outside world. In the novel we dream
> of, the setting will actually be the only character. Then the
> images and we ourselves will come to life. We do not float, nor
> do we sink. We live at the very heart of the universe, and
> the universe is all that exists. We ourselves have vanished.
> . . . The relationships between things have grown highly
> delicate, like ever-moving shadows, the light ebb and flow of
> a barely perceptible flux. Everything changes. Nothing is
> beyond understanding because the very idea of understanding,
> the calculated need to *explain,* has vanished. It is almost like
> an act of faith of which we do not know whether it is rooted
> in ourselves or in nature. Everything changes, but we are not
> even aware of it because, caught in the change, we ourselves
> have become the change and all points of reference have gone.
> Time and space become one. A single impulse carries all
> things toward a final aim that lies beyond our knowledge. . . .

The intensity of the tone indicates that such passages express
a genuine spiritual temptation that reaches well beyond momentary
influence or intellectual fashions. At more than forty years' distance, the Bergsonian fervor of this terminology may seem slightly
recondite, just as the attempts to put this aesthetic into practice
in the novel that Poulet published around the same time now appear dated.[4] Yet one should remember the movement as a constant,
one of the recurrent themes that reappear throughout the work.

It is perhaps a mistake to speak here of passivity. Pure passivity
would imply the complete loss of all spatial and temporal direction
in a universe both infinite and chaotic, comparable to the "neutralité identique du gouffre" that Mallarmé evokes in *Un Coup de
Dés.* In Poulet's text, the disappearance of all "points of reference"

4. Georges Thialet (pseudonym for Georges Poulet), *La Poule aux oeufs d'or*
(Emile Paul: Paris, 1927).

does not convey an entirely undifferentiated experience of reality. The fact that he uses terms such as "intention" or "élan," the persistence of a teleological vocabulary, indicates that the passivity is not a relaxation of consciousness but rather the reward a consciousness receives for being able to coincide with a truly originary movement. This makes it possible to speak, in such a case, of an authentic point of departure, instead of the false point of departure claimed by novelists who remain in fact dependent on the hidden presence of previous events.

The same fundamental temptation reappears, in various versions, in the criticism and the fiction of Georges Poulet until the publication, in 1949, of the first volume of *Etudes sur le temps humain*. Time already played a part in the 1924 article, although it appeared as a device by means of which the "classical" novelists concealed the artifice of an illusory continuity: "There are perhaps no novels that are more homogeneous, more continuous than [classical] novels. This is probably due to a third factor that artificially suspends the antinomy between space and duration. This is the *time* factor, perfectly artificial in itself, but the natural product of our intelligence. . . ." The conviction that temporality is a mask that the human intelligence can impose upon the face of reality will never reappear in the form of such a direct statement. But it remains another constant of Poulet's thought. He will forever preserve a degree of antinomy between time and duration, an antinomy that is in fact another version of the tension between the source (the origin of duration) and the center (the locus of temporal articulation).

In the still Bergsonian article of 1924, time appears as a degraded form of space and as an artifice of the mind. Not until the first volume of the *Etudes sur le temps humain* does it acquire a much deeper existential significance. The optimism of the earlier text, the act of faith which allows Poulet to speak of the creative impulse as if it were a spontaneous act of levitation ("we do not float, nor do we sink"), will be short-lived. The tone of the later text is much more somber; maybe the experience of the novelist in facing the internal difficulties of a genre of which he had so well understood the ambivalence played a part in this change of mood. Whatever the case may be, at the same moment that Poulet finds the format and the method that will allow for the full development of his critical powers, the confidence in a happy accord between the movements of the mind and those of the world is breaking down. It is replaced by an experience best expressed in a quotation from Nicole that appears in the introduction to the *Etudes sur le temps humain*: "We are like those birds that are air-borne but powerless to remain suspended without motion, hardly able to remain in the same place, because they lack something solid to support them and have insufficient strength and energy to overcome the weight that forces them downward." [5] Poulet seems to be sharing this very experience and to find it in most of the writers he studies, with increasing negativity as one progresses in the intellectual history of the West from the Middle Ages to the present. The awakening of consciousness always occurs as an awareness of the frailty of our link with the world. The *cogito*, in Poulet's thought, takes the form of a reawakened feeling of fundamental fragility, which is nothing else than the subjective experience of time. One should not forget, however, that this is not an original but a derived feeling, the correlative of an intent that aims at coinciding perfectly with the origin of things. The feeling of fragility and of contingency designates the mood of a consciousness in quest of its own movement of origination.

This explains why the kind of emotion that accompanies the *cogito*, the fact, for instance, that it occurs as a feeling of happiness or of distress, is of secondary importance. Some writers start out in a state of happiness. Rousseau's moment of initial sensation, for example, a moment of which the "state of nature" in his theoretical writings is a projection on a wider historical scale, is entirely positive: ". . . in the state of pure sensation which is at the same time pure activity and feeling of existence, man is perfectly happy. There are no tensions within him: he fills the universe and the universe fills him. . . . This tranquillity, a state of harmony with the self which is also a harmony with nature, constitutes the only true happiness, the only fulfillment that could be called absolute. . . ." [6] The same is true of a contemporary writer such as Julien Green:

5. *Etudes sur le temps humain* (Paris, 1950), vol. I, pp. xviii–xix.
6. *Ibid.* p. 163.

> In the novels of Julien Green, despite the somber and anxiety-ridden atmosphere, there always comes a moment in which consciousness and happiness, self-awareness and sensation are mysteriously joined in an experience which is the starting-point, the apogee, or even the endpoint of their history. Suddenly, and almost always without apparent reason, his characters literally wake up to a state of bliss. And in discovering happiness, they also discover themselves. They are suddenly stirred by a "happiness without cause, that comes from nowhere and that traverses the soul as the wind traverses the trees." [7]

In others, however, the same awakening of consciousness can be intensely painful. Thus for Marcel Proust ". . . the first moment is not a moment of plenitude or of vigor. He does not feel carried by his future possibilities or his present-day realities. His feeling of emptiness is not due to something that fails in his future, but to a gap in his past, something that *no longer* exists, not something that does *not as yet* exist. It resembles the first moment of a being that has lost everything, that has lost himself as if he were dead. . . ." [8] The same feeling of "le néant des choses humaines" (Rousseau) in a somewhat different form, appears as the point of departure of Benjamin Constant:

> What first appears in Benjamin Constant and threatens to become a permanent condition, is the absence of any desire to engage himself into life. . . . Man has no raison d'être. His existence has no meaning, and he is powerless to give it any. . . . Everything is settled from the start by the mere fact of his mortal condition. . . . The entire course of his life is determined by the event that marks its conclusion. Death and only death gives meaning to life—and this meaning is entirely negative.[9]

The initial mood, whether positive or negative, is the perceptible symptom of a change that takes place in the mind when it claims to have reached or rediscovered the place of its origin. In the deceptive stability of everyday consciousness which, in reality, is only a kind of stupor, the new departure acts like a sudden

7. *Mesure de l'instant* (Paris, 1968), p. 339.
8. *Etudes sur le temps humain*, vol. I, p. 364.
9. *Benjamin Constant (par lui-même)* (Editions du Seuil: Paris, 1968), p. 28.

reawakening, shocking us into the discontinuity of a genuine movement. Poulet finds himself in agreement with the French eighteenth-century usage of the word *mouvement* to designate any spontaneous emotion.[10] His "point of departure," experienced as a particularly strong emotional tension, is primarily a change, the discontinuous movement from one state of consciousness to another. It is not conceived as the setting-in-motion of a substance that had up till then been stationary, nor is it the movement of origination through which a nothingness turns into being; it appears much rather as the re-discovery of a permanent and pre-existent movement that constitutes the foundation of all things. Poulet often formulates this aspect of his thought most clearly with reference to eighteenth-century writers. Thus in the article on the abbé Prévost, in which the key-term of *instant de passage* (the moment as discontinuity) is defined in all its richness:

> The *instant de passage,* in Prévost, marks the sudden leap from one extreme to the other. It is the moment at which both extremes come together. It does not matter whether the leap occurs from the greatest joy to the deepest despair, or vice-versa. . . . In no way does the term describe a lasting state of mind; it is an *état de passage,* less a state than a movement, the motion by which, within the same moment, the mind passes from one situation to its precise opposite.[11]

The term is crucially important, not only as a theoretical concept among others that are perhaps more forcefully stated, but for Poulet's critical practice as well. Present from the beginning, it starts to take final shape from the first volume of the *Etudes sur le temps humain* on; in his introduction to this volume, Poulet had stated that "the major discovery of the eighteenth century was the phenomenon of memory," yet it is the concept of instantaneity that finally emerges, often against and beyond memory, as the main insight of the book. The *instant de passage* supplants memory or, to be more precise, supplants the naïve illusion that memory would be capable of conquering the distance that separates the present from the past moment. Poulet's moment is "precisely what

10. *Le Dictionnaire de l'Académie* of 1762 defines "mouvement" as follows: "Se dit . . . des différentes impulsions, passions ou affections de l'âme."
11. *Etudes . . . ,* pp. 148–52.

keeps different times from joining while nevertheless making it possible that they exist in succession . . . [man] lives in a present rooted in nothing, in a time that nowise relates to an earlier time. . . ." [12] Memory becomes important as failure rather than as achievement and acquires a negative value that gradually emerges from the critical essays of that period. The illusion that continuity can be restored by an act of memory turns out to be merely another moment of transition. Only the poetic mind can gather scattered fragments of time into a single moment and endow it with generative power.

Henceforth, Poulet's criticism will be organized around this moment, or around a sequence of such moments. His methodological assurance stems from the possibility of constructing and justifying a pattern that can encompass the entire work within the relatively narrow space of a coherent critical narrative, starting out from an initial situation and moving through a series of peripeties and discoveries to a conclusion that is satisfactory because it is prefigured. This narrative line does not follow that of the author's life, nor does it follow the chronological order of his writings; some of Poulet's books preserve the chronological order of traditional literary history and use it to some advantage, yet this order could be abandoned without anything essential being lost.[13] The critical narration has no reference to anything outside

12. *Ibid.* pp. 148–51.
13. The diachronic order of certain texts, such as the general introductions to the first *Etudes sur le temps humain* and especially to *Les Métamorphoses du cercle,* may create the impression that Poulet tends toward writing a general history of consciousness. But this is not really the case. The unity of his thought exists on the ontological and on the methodological level, not with regard to history. Since he conceives of literature as an eternally repeated sequence of new beginnings, no meaningful relationship can exist between the particularized narrative that traces the itinerary of a writer *ab ovo* and the collective narrative that aims to describe the cumulative movement of history. Some historical articulations can be described as if they were collective *moments de passage,* altogether similar in structure to the points of departure of an individual *cogito.* But the historical framework is kept only as a principle of classification without intrinsic significance. A rare attempt is made, as in the study on Proust that concludes the first volume of the *Études sur le temps humain,* to integrate an individual development within the historical scheme announced in the preface. The example, however, remains an isolated one. The light that Poulet's method can throw on literary history is at most a byproduct of its activity, certainly not its main principle.

the work and is constructed from the entirety of the writer's texts surveyed as in a panoramic view. It is articulated, however, around a number of centers without which it could not have taken shape. The plot of this critical narrative falls into an almost uniform pattern, which does not prevent individual or group variations but defines, in its uniformity, a literary consciousness as distinct from other forms of consciousness.

For all their basic uniformity, the various critical narratives are organized in terms of a series of dramatic events: reversals, repetitions, about-faces, and resolutions, each corresponding to a particular *moment de passage*. The original *cogito* is one of these moments. It is followed by a series of similar events in situations of greater or lesser complexity compared with the original impulse. Readers of Poulet are familiar with rebounding actions that, by a sudden change in direction, can turn the most desperate-looking impasse into an avenue of hope, or vice versa. In the study on Benjamin Constant, Constant's nihilism is so convincingly described that it seems impossible to imagine a force strong enough to rouse him from his prostration. Yet, a few pages later, we learn of a moment "that recurs from time to time and that enables him to break entirely with his former life." Constant seems to possess a faculty for radical reversal that cannot be explained, since it represents the very essence of discontinuity, but that can alter the most desperate situation. "We can say that every man carries within him the capacity to reverse the course of destiny an indefinite number of times" [14]—after which Constant finds himself "suddenly active and passionately interested, not only by the matter that holds his attention at the moment, but by everything that is alive in his vicinity." The reversal, brought about by mere chance, is followed by the reawakening of a consciousness reflecting on the miraculous nature of this event. By the same token, in a new *moment de passage,* "his thought passes from negative to positive, from a *no* to a *yes.*" [15] A period of great literary productivity ensues, until, in this particular case, a final reversal takes him back to the depressed indifference that existed at the beginning. The itinerary is made up of a sequence of moments, each

14. *Benjamin Constant,* p. 54.
15. *Ibid.* p. 67.

erasing entirely whatever came before. The critic, however, can only construct and cover this itinerary because he strings on the imaginary time-thread of his narrative discontinuous but successive states of mind, joined together by the *moments de passage* that lead from one state to the next.

The temporal structure of this process becomes particularly clear in the texts dealing with Marcel Proust. In a series of studies that stretch over several years, Poulet will come closer and closer to defining the movement of Proust's mind. The development of the essays (as well as Proust's own development) is presented as a sequence of reversals in the novelist's outlook on time. At first, caught in the barrenness of his consciousness, Proust turns toward the past in the hope of finding there a firm and natural link between himself and the world. Had this quest for the remembered past been successful, he would have discovered the power to make the past into the strongest possible support of his existence. In a first reversal, it soon appears that this is not the case. The power of memory does not reside in its capacity to resurrect a situation or a feeling that actually existed, but it is a constitutive act of the mind bound to its own present and oriented toward the future of its own elaboration. The past intervenes only as a purely formal element, as a reference or a leverage that can be used because it is different and distant rather than because it is familiar and near. If memory allows us to enter into contact with the past, it is not because the past acts as the source of the present, as a temporal continuity that had been forgotten and of which we are again made aware; the remembrance does not reach us carried by a temporal flux; quite to the contrary, it is a deliberate act establishing a relation between two distinct points in time between which no relationship of continuity exists. Remembrance is not a temporal act but an act that enables a consciousness "to find access to the intemporal" [16] and to transcend time altogether. Such transcendence leads to the rejection of all that precedes the moment of remembrance as misleading and sterile in its deceptive relationship to the present. The power of invention has entirely passed into the present subject as it shows itself capable of creating relationships

16. *Etudes* . . . , p. 394.

that are no longer dependent on past experience. The point of departure was originally a moment of anxiety and of weakness because it felt no longer supported by anything that came before; it has now freed itself from the deceptive weight under which it was laboring and has become the creative moment par excellence, the source of Proust's poetic imagination as well as the center of the critical narrative by means of which Poulet makes us share in the adventure of this creation. This critical narrative turns around the central affirmation: "time recovered is time transcended."

The transcendence of time can only become a positive force if it is capable of re-entering, in turn, into the temporal process. It has freed itself from a rejected past, but this negative moment is now to be followed by a concern with the future that engenders a new stability, entirely distinct from the continuous and Bergsonian duration of memory. In the volume entitled *Le Point de départ*, the priority of the creative moment over the past, transposed into literary history, becomes an explicit concern with the future existence of the work. Such a concern was entirely lacking in the 1949 essay in which Proust's novel is said to be "without duration" or "covering the duration of a retrospective existence." Whereas, in the 1968 essay, "the work of literature . . . reveals how it passes from an instantaneous temporality, i.e. a sequence of detached events that make up the narrative, to a structural temporality, i.e. the gradual cohesion that unites the different parts. . . ." "The time of the work of art is the very movement by which the work passes from a formless and instantaneous to a formed and lasting state." [17] We are, in fact, witnessing a new *moment de passage* that will again reverse the perspective. At the start, a deceptive priority of the past over present and future was being asserted; this stage was followed by the discovery that the actual poetic power resides in a time-transcending moment: "It is not time that is given us, but the moment. With the given moment, it is up to us to make time." But since the moment then becomes reintegrated within time, we return in fact to a temporal activity, no longer based on memory but on the future-engendering

17. *Le Point de départ* (Paris, 1964), p. 40.

power of the mind. Thus the 1968 study on Marcel Proust is the exact reversal of its 1949 predecessor. The outlook toward the past is replaced by an equally passionate outlook toward the future which will have to experience its own disappointments, find its own strategies, and reach its own tentative solutions. Yet it could not be said that these two texts are in any way contradictory. They do not set up scales of value or make normative statements about an assumed superiority of future over past. Their interest stems instead from the movement generated by their dialectical interplay. The assertion of a future-engendering time, capable of duration, is certainly an important statement in itself, but it counts less by what it asserts than by what it represents: another *moment de passage* allowing for a new episode in the unending narrative of literary invention.

By thus singling out the notion of *moment de passage* as the main structural principle of Poulet's criticism, it may seem that we have definitely substituted the center for the source. We may have reintroduced time in a manner that was already being denounced in Poulet's earliest articles as contrary to his deepest spiritual leanings. Although the writer's experience of his past is being rejected, the fact remains that no critical discourse could come into being without the intervention of this past—just as the 1924 novelist could not construct a narrative that would not be founded, whether he wanted it or not, on a pattern that, for being prefigurative, nonetheless originated prior to the actual work. Should we conclude that Poulet had to forsake his fundamental project out of methodological necessity, that he had to renounce his desire to coincide with originating movements of thought in order to construct a coherent critical narrative?

The question cannot be considered without taking into account the complex relation in Poulet's work between the author and the reader of a given text. Like all truly literary works, his takes as its theme the choice it had to make between various modes of literary expression; no wonder, therefore, that it reflects the latent tension between poet (or novelist) and critic, especially with regard to their respective experiences of human time.

A critic has the possibility of seeing himself as a mediator who gives presence to an originating force. Something that predates

him in time is given him *a priori:* there can be no criticism without the prior existence of a text. And the tension between origin
and anteriority develops only when the source as well as the events
that are prior to it are located within the same person, when origin
and anteriority stem from a mind that is itself in quest of its
origin. This was the case in the earlier texts in which Poulet is
both novelist and critic. One remembers how the young novelist
of 1924 rebelled most of all against the deliberate and self-willed
aspects of the hidden world that preceded the beginning of his
narrative. An almost perverse streak of the human mind seems to
prevent an origin from coming into being; whenever this is about
to occur, the mind feels compelled to invent an earlier past that
deprives the event of its status origin. The novel that seemed to
flow freely from its own source thus lost all spontaneity, all genuine
originality. Things are quite different when the earlier past, the
passé antérieur, is initiated by someone else. The source is then
transferred from our own mind into that of another, and nothing
prevents us from considering this other mind as a genuine origin.
This happens in literary criticism, especially when one stresses the
element of identification that is part of all critical reading.

In the more general essays on method that Poulet has recently
been writing[18] the notion of identification plays a very prominent
part. Reading becomes an act of self-immolation in which the
initiative passes entirely into the hands of the author. The critic,
in Poulet's words, becomes the "prey" of the author's thought and
allows himself to be entirely governed by it. This complete surrender to the movement of another mind is the starting point of
the critical process. "I begin by letting the thought that invades
me . . . reoriginate within my own mind, as if it were reborn
out of my own annihilation." [19] This is said with reference to
Charles du Bos, but there can be little doubt that, in this essay
on one of his predecessors, Poulet speaks more than anywhere
else in his own name. In criticism, the *moment de passage* changes

18. Written as studies of individual critics (Rivière, Du Bos, Bachelard,
Blanchot, Marcel Raymond, Starobinski, etc.), these essays will eventually be
gathered into a volume on contemporary criticism.
19. "La pensée critique de Charles du Bos," *Critique,* 217, June 1965, pp. 491–
516.

from a temporal into an intersubjective act or, to be more precise, into the total replacement of one subject by another. We are, in fact, dealing with a substitutive relationship, in which the place of a self is usurped by another self. Proclaiming himself a passage-way (*lieu de passage*) for another person's thought, the critic evades the temporal problem of an anterior past. Nothing pre-vents the work from acquiring the status of an absolute origin. Poulet can then legitimately apply to the critic what Du Bos said of the poet: "He is the one who receives or, better, who endures. He is a meeting point (*point d'intersection*) rather than a center." With the experience of identification so defined, the problem of the center has, in fact, been eliminated, since the center is now entirely replaced by the authority of the originary source, which determines all the aspects and dimensions of the work. Poulet nevertheless continues to speak of the critic's relationship with his source in a vocabulary that derives from interpersonal relation-ships. He avoids all reference to biographical or psychological ele-ments, yet a literary work remains for him quite unambiguously the production of a person. Hence the presence, in his theoretical articles, of a hierarchical language in which the relationship be-tween author and reader is stated in terms of superiority and in-feriority: "the relationship [between author and reader] necessarily implies a special distinction between the one who gives and the one who receives, a relationship of superiority and inferiority." [20] "By becoming a critic . . . I find access to a new subjectivity. We could say that I allow myself to be replaced by some one better than myself." [21] Hence also some allusions that confer upon criti-cism a redeeming power that makes it akin to an act of personal grace. For if it is true that the particular subject that presides over the invention of a work is present in this work as a unique and absolute source, and if we can, in our turn, coincide entirely with this source in the act of critical identification, then literature would indeed be "the place where the person must be metamorphosed into a temple." [22] The fulfillment that was expected, in 1924, from abandoning oneself passively to the *élan vital* that animates

20. *Ibid.* p. 501.
21. *Les Chemins actuels de la critique* (Plon: Paris, 1967), p. 478.
22. "La pensée . . . ," *op. cit.* p. 515.

the universe finds its exact equivalence, after forty years, in the abandon with which the critic relinquishes his own self in his encounter with the work. In each case, the same quest for the experience of origination is lived with all the intensity of a truly spiritual aspiration.

But these theoretical texts on fellow critics or on criticism in general fail to define Poulet's own critical practice. The originality of his approach stems from the fact that he does not content himself with merely receiving works as if they were gifts, but that he participates, much more than he claims to do, in the problematic possibility of their elaboration. If one can speak of identification in his case, it is in a very different way than one would for Du Bos or Jean-Pierre Richard who can, at times, become one with the material or spiritual substance of the work. Whereas Poulet identifies himself with the project of its constitution; this is to say, his point of view is not so much that of the critic—as he himself defines it—as that of the writer. Consequently, the entire problem of anteriority and origin is not met as in the substitutive scheme which calls upon another to intervene, but is experienced from the inside, as seen by a subject that has delegated none of its inventive power to anyone else. Poulet often succeeds, in the course of a single article, in renewing entirely the interpretation of a given author. He can do so because he reaches as by instinct into the nearly inaccessible zone where the possibility of a work's existence is being decided. His criticism allows us to take part in a process that, far from being the inexorable development of an impulse that none could resist, appears as extremely vulnerable, likely to go astray at any moment, always threatened with error and aberration, risking paralysis or self-destruction, and forever obliged to start again on the road that it had hoped to have covered. It succeeds best of all when it deals with writers who have felt this fragility most acutely. Poulet can reach the quality of genuine subjectivity because, in his criticism, he is willing to undermine the stability of the subject and because he refuses to borrow stability for the subject from outside sources.

Significantly enough, in the most revealing passage of the Du Bos study, the presumed identification with another turns out to be the outward symptom of a division that takes place within the self: "It often happens . . . that the outburst of life that occurs with such admirable consequences, no longer seems to be the result of an outside influence, but the manifestation within the actual, inferior self of some earlier and superior self identified with our very soul." [23] But how are we to understand a movement which allows for a superior or "deeper" self to take the place of an actual self, in accordance with a scheme of which the encounter between author and critic was only the symbolical prefiguration? One can say, with Poulet, that between these two selves, "relationships are born, revelations carried over and a marvelous receptivity from mind to mind made to prevail." [24] Nevertheless, this relationship exists first of all in the form of a radical questioning of the actual, given self, extending to the point of annihilation. And the medium within which and by means of which this questioning can take place can only be language, although Poulet hardly ever designates it explicitly by that name. What was here being described as a relationship between two subjects designates in fact the relationship between a subject and the literary language it produces.

A far-reaching change of the temporal structure results from this. The *instant de passage,* the decisive importance of which has been so strongly in evidence, now turns out to create a disjunction within the subject. On the temporal level, this disjunction takes the form of a sudden reversal from a retrospective to a future-oriented attitude of mind. However, the dimension of futurity that is thus being engendered exists neither as an empirical reality nor in the consciousness of the subject. It exists only in the form of a written language that relates, in its turn, to other written languages in the history of literature and criticism. In this way we can see Marcel Proust clearly separate a past or a present that precedes the act of writing from a future that exists only in a purely literary form. Proust mentions certain sensations or emotions that will only become important in retrospect when these same events will recur as part of an interpretative process. "If, in the *Recherche,* the hero's experience is already over at the time that the novel begins, the knowledge of this experience, its mean-

23. *Ibid.* p. 502.
24. *Ibid.* p. 503.

ing and the use that can be made of it remain in suspense until the end, that is to say until a certain event has taken place that makes the future into more than just the point of arrival of the past, but into the point from where the past, seen in retrospect, gains meaning and intention." [25] In Proust's case, we know exactly what this decisive event was: the decision to write *A la recherche du temps perdu,* to pass from experience to writing, with all the risks this involves for the person of the writer. The explicit decision of Marcel Proust recurs in each writer; each one has invested his future existence once and forever into the project of his work.[26]

Why then does Poulet treat language, as a constitutive category of the literary consciousness, with a discretion that amounts to distrust? It takes a certain amount of interpretative labor to show that his criticism is actually a criticism of language rather than a criticism of the self.[27] His reserve can partly be explained by tactical considerations and by the desire to avoid misunderstandings. Poulet seems very eager to separate himself from other methods that give a prominent place to literary language, albeit for very different reasons. He is as remote from an impressionistic aestheticism that uses language as an object of sensation and pleasure, as from a formalism that would give it an autonomous and

25. *Mesure* . . . , pp. 334–35.
26. Things seemed to be different in an earlier, more clearly theocentric period, when literary language could put itself directly in the service of religious experience. In the historical scheme presented by Poulet, this is no longer the case, ever since the increased secularization that took place in the eighteenth century. This historical view, certainly far from original in itself, is perhaps only brought in to justify Poulet's fundamental commitment to the literary vocation, a commitment that never wavers. If, during the seventeenth century, no incompatibility exists between the quest for the true Self that takes place in literature and in religious thought, this raises the dignity and the effectiveness of the literary act to a level that no subsequent event will be able to lower. Poulet's thought does not spring from a nostalgia for the theological vigor of the seventeenth century that he knows and understands so well; much rather, it asserts the fact that the main part of this energy is preserved later on in the manifestations of literary genius. Racine could still be theologian as well as poet; the same could no longer be true of Rousseau, less still of Proust. Yet, what Racine, Rousseau, and Proust have in common and what gives their work the power to last, belongs properly to their vocation as writers and is therefore irrevocably bound up with their literary project.
27. This is also the opinion of Gérard Genette, who rates Georges Poulet among the critics of interpretation (*Figures,* Paris 1966, p. 158).

objective status. And, in the present historical picture, these may well be the first tendencies that come to mind when one speaks of critical methods that put the main emphasis on language.

Yet his distrust of language has other causes that take us back to his more fundamental problems. Language clearly matters to him only when it gives access to a deeper subjectivity, as opposed to the scattered mood of common, everyday existence. The question remains whether this deeper self must be considered as an origin or as a center, as a source or as a reorientation of the mind from the past toward the future. In the first case, the self could coincide with a movement of origination and language could disappear into pure transparency. Literature would then tend to consume itself and become superfluous in the assertion of its own success. The only thing that jeopardizes it would be its dispersion within the facticity of the world, but this does not threaten its real core.

A conception of literature as a language of authenticity, similar to what is found, for example, in some of Heidegger's texts after *Sein und Zeit* is not Poulet's. He remains far removed from any form of prophetic poeticism. The quest for the source, which we have found constantly operative in his thought, can never be separated from the concern for the self that is the carrier of this quest. Yet this self does not possess the power to engender its own duration. This power belongs to what Poulet calls "the moment," but "the moment" designates, in fact, the point in time at which the self accepts language as its sole mode of existence. Language, however, is not a source; it is the articulation of the self and language that acquires a degree of prospective power. Self and language are the two focal points around which the trajectory of the work originates, but neither can by itself find access to the status of source. Each is the anteriority of the other. If one confers upon language the power to originate, one runs the risk of hiding the self. This Poulet fears most of all, as when he asserts: "I want at all costs to save the subjectivity of literature." [28] But if the subject is, in its turn, given the status of origin, one makes it coincide with Being in a self-consuming identity in which lan-

28. *Chemins actuels* . . . , p. 251.

guage is destroyed. Poulet rejects this alternative just as cate-
gorically as he rejects the other, although much less explicitly.
The concern for language can be felt in the tone of anguish that
inhabits the whole of his work and expresses a constant solicitude
for literary survival. The subject that speaks in the criticism of
Georges Poulet is a vulnerable and fragile subject whose voice can
never become established as a presence. This is the very voice of
literature, here incarnated in one of the major works of our time.

VII

The Rhetoric of Blindness:
Jacques Derrida's Reading of Rousseau

> ". . . einen Text als Text ablesen zu können, ohne eine In-
> terpretation dazwischen zu mengen, ist die späteste Form der
> 'inneren Erfahrung,'—vielleicht eine kaum mögliche. . . ."
>
> (". . . to be able to read a *text as text* without the inter-
> ference of an interpretation is the latest-developed form of
> "inner experience,"—perhaps one that is hardly possible. . . ."
> (Nietzsche, *Der Wille zur Macht,* 479)

Looking back over this first group of essays as a representative though deliberately one-sided selection from contemporary
literary criticism, a recurrent pattern emerges. A considerable
amount of insight into the distinctive nature of literary language
can be gained from writers such as Lukács, Blanchot, Poulet, or
the American New Critics, but not by way of direct statement, as
the explicit assertion of a knowledge derived from the observation
or understanding of literary works. It is necessary, in each case,
to read beyond some of the more categorical assertions and balance
them against other much more tentative utterances that seem to
come close, at times, to being contradictory to these assertions. The
contradictions, however, never cancel each other out, nor do they
enter into the synthesizing dynamics of a dialectic. No contradiction or dialectical movement could develop because a fundamental

difference in the level of explicitness prevented both statements from meeting on a common level of discourse; the one always lay hidden within the other as the sun lies hidden within a shadow, or truth within error. The insight seems instead to have been gained from a negative movement that animates the critic's thought, an unstated principle that leads his language away from its asserted stand, perverting and dissolving his stated commitment to the point where it becomes emptied of substance, as if the very possibility of assertion had been put into question. Yet it is this negative, apparently destructive labor that led to what could legitimately be called insight.

Even among the few examples of this short list, significant variations occur in the degree of complexity of the process. In a case such as Lukács's *Essay on the Novel,* we came close to open contradiction. Two explicit and irreconcilable statements face each other in a pseudo-dialectic. The novel is first defined as an ironic mode condemned to remain discontinuous and contingent; the type of totality claimed for the form therefore has to differ in essence, and even in appearance, from the organic unity of natural entities. Yet the tone of the essay itself is not ironical but elegiac: it never seems able to escape from a concept of history that is itself organic, tributary of an original source—the Hellenic epic—that knew neither discontinuity nor distance and, potentially, contained the entirety of the later development within itself. This nostalgia ultimately leads to a synthesis in the modern novel—Flaubert's *Education sentimentale*—in which the unity is recaptured beyond all the negative moments it contains. The second assertion, that "Time confers upon it [the *Education sentimentale*] the appearance of organic growth," stands in direct contradiction to the first, which allows for no such apparent or actual resemblance with organic forms.

It is not a matter of indifference that the mediating category through which this synthesis is presumably achieved is precisely time. Time acts as the healing and reconciling force against an estrangement, a distance that seems to be caused by the arbitrary intervention of a transcendental force. A slightly tighter exegetic pressure on the text reveals that this transcendental agent is itself temporal and that what is being offered as a remedy is in fact the

disease itself. A negative statement about the essentially problematical and self-destructive nature of the novel is disguised as a
positive theory about its ability to rejoin, at the end of its dialectical
development, a state of origin that is purely fictional, though fal-
laciously presented as having historical existence. A certain concept, time, is made to function on two irreconcilable levels: on the
organic level, where we have origin, continuity, growth, and
totalization, the statement is explicit and assertive; on the level
of ironic awareness, where all is discontinuous, alienated, and
fragmentary, it remains so implicit, so deeply hidden behind error
and deception, that it is unable to rise to thematic assertion. The
crucial link between irony and time is never made in Lukács's
essay. And yet, it is the existence of this link that the text finally
conveys to the mind of the reader. The three crucial factors in
the problem have been identified and brought into relationship
with each other: organic nature, irony, and time. To reduce the
novel, as an instance of literary language, to the interplay among
these three factors is an insight of major magnitude. But the manner in which the three factors are said to relate to each other, the
plot of the play they are made to perform, is entirely wrong. In
Lukács's story, the villain—time—appears as the hero, when he
is in fact murdering the heroine—the novel—he is supposed to
rescue. The reader is given the elements to decipher the real plot
hidden behind the pseudo-plot, but the author himself remains
deluded.

In the other instances, the pattern, though perhaps less clear,
is closely similar. The American New Critics arrived at a description of literary language as a language of irony and ambiguity
despite the fact that they remained committed to a Coleridgian
notion of organic form. They disguised a foreknowledge of
hermeneutic circularity under a reified notion of a literary text
as an objective "thing." Here it is the concept of form that is made
to function in a radically ambivalent manner, both as a creator
and undoer of organic totalities, in a manner that resembles the
part played by time in Lukács's essay. The final insight, here
again, annihilated the premises that led up to it, but it is left to
the reader to draw a conclusion that the critics cannot face if they
are to pursue their task.

Similar complications arise when the question of the specificity of literary language is seen from a perspective that is neither historical, as in Lukács, nor formal, as in the American New Criticism, but centered in a self, in the subjectivity of the author or of the author-reader relationship. The category of the self turns out to be so double-faced that it compels the critic who uses it to retract implicitly what he affirms and to end up by offering the mystery of this paradoxical movement as his main insight. Acutely aware of the frailty and fragmentation of the self in its exposure to the world, Binswanger tries to establish the power of the work of art as a sublimation that can lead, despite persistent dangers, to a balanced structurization of multiple tensions and potentialities within the self. The work of art thus becomes an entity in which empirical experiences and their sublimation can exist side by side, through the mediating power of a self that possesses sufficient elasticity to encompass both. In the end he suggests the existence of a gap separating the artist as an empirical subject from a fictional "self." This fictional self seems to exist in the work, but can only be reached at the cost of reason. In this way the assertion of a self leads by inference to its disappearance.

Writing on a more advanced level of awareness, the disappearance of the self becomes the main theme of Blanchot's critical work. Whereas it seems impossible to assert the presence of a self without in fact recording its absence, the thematic assertion of this absence reintroduces a form of selfhood, albeit in the highly reductive and specialized form of a self-reading. And if the act of reading, potential or actual, is indeed a constitutive part of literary language, then it presupposes a confrontation between a text and another entity that seems to exist prior to the elaboration of a subsequent text and that, for all its impersonality and anonymity, still tends to be designated by metaphors derived from selfhood. Claiming to speak for this universal but strictly literary subject, Poulet asserts its power to originate its own temporal and spatial world. It turns out, however, that what is here claimed to be an origin always depends on the prior existence of an entity that lies beyond reach of the self, though not beyond the reach of a language that destroys the possibility of origin.

All these critics seem curiously doomed to say something quite

different from what they meant to say. Their critical stance—
Lukács's propheticism, Poulet's belief in the power of an original
cogito, Blanchot's claim of meta-Mallarméan impersonality—is
defeated by their own critical results. A penetrating but difficult
insight into the nature of literary language ensues. It seems,
however, that this insight could only be gained because the critics
were in the grip of this peculiar blindness: their language could
grope toward a certain degree of insight only because their method
remained oblivious to the perception of this insight. The insight
exists only for a reader in the privileged position of being able
to observe the blindness as a phenomenon in its own right—the
question of his own blindness being one which he is by definition
incompetent to ask—and so being able to distinguish between
statement and meaning. He has to undo the explicit results of a
vision that is able to move toward the light only because, being
already blind, it does not have to fear the power of this light.
But the vision is unable to report correctly what it has perceived in
the course of its journey. To write critically about critics thus
becomes a way to reflect on the paradoxical effectiveness of a
blinded vision that has to be rectified by means of insights that it
unwittingly provides.

Several questions at once arise. Is the blindness of these critics
inextricably tied up with the act of writing itself and, if this is
so, what characteristic aspect of literary language causes blindness
in those who come into close contact with it? Or could the considerable complication of the process be avoided by writing about
literary texts instead of about critics, or about other, less subjective
critics? Are we perhaps dealing with pseudo-complexities, resulting
from an aberration restricted to a small group of contemporary
critics?

The present essay strives for a tentative answer to the first of
these questions. As for the others, they touch upon a recurrent
debate that underlies the entire history of literary criticism: the
latent opposition between what is now often called instrinsic versus
extrinsic criticism. The critics here assembled all have in common
a certain degree of immanence in their approach. For all of them,
the encounter with the language of literature involves a mental
activity which, however problematical, is at least to a point gov-

erned by this language only. All strive for a considerable degree of generality, going so far that they can be said to be writing, not about particular works or authors, but about literature as such. Nevertheless, their generality remains grounded in the initial act of reading. Prior to any generalization about literature, literary texts have to be read, and the possibility of reading can never be taken for granted. It is an act of understanding that can never be observed, nor in any way prescribed or verified. A literary text is not a phenomenal event that can be granted any form of positive existence, whether as a fact of nature or as an act of the mind. It leads to no transcendental perception, intuition, or knowledge but merely solicits an understanding that has to remain immanent because it poses the problem of its intelligibility in its own terms. This area of immanence is necessarily part of all critical discourse. Criticism is a metaphor for the act of reading, and this act is itself inexhaustible.

Attempts to circumvent or to resolve the problem of immanence and to inaugurate a more scientific study of literature have played an important part in the development of contemporary criticism. Perhaps the most interesting cases are authors such as Roman Jakobson, Roland Barthes, and even Northrop Frye, who are on the borderline between the two camps. The same is true of certain structuralist tendencies, which try to apply extrinsic methods to material that remains defined intrinsically and selectively as literary language. Since it is assumedly scientific, the language of a structuralist poetics would itself be definitely "outside" literature, extrinsic to its object, but it would prescribe (in deliberate opposition to describe) a generalized and ideal model of a discourse that defines itself without having to refer to anything beyond its own boundaries; the method postulates an immanent literariness of literature that it undertakes to prescribe.[1] The question remains whether the logical difficulties inherent in the act of interpretation can be avoided by thus moving from an actual, particular text to an ideal one. The problem has not always been correctly perceived, partly because the model for the act of interpretation is being constantly oversimplified.

1. T. Todorov, *Qu'est-ce que le structuralisme?* (Editions du Seuil: Paris, 1968), p. 102.

A recent example can serve as illustration. In a cogently argued and convincing plea for a structural poetics, Tszvestan Todorov dismisses intrinsic criticism in the following manner:

> . . . if one introduces the concept of immanence, a limitation quickly appears and puts into question the very principle of the description. To describe a work, whether literary or not, for itself and in itself, without leaving it for a moment, without projecting it on anything but itself—this is properly speaking impossible. Or rather: the task is possible, but it would make the description into a mere word-for-word repetition of the work itself. . . . And, in a sense, every work is itself its best description.[2]

The use of the term "description," even when taken with full phenomenological rigor, is misleading here. No interpretation pretends to be the description of a work, as one can speak of the description of an object or even of a consciousness, the work being at most an enigmatic appeal to understanding. Interpretation could perhaps be called the description of an understanding, but the term "description," because of its intuitive and sensory overtones, would then have to be used with extreme caution; the term "narration" would be highly preferable. Because the work cannot be said to understand or to explain itself without the intervention of another language, interpretation is never mere duplication. It can legitimately be called a "repetition," but this term is itself so rich and complex that it raises at once a host of theoretical problems. Repetition is a temporal process that assumes difference as well as resemblance. It functions as a regulative principle of rigor but asserts the impossibility of rigorous identity, etc. Precisely to the extent that all interpretation has to be repetition it also has to be immanent.

Todorov rightly perceives the very close connection between interpretation and reading. As he is, however, the captive of the notion of interpretation as duplication, Todorov blames the interpretative process for producing the divergence, the margin of error that is in fact its *raison d'être*:

> What comes closest of all to this ideal but invisible description is simply reading itself. . . . Yet the mere process of reading

2. *Ibid.* p. 100.

is not without consequence: no two readings of the same book are ever identical. In reading, we trace a passive type of writing, we add and suppress what we wish to find or to avoid in the text. . . . What to say then of the no longer passive but active form of reading that we call criticism? . . . How could one write a text that remains faithful to another text and still leaves it untouched; how could one articulate a discourse that remains immanent to another discourse? From the moment there is writing and no longer mere reading, the critic is saying something that the work he studies does not say, even if he claims to be saying the same thing.[3]

Our readings have revealed even more than this: not only does the critic say something that the work does not say, but he even says something that he himself does not mean to say. The semantics of interpretation have no epistemological consistency and can therefore not be scientific. But this is very different from claiming that what the critic says has no immanent connection with the work, that it is an arbitrary addition or subtraction, or that the gap between his statement and his meaning can be dismissed as mere error. The work can be used repeatedly to show where and how the critic diverged from it, but in the process of showing this our understanding of the work is modified and the faulty vision shown to be productive. Critics' moments of greatest blindness with regard to their own critical assumptions are also the the moments at which they achieve their greatest insight. Todorov correctly states that naïve and critical reading are in fact actual or potential forms of "écriture" and, from the moment there is writing, the newly engendered text does not leave the original text untouched. Both texts can even enter into conflict with each other. And one could say that the further the critical text penetrates in its understanding, the more violent the conflict becomes, to the point of mutual destruction: Todorov significantly has to have recourse to an imagery of death and violence in order to describe the encounter between text and commentary.[4] One could

3. *Ibid.* p. 100.
4. *Ibid.* p. 101. ". . . pour laisser la vie à l'oeuvre, le texte descriptif doit mourir; s'il vit lui-même, c'est qu'il tue l'oeuvre qu'il dit."

even go further still and see the murder become suicide as the critic, in his blindness, turns the weapon of his language upon himself, in the mistaken belief that it is aimed at another. In saying all this, however, no argument has been presented against the validity of intrinsic criticism; on the contrary, not only is the discrepancy between the original and the critical text granted, but it is given immanent exegetic power as the main source of understanding. Since they are not scientific, critical texts have to be read with the same awareness of ambivalence that is brought to the study of non-critical literary texts, and since the rhetoric of their discourse depends on categorical statements, the discrepancy between meaning and assertion is a constitutive part of their logic. There is no room for Todorov's notions of accuracy and identity in the shifting world of interpretation. The necessary immanence of the reading in relation to the text is a burden from which there can be no escape. It is bound to stand out as the irreducible philosophical problem raised by all forms of literary criticism, however pragmatic they may seem or want to be. We encounter it here in the form of a constitutive discrepancy, in critical discourse, between the blindness of the statement and the insight of the meaning.

The problem occupies, of course, a prominent place in all philosophies of language, but it has rarely been considered within the humbler, more artisan-like context of practical interpretation. "Close reading" can be highly discriminating and develop a refined ear for the nuances of self-conscious speech, but it remains curiously timid when challenged to reflect upon its own self-consciousness. On the other hand, critics like Blanchot and Poulet who make use of the categories of philosophical reflection tend to erase the moment of actual interpretative reading, as if the outcome of this reading could be taken for granted in any literate audience. In France it took the rigor and intellectual integrity of a philosopher whose main concern is not with literary texts to restore the complexities of reading to the dignity of a philosophical question.

Jacques Derrida makes the movements of his own reading an integral part of a major statement about the nature of language in general. His knowledge stems from the actual encounter with texts, with a full awareness of the complexities involved in such an encounter. The discrepancy implicitly present in the other critics here becomes the explicit center of the reflection. This means that Derrida's work is one of the places where the future possibility of literary criticism is being decided, although he is not a literary critic in the professional sense of the term and deals with hybrid texts—Rousseau's *Essai sur l'origine des langues,* Plato's *Phaedrus*—that share with literary criticism the burden of being partly expository and partly fictional. His commentary on Rousseau[5] can be used as an exemplary case of the interaction between critical blindness and critical insight, no longer in the guise of a semiconscious duplicity but as a necessity dictated and controlled by the very nature of all critical language.

Rousseau is one of the group of writers who are always being systematically misread. I spoke above of the blindness of critics with regard to their own insights, of the discrepancy, hidden to them, between their stated method and their perceptions. In the history as well as in the historiography of literature, this blindness can take on the form of a recurrently aberrant pattern of interpretation with regard to a particular writer. The pattern extends from highly specialized commentators to the vague *idées reçues* by means of which this writer is identified and classified in general histories of literature. It can even include other writers who have been influenced by him. The more ambivalent the original utterance, the more uniform and universal the pattern of consistent error in the followers and commentators. Despite the apparent alacrity with which one is willing to assent in principle to the notion that all literary and some philosophical language is essentially ambivalent, the implied function of most critical commentaries and some literary influences is still to do away at all costs with these ambivalences; by reducing them to contradictions, blotting out the disturbing parts of the work or, more subtly, by manipulating the systems of valorization that are operating within the texts. When, especially as in the case of Rousseau, the ambivalence is itself a part of the philosophical statement, this is

5. Jacques Derrida, *De la Grammatologie* (Éditions de Minuit: Paris, 1967), Part II, pp. 145–445. Henceforth referred to as *Gr.*

very likely to happen. The history of Rousseau interpretation is particularly rich in this respect, both in the diversity of the tactics employed to make him say something different from what he said, and in the convergence of these misreadings toward a definite configuration of meanings. It is as if the conspiracy that Rousseau's paranoia imagined during his lifetime came into being after his death, uniting friend and foe alike in a concerted effort to misrepresent his thought.

Any attempt to explain why and how this distortion took place would lead afield to considerations that do not belong in this context. We can confine ourselves to a single, trivial observation: in Rousseau's case, the misreading is almost always accompanied by an overtone of intellectual and moral superiority, as if the commentators, in the most favorable of cases, had to apologize or to offer a cure for something that went astray in their author. Some inherent weakness made Rousseau fall back into confusion, bad faith, or withdrawal. At the same time, one can witness a regaining of self-assurance in the one who utters the judgment, as if the knowledge of Rousseau's weakness somehow reflected favorably on his own strength. He knows exactly what ails Rousseau and can therefore observe, judge, and assist him from a position of unchallenged authority, like an ethnocentric anthropologist observing a native or a doctor advising a patient. The critical attitude is diagnostic and looks on Rousseau as if he were the one asking for assistance rather than offering his counsel. The critic knows something about Rousseau that Rousseau did not wish to know. One hears this tone of voice even in so sympathetic and penetrating a critic as Jean Starobinski, who did more than anyone else to free Rousseau studies from accumulated decades of wrong *idées reçues*. "No matter how strong the duties of his sympathy may be, the critic must understand [what the writer can not know about himself] and not share in this ignorance," [6] he writes, and although this claim is legitimate, especially since it applies, in this passage, to Rousseau's experiences of childhood, it is perhaps stated with a little too much professional confidence. The same critic goes on to suggest that the more paradoxical statements of Rousseau should not really be taken at face value:

6. Jean Starobinski, "Jean-Jacques Rousseau et le péril de la réflexion" in *L'Oeil vivant* (Gallimard: Paris, 1961), p. 98.

. . . it often happens that he overstates his aim and forces
the meaning, in splendid sentences that can hardly stand the
test of being confronted with each other. Hence the frequently
repeated accusations of sophistry. . . . Should we take those
lapidary maxims, those large statements of principle at face
value? Should we not rather be looking beyond Jean-Jacques's
words toward certain demands made by his soul, toward the
vibration of his feelings? We do him perhaps a disservice
when we expect him to provide rigorous coherence and systematic thought; his true presence is to be found, not in his
discourse, but in the live and still undefined movements that
precede his speech. . . .[7]

Benevolent as it sounds, such a statement reduces Rousseau from
the status of philosopher to that of an interesting psychological
case; we are invited to discard his language as "des phrases
splendides" that function as a substitute for pre-verbal emotional
states into which Rousseau had no insight. The critic can describe
the mechanism of the emotions in great detail, drawing his evidence from these very "phrases splendides" that cover up a by no
means splendid personal predicament.

At first sight, Derrida's attitude toward Rousseau seems hardly
different. He follows Starobinski in presenting Rousseau's decision
to write as an attempt at the fictional recovery of a plenitude, a
unity of being that he could never achieve in his life.[8] The writer
"renounces" life, but this renunciation is hardly in good faith: it
is a ruse by means of which the actual sacrifice, which would imply the literal death of the subject, is replaced by a "symbolic"
death that leaves intact the possibility of enjoying life, adding to
it the possibility of enjoying the ethical value of an act of renunciation that reflects favorably on the person who performs it. The
claim of the literary language to truth and generality is thus suspect from the start, based on a duplicity within a self that willfully
creates a confusion between literal and symbolic action in order
to achieve self-transcendence as well as self-preservation. The
blindness of the subject to its own duplicity has psychological roots
since the unwillingness to see the mechanism of self-deception is
protective. A whole mythology of original innocence in a pre-

7. *Ibid.* p. 184.
8. *Gr.*, pp. 204–5.

reflective state followed by the recovery of this innocence on a more impersonal, generalized level—the story so well described by Starobinski in the Rousseau essay of *L'Oeil vivant*—turns out to be the consequence of a psychological ruse. It collapses into nothingness, in mere "phrases splendides," when the stratagem is exposed, leaving the critic to join ranks with the numerous other "juges de Jean-Jacques."

Even on this level, Derrida's reading of Rousseau diverges fundamentally from the traditional interpretation. Rousseau's bad faith toward literary language, the manner in which he depends on it while condemning writing as if it were a sinful addiction, is for Derrida the personal version of a much larger problem that cannot be reduced to psychological causes. In his relationship to writing, Rousseau is not governed by his own needs and desires, but by a tradition that defines Western thought in its entirety: the conception of all negativity (non-being) as absence and hence the possibility of an appropriation or a reappropriation of being (in the form of truth, of authenticity, of nature, etc.) as presence. This ontological assumption both conditions and depends on a certain conception of language that favors oral language or voice over written language (*écriture*) in terms of presence and distance: the unmediated presence of the self to its own voice as opposed to the reflective distance that separates this self from the written word. Rousseau is seen as one link in a chain that closes off the historical era of Western metaphysics. As such, his attitude toward language is not a psychological idiosyncrasy but a typical and exemplary fundamental philosophical premise. Derrida takes Rousseau seriously as a thinker and dismisses none of his statements. If Rousseau nevertheless stands, or seems to stand, indicted, it is because the entirety of Western philosophy is defined as the possibility of self-indictment in terms of an ontology of presence. This would suffice to exclude any notion of superiority on Derrida's part, at least in the interpersonal sense of the term.

Rousseau's assertion of the primacy of voice over the written word, his adherence to the myth of original innocence, his valorization of unmediated presence over reflection—all these are characteristics that Derrida could legitimately have derived from a long tradition of Rousseau interpreters. He wishes, however, to set himself apart from those who reduce these myths to self-centered strategies of Rousseau's psyche and prefers to approach him by way of a disciple who is more orthodox than Rousseau himself in accepting at face-value dreams of the innocence and integrity of oral language. Derrida's main theme, the recurrent repression, in Western thought, of all written forms of language, their degradation to a mere adjunct or supplement to the live presence of the spoken word, finds a classical example in the works of Lévi-Strauss. The pattern in the passages from Lévi-Strauss that Derrida singles out for comment is consistent in all its details, including the valorization of music over literature and the definition of literature as a means to recoup a presence of which it is a distant and nostalgic echo, unaware that literature is itself a cause and a symptom of the separation it bewails.

Naïve in Lévi-Strauss, the same assumptions become a great deal more devious and ambivalent when they appear in Rousseau himself. Whenever Rousseau designates the moment of unity that exists at the beginning of things, when desire coincides with enjoyment, the self and the other are united in the maternal warmth of their common origin, and consciousness speaks with the voice of truth, Derrida's interpretation shows, without leaving the text, that what is thus designated as a moment of presence always has to posit another, prior moment and so implicitly loses its privileged status as a point of origin. Rousseau defines voice as the origin of written language, but his description of oral speech or of music can be shown to possess, from the start, all the elements of distance and negation that prevent written language from ever achieving a condition of unmediated presence. All attempts to trace writing back to a more original form of vocal utterance lead to the repetition of the disruptive process that alienated the written word from experience in the first place. Unlike Lévi-Strauss, Rousseau *"in fact,* experienced the disappearance [of full presence] in the word itself, in the illusion of immediacy," [9] and he "recognized and analyzed [this disappearance] with incomparable astuteness." But Rousseau never openly declares this; he never asserts the disappearance of presence outright or faces its consequences. On the

9. *Gr.*, p. 203.

contrary, the system of valorization that organizes his writings favors the opposite trend, praises nature, origin, and the spontaneity of mere outcry, over their opposites, not only in the nostalgic, elegiac manner of a poetic statement that makes no claim to truth, but as a philosophical system. In the *Discours sur l'origine de l'inégalité*, in the *Essai sur l'origine des langues* and also later in *Emile* and the *Confessions*, Rousseau expounds the philosophy of unmediated presence that Lévi-Strauss took over uncritically and that Starobinski tries to demystify in the name of a later, perhaps less enlightened, version of the same philosophy. Derrida's considerable contribution to Rousseau studies consists in showing that Rousseau's own texts provide the strongest evidence against his alleged doctrine, going well beyond the point reached by the most alert of his modern readers. Rousseau's work would then reveal a pattern of duplicity similar to what was found in the literary critics: he "knew," in a sense, that his doctrine disguised his insight into something closely resembling its opposite, but he chose to remain blind to this knowledge. The blindness can then be diagnosed as a direct consequence of an ontology of unmediated presence. It remains for the commentator to undo, with some violence, the historically established pattern or, as Derrida puts it, the "orbit" of significant misinterpretation—a pattern of which the first example is to be found in Rousseau's own writings—and thus, by a process of "deconstruction," to bring to light what had remained unperceived by the author and his followers.

Within the orbit of my own question, the attention has to be directed toward the status of this ambivalent "knowledge" that Derrida discovers in Rousseau. The text of *De la Grammatologie* necessarily fluctuates on this point. At times, it seems as if Rousseau were more or less deliberately hiding from himself what he did not want to know: "Having, in a way . . . identified this power which, by opening up the possibility of speech, disrupts the subject that it creates, prevents it from being present to its own signs, saturates its speech with writing, Rousseau is nevertheless more eager to conjure it out of existence than to assume the burden of its necessity." [10] "Conjurer" (as well as the weaker

---

10. *Gr.*, p. 204.

"effacer" that is used elsewhere in the same context) supposes some awareness and, consequently, a duplicity within the self, a degree of deliberate self-deception. The ethical overtone of deceit, implying some participation of the will, is apparent in several other descriptions that use a vocabulary of transgression: "The replacement of mere stressed sound by articulated speech is the origin of language. The modification of speech by writing took place as an extrinsic event at the very beginning of language. It is the origin of language. Rousseau describes this without openly saying so. In contraband."[11] But at other moments it appears instead as if Rousseau were in the grip of a fatality that lies well beyond the reach of his will: "Despite his avowed intent [to speak of origins] Rousseau's discourse is governed (se laisse contraindre) by a complication that always takes on the form of an excess, a "supplement" to the state of origin. This does not eliminate the declared intent but *inscribes* it within a system that it no longer controls (qu'elle ne domine plus)."[12] "Se laisser contraindre" unlike "conjurer" or "effacer" is a passive process, forced upon Rousseau by a power that lies beyond his control. As the word, "inscrite" (italicized by Derrida), and the next sentence[13] make clear, this power is precisely that of written language whose syntax undermines the declarative assertion. Yet the act of "conjurer" also occurred by means of written language, so the model is not simply that of a pre-lingual desire that would necessarily be corrupted or overtaken by the transcendental power of language: language is being smuggled into a presumably languageless state of innocence, but it is by means of the same written language that it is then made to vanish: the magic wand that should "conjure" the written word out of existence is itself made of language. This double valorization of language is willed and controlled as the crux of Derrida's argument: only by language can Rousseau conquer language, and this paradox is responsible for the ambivalence of his attitude toward writing.[14] The exact epistemological status of

11. *Gr.*, p. 443.
12. *Gr.*, p. 345.
13. *Gr.*, p. 345. "The desire for origin becomes a necessary and unavoidable function [of language], but it is governed by a syntax that is without origin."
14. *Gr.*, p. 207.

this ambivalence cannot be clarified: things do not happen as if Rousseau were at least semi-conscious when engaged in the recovery of an unmediated presence and entirely passive when engaged in undermining it. A terminology of semi-consciousness is made to apply to the two contrary impulses: to eliminate awareness of non-presence (*conjurer*) as well as to assert it (*en contrebande*). Derrida's text does not function as if the discrimination that concerns us, namely, the mode of knowledge governing the implicit as opposed to the explicit statement, could be made in terms of the orientation of the thought (or the language) away from or toward the recouping of presence. The awareness of distance, in Rousseau, is at times stated in a blind, at times in a semi-conscious language, and the same applies to the awareness of presence. Rousseau truly seems to want it both ways, the paradox being that he wants wanting and not-wanting at the same time. This would always assume some degree of awareness, though the awareness may be directed against itself.

The "difference between an implied meaning, a nominal presence and a thematic exposition" [15] and all such distinctions within the cognitive status of language are really Rousseau's central problem, but it remains questionable whether he approached the problem explicitly or implicitly in terms of the categories of presence and distance. Derrida is brought face to face with the problem, but his terminology cannot take him any further. The structurization of Rousseau's text in terms of a presence-absence system leaves the cognitive system of deliberate knowledge versus passive knowledge unresolved and distributes it evenly on both sides.

This observation should by no means be construed as a criticism of Derrida; on the contrary. His aim is precisely to show, by a demonstration *ad absurdum,* that a crucial part of Rousseau's statement lies beyond the reach of a categorization in terms of presence and absence. On the all-important point of the cognitive status of Rousseau's language, these categories fail to function as effective indicators; Derrida's purpose in discrediting their absolute value as a base for metaphysical insight is thus achieved. Terms such as "passive," "conscious," "deliberate," etc., all of which postulate a

15. *Gr.,* p. 304. "C'est cette différence entre l'implication, la présence nominale et l'exposition thématique qui nous intéresse ici."

notion of the self as self-presence, turn out to be equally relevant
or irrelevant when used on either side of the differential scale. This
discredits the terms, not the author who uses them with an intent
similar to that of parody: to devalue their claim to universal discriminatory power. The key to the status of Rousseau's language
is not to be found in his consciousness, in his greater or lesser
awareness or control over the cognitive value of his language. It
can only be found in the knowledge that this language, as language, conveys about itself, thereby asserting the priority of the
category of language over that of presence—which is precisely
Derrida's thesis. The question remains why he postulates within
Rousseau a metaphysics of presence which can then be shown not
to operate, or to be dependent on the implicit power of a language which disrupts it and tears it away from its foundation.
Derrida's story of Rousseau's getting, as it were, a glimpse of the
truth but then going about erasing, conjuring this vision out of
existence, while also surreptitiously giving in to it and smuggling
it within the precinct he was assigned to protect, is undoubtedly
a good story. It reverses the familiar pattern of "le bráconnier
devenu garde-chasse," since it is rather the gamekeeper himself
who is here doing the poaching. We should perhaps not even ask
whether it is accurate, for it may well be offered as parody or
fiction, without pretending to be anything else. But, unlike epistemological statements, stories do not cancel each other out, and
we should not let Derrida's version replace Rousseau's own story
of his involvement with language. The two stories are not
quite alike and their differences are worth recording; they are instructive with regard to the cognitive status, not only of Rousseau's
but also of Derrida's language and beyond that, of the language
of criticism in general.

We should not be detained too long by differences in emphasis
that could lead to areas of disagreement within the traditional field
of Rousseau interpretation. Having deliberately bracketed the
question of the author's knowledge of his own ambivalence, Derrida proceeds as if Rousseau's blindness did not require further
qualification. This leads to simplifications in the description of
Rousseau's stated positions on matters of ethics and history. In a

Nietzschean passage in which he claims to have freed the question of language from all ethical valorization,[16] Derrida implies a single-minded, unalterable basis for moral judgment in Rousseau —the notion of a reliable "voice" of moral consciousness—that fails to do justice to the moral intricacies of the *Nouvelle Héloïse,* or even to Derrida's own illuminating comments on the nature of pity in the *Discours sur l'origine de l'inégalité.* Having convincingly demonstrated that an arbitrary inside-outside dichotomy is used in *Essai sur l'origine des langues* to make it appear as if the hardships of distance and alienation were wrought upon man by an external catastrophical event, he makes it appear as if Rousseau understood this catastrophe in a literal sense, as an actual event in history or as the act of a personal god. Whenever a delicate transposition from the literary statement to its empirical referent occurs, Derrida seems to bypass Rousseau's complexities. Thus on the valorization of historical change or the possibility of progress, Derrida writes: "Rousseau wants to say that progress, however ambivalent, moves *either* towards deterioration, *or* toward improvement, the one or the other. . . . But Rousseau describes what he does not want to say: that progress moves in both directions, toward good and evil at the same time. This excludes eschatological and teleological endpoints, just as difference—or articulation at the source—eliminates the archeology of beginnings." [17] In fact, it would be difficult to match the rigor with which Rousseau always asserts, at the same time and at the same level of explicitness, the simultaneous movement toward progress and retrogression that Derrida here proclaims. The end of the state of nature leads to the creation of societies and their infinite possibilities of corruption—but this apparent regression is counterbalanced, at the same time, by the end of solitude and the possibility of human love. The development of reason and consciousness spells the end of tranquillity, but this tranquillity is also designated as a state of intellectual limitation similar to that of an imbecile. In such descriptions, the use of progressive and regressive terms is evenly balanced: "perfectionner la raison humaine" balances with "détériorer l'espèce," "rendre méchant" with "rendre

16. *Gr.,* p. 442.
17. *Gr.,* p. 326.

sociable." [18] The evolution of society toward inequality is far from being an unmitigated evil: we owe to it "ce qu'il y a de meilleur et de pire parmi les hommes." The end of history is seen as a relapse into a state that is undistinguishable from the state of nature, thus making the starting-point, the outcome, and the trajectory that leads from one to the other all equally ambivalent. Perhaps most typical of all is the curious movement of a long foot-note to the *Discours sur l'origine de l'inégalité* in which, after hav-ing denounced with eloquence all the perils of civilization ("These are the manifest causes of all the miseries that opulence brings in the end to even the most admired of nations . . ."), Rousseau then demands from us, without any trace of irony, the utmost in civic obedience, while nevertheless despising the neces-sary recourse to a political order that generates its own abuses.[19] The paradoxical logic of a simultaneously positive and negative evaluation, whenever the movement of history is involved, could not be more consistent. There can be some debate as to whether the progressive and regressive movements are indeed equally balanced: in less descriptive passages, Rousseau tends to see his-tory as a movement of decline, especially when he speaks from the point of view of the present. But whenever the double valoriza-tion occurs, the structure is simultaneous rather than alternating. Derrida's conclusion is based on an inadequate example, nor is there much evidence to be found elsewhere in Rousseau's works for such an alternating theory of historical change.[20]

None of these points is substantial. Derrida could legitimately

18. J. J. Rousseau, *Discours sur l'origine et les fondements de l'inégalité parmi les hommes* in *Oeuvres complètes*, vol. III (Ecrits politiques), Bernard Gagnebin and Marcel Raymond, eds. (Bibliothèque de la Pléiade: Paris, 1964), p. 189.
19. *Ibid.* Note IX, pp. 207–8.
20. Derrida (Gr., p. 236) quotes the sentence from the *Essai sur l'origine des langues:* "La langue de convention n'appartient qu'à l'homme. Voilà pourquoi l'homme fait des progrès, soit en bien, soit en mal, et pourquoi les animaux n'en font point." Rousseau here distinguishes man from the animal in terms of historical mutability. "Soit en bien, soit en mal" indicates that the change is morally ambivalent but does not describe an alternating movement. In the *Discours sur l'économie politique* or in the second part of the *Discours sur l'origine de l'inégalité*, the dialectical movement takes place between the prin-ciples of law and freedom, on the one hand, as opposed to the necessary de-cline of all human political order on the other. No alternating movement of reversal from a progressive to a regressive pattern is suggested.

claim that passages in Rousseau on moral ambiguity, on the fictional (and therefore "inward") quality of the external cause for
the disruption of the state of nature, on the simultaneity of historical decline and historical progress, do not in the least invalidate
his reading. They are the *descriptive* passages in which Rousseau
is compelled to write the reverse of what he wants to say. The
same would apply to a more complex aspect of Derrida's reading:
the strange economy of Rousseau's valorization of the notion of
origin and the manner in which it involves him in an infinitely
regressive process; he always has to substitute for the discarded
origin a "deeper," more primitive state that will, in turn, have to
be left behind. The same pattern appears in Derrida when he
chooses to maintain a vocabulary of origin to designate the non-
original quality of all so-called beginnings—as when we are told
that the articulation is the origin of language, when articulation is
precisely the structure that prevents all genuine origination from
taking place. The use of a vocabulary of presence (or origin, nature, consciousness, etc.) to explode the claims of this vocabulary,
carrying it to the logical dead-end to which it is bound to lead, is
a consistent and controlled strategy throughout *De la Grammatologie*. We would be falling into a trap if we wanted to show
Derrida deluded in the same manner that he claims Rousseau to
be deluded. Our concern is not so much with the degree of blindness in Rousseau or in Derrida as with the rhetorical mode of
their respective discourses.

It is not surprising that Derrida should be more detailed and
eloquent in expounding the philosophy of written language and
of "difference" that Rousseau rejects than in expounding the philosophy of plenitude that Rousseau wants to defend. He has, after
all, a massive tradition of Rousseau interpretation behind him to
support his view of him as an avowed philosopher of unmediated
presence. In this respect, his image of Rousseau is so traditional
that it hardly needs to be restated. The main bulk of his analysis
therefore deals with the gradual chipping away of Rousseau's
theory of presence under the onus of his own language. On at
least two points, however, Derrida goes out of his way to demonstrate the strict orthodoxy of Rousseau's position with regard to
the traditional ontology of Western thought, and in at least one

of these instances, he can do so only at the expense of a considerable and original interpretative effort that has to move well beyond and even against the face-value of Rousseau's own statement.[21] Significantly, the two passages have to do with Rousseau's use and understanding of rhetorical figures. On the questions of nature, of self, of origin, even of morality, Derrida starts out from the current view in Rousseau interpretation and then proceeds to show how Rousseau's own text undermines his declared philosophical allegiances. But on the two points involving rhetoric, Derrida goes the tradition one better. It is obviously important for him that Rousseau's theory and practice of rhetoric would also fall under the imperatives of what he calls a "logocentric" ontology that privileges the spoken word over the written word. This is also the point at which we have to reverse the interpretative process and start reading Derrida in terms of Rousseau rather than vice versa.

The two closely related rhetorical figures discussed by Derrida, both prominently in evidence in the *Essai sur l'origine des langues,* are imitation (mimesis) and metaphor. In order to demonstrate the logocentric orthodoxy of Rousseau's theory of metaphor, Derrida has to show that his conception of representation is based on an imitation in which the ontological status of the imitated entity is not put into question. Representation is an ambivalent process that implies the absence of what is being made present again, and this absence cannot be assumed to be merely contingent. However, when representation is conceived as imitation, in the classical sense of eighteenth-century aesthetic theory, it confirms rather than undermines the plenitude of the represented entity. It functions as a mnemotechnic sign that brings back something that happened not to be there at the moment, but whose existence in another place, at another time, or in a different mode of consciousness is not challenged. The model for this idea of representation is the painted image, restoring the object to view as if it were present and thus assuring the continuation of its presence. The power of the image reaches beyond duplication of sense data: the mimetic imagination is able to convert non-sensory, "inward" patterns of ex-

21. I am referring to the passage on metaphor (*Gr.,* pp. 381–97) here discussed on pp. 133–35.

perience (feelings, emotions, passions) into objects of perception
and can therefore represent as actual, concrete presences, experiences of consciousness devoid of objective existence. This possibility is often stressed as the main function of non-representational
art forms such as music: they imitate by means of signs linked by
natural right with the emotions which they signify. A representative eighteenth-century aesthetician, the abbé Du Bos, writes:

> Just as the painter imitates the lines and colors of nature, the
> musician imitates the tone, the stresses, the pauses, the voice-
> inflections, in short all the sounds by means of which nature
> itself expresses its feelings and emotions. All these sounds
> . . . are powerfully effective in conveying emotions, because
> they are the signs of passion instituted by nature itself. They
> receive their strength directly from nature, whereas articulated
> words are merely the arbitrary signs of the passions. . . .
> Music groups the natural signs of the passions and uses them
> artfully to increase the power of the words it makes into song.
> These natural signs have an amazing power in awakening
> emotions in those who hear them. They receive this power
> from nature itself.[22]

Classical eighteenth-century theories of representation persistently strive to reduce music and poetry to the status of painting.[23]
"La musique peint les passions" and ut pictura poesis are the great
commonplaces of an aesthetic creed that involves its proponents
in an interesting maze of problems, without, however, leading
them to revise their premises. The possibility of making the invisible visible, of giving presence to what can only be imagined, is
repeatedly stated as the main function of art. The stress on subject-
matter as the basis for aesthetic judgment stems from such a creed.
It involves the representation of what lies beyond the senses as a
means to confer upon it the ontological stability of perceived
objects. One is interested in the subject-matter primarily because it

22. Jean Baptiste (abbé) Du Bos, Réflexions critiques sur la poésie et sur la
peinture (Paris, 1740) vol. I, pp. 435–36, 438.
23. Ibid. "Il n'y a de la vérité dans une symphonie, composée pour imiter une
tempête, que lorsque le chant de la symphonie, son harmonie et son rhythme
nous font entendre un bruit pareil au fracas que les vents font dans l'air et au
mugissement des flots qui s'entrechoquent, ou qui se brisent contre les rochers."
(Du Bos, op. cit. p. 440.)

confirms that the unseen can be represented: representation is the condition that confirms the possibility of imitation as universal proof of presence. The need for the reassurance of such a proof stands behind many characteristic statements of the period [24] and confirms its orthodoxy in terms of a metaphysics of presence.

At first sight, Rousseau seems to continue the tradition, specifically in the passages from the *Essai* that deal with the characterization of music and that differ little from the classical statements of his predecessors. His stress on the inwardness of music is entirely compatible with his proclaimed theory of music as imitation: "The sounds in a melody do not only affect us as sounds, but as signs of our emotions, of our feelings. This is how they produce within us the responses they express and how we recognize the image of our emotions in them." [25] From the point of view of imitation, there is no difference between the outward physical impressions and the "impressions morales." "Passions" and "objets" can be used interchangeably without modifying the nature of imitation.

> Beautiful, well-shaded colors please our sight, but this pleasure is purely of the senses. Colors come to life and move us because of the design (le dessin), the imitation. We are affected by the objects represented and by the passions expressed in the design of the painting. The interest and the seductiveness of the picture does not stem from the colors. We will still be moved by the outline (les traits) of a painting that has been

24. The following passage from Du Bos is a typical example: "Un peintre peut donc passer pour un grand artisan, en qualité de dessinateur élégant ou de coloriste rival de la nature, quand même il ne saurait pas faire usage de ses talents pour représenter des objets touchants, et pour mettre dans ses tableaux l'âme et la vraisemblance qui se font sentir dans ceux de Raphaël et du Poussin. Les tableaux de l'école Lombarde sont admirés, bien que les peintres s'y soient bornés souvent à flatter les yeux par la richesse et par la vérité de leurs couleurs, sans penser peut-être que l'art fut capable de nous attendrir: mais leurs partisans les plus zélés tombent d'accord qu'il manque une grande beauté aux tableaux de cette école, et que ceux du Titien, par exemple, seraient encore bien plus précieux s'il avait traité toujours de sujets touchants, et s'il eut joint plus souvent les talents de son Ecole aux talents de l'Ecole romaine." (Du Bos, *op. cit.* p. 69.)

25. J. J. Rousseau, *Essai sur l'origine des langues*, texte reproduit d'après l'édition A. Belin de 1817 (Bibliothèque du Graphe: Paris, n.d.), p. 534. Henceforth designated as *Essai*.

reduced to a print but, if we remove the outline, the colors will lose all their power.

Melody does for music exactly what design does for painting. . . .[26]

Derrida seems altogether justified in seeing Rousseau as a traditional expounder of a theory of imitation that bridges the distinction between external and inward themes.

> Rousseau remains faithful to a tradition that is unaffected by his thought: he stays convinced that the essence of art is imitation (*mimesis*). Imitation duplicates presence: it is added to the presence of the entity which it replaces. It transposes what is present into an "outside" version of this presence (elle fait donc passer le présent dans son dehors). In the inanimate arts, the "outside" version of the entity is being duplicated: we have the "outside" reproduction of an "outside" version (la reproduction du dehors dans le dehors). . . . In animate art, most emphatically in song, the "outside" imitates an "inside" (le dehors imite le dedans). It is *expressive*. It "paints" the passions. The metaphor that transforms song into painting can force the inwardness of its power into the outwardness of space only under the aegis of the concept of imitation, shared alike by music and by painting. Whatever their differences, music and painting both are duplications, representations. Both equally partake of the categories of outside and inside. The expression has already begun to move the passion outside itself into the open and has already begun to paint it.[27]

The rest of Derrida's analysis will then show how imitation, which expresses an avowed desire for presence, surreptitiously functions, in Rousseau's text, as the undoing of a desire that it reduces to absurdity by its very existence: there never would be a need for imitation if the presence had not been *a priori* pre-empted (entamée).

Turning with this reading in mind to the section of the *Essai* that deals with music, we find something different, especially if we take into account some of the passages that Derrida does not

26. *Essai*, pp. 530–31.
27. *Gr.*, pp. 289–90.

include in his commentary.* In Chapters XIII to XVI of the *Essai*, Rousseau is not so much bent on showing that music, painting and art in general do not involve sensation (as seems to be the thrust of his polemical argument against sensualist aesthetics), but that the sensory element that is necessarily a part of the pictorial or musical sign plays no part in the aesthetic experience. Hence the priority of drawing (le trait, le dessin) over color, of melody over sound, because both are oriented toward meaning and less dependent on seductive sensory impressions. Like Du Bos, Rousseau seems eager to safeguard the importance of subject matter (or, in the case of literature, of meaning) over the sign. When he pays attention, at moments, to the sign, as in the statement: "Les couleurs et les sons peuvent beaucoup comme représentation et signes, peu de chose comme simples objets de sens," [28] this does not imply any willingness to dissociate the sign from the sensation or to state its autonomy. The sign never ceases to function as *signifiant* and remains entirely oriented toward a meaning.[29] Its own sensory component is contingent and distracting. The reason for this, however, is not, as Derrida suggests, because Rousseau wants the meaning of the sign, the *signifié*, to exist as plenitude and as presence. The sign is devoid of substance, not because it has to be a transparent indicator that should not mask a plenitude of meaning, but because the meaning itself is empty; the sign should not offer its own sensory richness as a substitute for the void that it signifies. Contrary to Derrida's assertion, Rousseau's theory of representation is not directed toward meaning as presence and plenitude but toward meaning as void.

The movement of the sixteenth chapter of the *Essai*, entitled, "Fausse analogie entre les couleurs et les sons" bears this out. Reversing the prevailing hierarchy of eighteenth-century aesthetic theory, it states the priority of music over painting (and, within music, of melody over harmony) in terms of a value-system that is structural rather than substantial: music is called superior to

---

* With perfect right, within the logic of his own argument, which would consider these passages as redundant or dealt with elsewhere in the commentary. The validity of my emphasis has to stand on its own merits and be responsible for it own omissions, not less blatant than Derrida's for being different.

28. *Essai*, p. 535.

29. As stated by Derrida, *Gr.*, p. 296.

painting despite and even because of its lack of substance. With remarkable foresight, Rousseau describes music as a pure system of relations that at no point depends on the substantive assertions of a presence, be it as a sensation or as a consciousness. Music is a mere play of relationships:

> . . . for us, each sound is a relative entity. No sound by itself possesses absolute attributes that allow us to identify it: it is high or low, loud or soft with respect to another sound only. By itself, it has none of these properties. In a harmonic system, a given sound is nothing by natural right (un son quelconque n'est *rien* non plus *naturellement*). It is neither tonic, nor dominant, harmonic or fundamental. All these properties exist as relationships only and since the entire system can vary from bass to treble, each sound changes in rank and place as the system changes in degree.[30]

"Un son n'est rien . . . naturellement." Are we entitled to italicize and isolate this passage as proof of the negation of the substantiality of meaning in Rousseau? Not on the basis of the sentence just quoted, but with greater semblance of truth if we take the neighboring passages into account, for it seems that Rousseau fully understood the implications and consequences of what he was saying. Music is not reduced to a system of relationships because it functions as a mere structure of sounds independently of meaning, or because it is able to obscure the meaning by seducing the senses. There is no vacillation in Rousseau as to the semiotic and non-sensory status of the sign. Music becomes a mere structure because it is hollow at the core, because it "means" the negation of all presence. It follows that the musical structure obeys an entirely different principle from that of structures resting on a "full" sign, regardless of whether the sign refers to sensation or to a state of consciousness. Not being grounded in any substance, the musical sign can never have any assurance of existence. It can never be identical with itself or with prospective repetitions of itself, even if these future sounds possess the same physical properties of pitch and timbre as the present one. The identities of physics have no bearing on the mode of

30. *Essai*, p. 536.

being of a sign that is, by definition, unaffected by sensory attributes. "Colors remain but sounds faint away and we can never be certain that the sounds reborn are the same as the sounds that vanished." [31]

Unlike the stable, synchronic sensation of "painting," [32] music can never rest for a moment in the stability of its own existence: it steadily has to repeat itself in a movement that is bound to remain endless. This movement persists regardless of any illusion of presence, regardless of the manner in which the subject interprets its intentionality: it is determined by the nature of sign as *signifiant*, by the nature of music as language. The resulting repetitive pattern is the ground of temporality: "The field of music is time, that of painting space." The duration of the colors, in painting, is spatial and constitutes therefore a misleading analogy for the necessarily diachronic structure of music. On the one hand, music is condemned to exist always as a moment, as a persistently frustrated intent toward meaning; on the other hand, this very frustration prevents it from remaining within the moment. Musical signs are unable to coincide: their dynamics are always oriented toward the future of their repetition, never toward the consonance of their simultaneity. Even the apparent harmony of the single sound, *à l'unisson,* has to spread itself out into a pattern of successive repetition; considered as a musical sign, the single sound is in fact the melody of its potential repetition. "Nature does not analyze [sound] into its harmonic components: it hides them instead under the illusion of unison (l'apparence de l'unisson). . . ."

Music is the diachronic version of the pattern of non-coincidence within the moment. Rousseau attributes to nature the imaginative power to create melody when it refers to noises such as the song of the birds, but it becomes distinctively human in reference to music: ". . . if nature sometimes breaks down [the song into its harmonic components] in the modulated song of man

31. *Ibid.* p. 536.
32. "Painting" here designates the general prejudice in favor of the image as presence in eighteenth-century aesthetics. It goes without saying that when painting is conceived as art, the illusion of plenitude can be undermined in the plastic arts as well as in poetry or music; the problem, as is well known, figures prominently in contemporary discussions about non-representational painting.

or in the song of birds, it does so sequentially, putting one sound after the other: it inspires song, not chords; it dictates melody, not harmony." [33] Harmony is rejected as a mistaken illusion of consonance within the necessarily dissonant structure of the moment. Melody does not partake of this mystification: it does not offer a resolution of the dissonance but its projection on a temporal, diachronic axis.

The successive structure of music is therefore the direct consequence of its non-mimetic character. Music does not imitate, for its referent is the negation of its very substance, the sound. Rousseau states this in a remarkable sentence that Derrida does not quote: "It is one of the main privileges of the musician to be able to paint things that are inaudible, whereas the painter cannot represent things that are invisible. An art that operates entirely by means of motion can accomplish the amazing feat of conveying the very image of repose. Sleep, the quiet of night, solitude and even silence can enter into the picture that music paints. . . ." [34] The sentence starts off by reaffirming that music is capable of imitating the most inward, invisible, and inaudible of feelings; the use of the pictorial vocabulary suggests that we have re-entered the orthodoxy of eighteenth-century representational theory. But as the enumeration proceeds, the content of the sentiment which, in Du Bos, was rich in all the plenitude and interest of experience, is increasingly hollowed out, emptied of all trace of substance. The idyllic overtones of tranquillity tend to disappear if one remembers to what extent music itself depends on motion; the "repos" should also be understood negatively as loss

33. *Essai*, p. 536. See also, p. 537: "les oiseaux sifflent, l'homme seul chante. . . ."
34. *Ibid*. p. 537. Cf. the passage on silence in Du Bos, *op. cit.* pp. 447–48. Rousseau's allusion to "une lecture égale et monotone à laquelle on s'endort" parallels Du Bos: "Un homme qui parle longtemps sur le même ton, endort les autres . . .", possibly suggesting a direct echo in Rousseau, certainly a very similar point of departure. But Rousseau does not simply refer to a mechanical effect that would allow for a musical "imitation" of silence: he distinguishes at once between this automatic action and a much closer affinity between music and silence: "la musique agit plus intimement sur nous. . . ." The rest of the paragraph complicates matters further by bringing in notions of irreversible synaesthesia between music and painting, but does not pursue the paradox of a "music of silence" that has just been stated.

of motion and therefore as a restatement of the inherent fragility, impermanence, and self-destructiveness of music. The solitude is equally disquieting since much has been made elsewhere in the text of music as the element that sets man apart from nature and unites him with other men. And the radically paradoxical formulation that the musical sign can refer to silence would have for its equivalent, in the other arts, that painting refers to the absence of all light and color, and that language refers to the absence of meaning.[35] The passage prefigures its later, more extreme version in *La Nouvelle Héloïse*: "tel est le néant des choses humaines qu'hors l'Etre existant par lui-même, il n'y a rien de beau que ce qui n'est pas." [36]

It would not be fruitful to dispute these statements on the basis of a different phenomenology of music: the avowed thesis of the *Essai* equates music with language and makes it clear that, throughout the text, Rousseau never ceased to speak about the nature of language. What is here called language, however, differs entirely from an instrumental means of communication: for that purpose, a mere gesture, a mere cry would suffice. Rousseau acknowledges the existence of language from the moment speech is structured according to a principle similar to that of music. Like music, language is a diachronic system of relationships, the succesive sequence of a *narrative*. "The sequential effect of discourse, as it repeats its point again and again, conveys a much stronger emotion than the presence of the object itself, where the full meaning is revealed in one single stroke. Let us assume that we confront a familiar situation of grief. The sight of the bereaved person will hardly move us to tears, but if we give him time to tell all that he feels, our tears will soon begin to flow." [37] The structural characteristics of language are exactly the same as those attributed to music: the misleading synchronism of the visual perception which creates a false illusion of presence has to be replaced by a succession of discontinuous moments that

35. "Musicienne du silence . . ." is a famous line from Mallarmé ("Sainte"). It could be argued that Mallarmé went less far than Rousseau in seeing the implications of this line for a representational theory of poetry.
36. Rousseau, *La Nouvelle Héloïse*, Pléiade edition, *Oeuvres complètes*, vol. II, p. 693.
37. *Essai*, p. 503.

create the fiction of a repetitive temporality. That this diachrony is indeed a fiction, that it belongs to the language of writing and of art and not to a language of needs is made clear by the choice of an example taken, not from life, but from a dramatic performance: "Scenes from a tragedy reach their effect [by sequential discourse] only. Mere pantomime without words will leave us nearly cold, but speech even without gestures will make us weep." [38] All sequential language is dramatic, narrative language. It is also the language of passion because passion, in Rousseau, is precisely the manifestation of a will that exists independently of any specific meaning or intent and that therefore can never be traced back to a cause or origin. "A man will weep at the sight of a tragic performance even though he never felt pity for a person in need." [39] But pity, the arch passion in Rousseau is itself, as Derrida has very well perceived, inherently a fictional process that transposes an actual situation into a world of appearance, of drama and literary language: all pity is in essence theatrical. It follows that the diachronic pattern of narrative discourse, which confers upon this discourse the semblance of a beginning, of a continuity, and of an ending, by no means implies a quest for origin, not even the metaphorical representation of such a quest. Neither the *Discours sur l'origine de l'inégalité* nor the *Essai sur l'origine des langues* is the history of a genetic movement, of an organic process of birth and decay: Rousseau's famous statement "Commençons donc par écarter tous les faits . . ." cannot be taken too radically and applies to the mode of language used throughout the two texts. They do not "represent" a successive event, but are the melodic, musical, successive projection of a single moment of radical contradiction—the present—upon the temporal axis of a diachronic narrative. The only point at which they touch upon an empirical reality is in their common rejection of any present as totally intolerable and devoid of meaning.[40] Diachronic structures such as music, melody, or allegory are favored over pseudo-syn-

38. *Ibid*. p. 503.
39. *Ibid*. p. 503 (Rousseau's own footnote).
40. Clearly stated in the last chapter of the *Essai* entitled "Rapport des langues aux gouvernements," the true point of departure of the text. The same applies, in a somewhat more diffuse way, to the *Discours sur l'origine de l'inégalité*.

chronic structures such as painting, harmony, or mimesis because the latter mislead one into believing in a stability of meaning that does not exist. The elegiac tone that is occasionally sounded does not express a nostalgia for an original presence but is a purely dramatic device, an effect made possible and dictated by a fiction that deprives the nostalgia of all foundation.[41] It does not suffice to say that, in these texts, origin is merely a metaphor that "stands for" a beginning, even if one makes it clear that Rousseau's theory of figural language breaks with any idea of representation. The origin here "precedes" the present for purely structural and not chronological reasons. Chronology is the structural correlative of the necessarily figural nature of literary language.

It is in that sense that the title of the third chapter of the *Essai* must be understood: "Que le premier langage dut être figuré." The only literal statement that says what it means to say is the assertion that there can be no literal statements. In the narrative rhetoric of Rousseau's text, this is what is meant by the chronological fiction that the "first" language had to be poetic language. Derrida, who sees Rousseau as a representational writer, has to show instead that his theory of metaphor is founded on the priority of the literal over the metaphorical meaning, of the "sens propre" over the "sens figuré." And since Rousseau explicitly says the opposite, Derrida has to interpret the chapter on metaphor as a moment of blindness in which Rousseau says the opposite of what he means to say.

The argument on this point duplicates the line of reasoning applied to representation: Rousseau no longer locates the literal meaning in the referent of the metaphor as an object, but he interiorizes the object and makes the metaphor refer to an inner state of consciousness, a feeling or a passion. "Rousseau bestows upon the expression of emotions a literal meaning that he is willing to relinquish, from the start, in the designation of objects." [42] In accordance with Derrida's general image of Rous-

41. The point should be developed in terms of the *Discours sur l'origine de l'inégalité*, showing that elegiac passages are associated with a deluded primitivism unequivocally condemned in the text as a whole. (See, for example, the section on p. 133 beginning "Les temps dont je vais parler sont bien éloignés. . . .")
42. *Gr.*, p. 389.

seau's place in the history of Western thought—the moment
when the postulate of presence is taken out of the external world
and transposed within the self-reflective inwardness of a consciousness—the recovery of presence is shown to occur along
the axis of an inner-outer polarity. Derrida can use Rousseau's
own example of metaphor to prove his case: the primitive man
who designates the first other men he encounters by the term
"giants," blindly coins a metaphorical term to state a literal meaning, the inner experience of fear. The statement, "I see a giant"
is a metaphor for the literal statement, "I am frightened," a feeling
that could not be expressed by saying, "I see a man (like myself)."
Rousseau uses this example to indicate that the transposed meaning can "precede" the literal one. But the example is badly chosen,
possibly, as Derrida suggests,[43] under the influence of Condillac,
to whose *Essai sur l'origine des connaissances humaines* Rousseau
is alluding in the chapter on metaphor. The "babes in the woods"
topos is used by Condillac to make language originate out of a
feeling of fear.[44] In Rousseau's vocabulary, language is a product
of passion and not the expression of a need; fear, the reverse side
of violence and agression, is distinctively utilitarian and belongs
to the world of "besoins" rather than "passions." Fear would hardly
need language and would be best expressed by pantomime, by
mere gesture. All passion is to some degree *passion inutile,* made
gratuitous by the non-existence of an object or a cause. The
possibility of passion distinguishes man from the animal: "The
need for subsistence forces man apart from other men, but the
passions draw them together. The first speech was not caused by
hunger or thirst, but by love, hatred, pity and anger." [45] Fear is

43. *Ibid.* p. 393. The argument on the same page in which Derrida tries to
show the priority of fear over pity as the "earlier" passion, loses what was gained
by the masterful insight in the nature of pity as an element of distance and
difference (*Gr.,* p. 262). The distinction between "passion" and "besoin" cannot be made in terms of origin but of substance: the substantial referent of the
need is missing in the case of the passion.
44. Condillac, *Essai sur l'origine des connaissances humaines,* Part II, Section I
(De l'origine et des progrès du langage): "Celui [des deux enfants abandonnés
dans le désert] qui voyait un lieu où il avait été effrayé, imitait les cris et les
mouvements qui étaient les signes de la frayeur, pour avertir l'autre de ne pas
s'exposer au danger qu'il avait connu." *Oeuvres* (Paris, 1798), vol. I, p. 263.
45. *Gr.,* p. 505.

on the side of hunger and thirst and could never, by itself, lead to the supplementary figuration of language; it is much too practical to be called a passion. The third chapter of the *Essai*, the section on metaphor, should have been centered on pity, or its extension: love (or hate). When the story of the "birth" of figural language is told later in the text (Chapter IX, p. 525) it is directly associated with love, not with fear. The definitive statement, here again, is to be found in the *Nouvelle Héloïse*: "Love is mere illusion. It invents, so to speak, another universe; it surrounds itself with objects that do not exist or to which only love itself has given life. Since it expresses all its feelings by means of images it speaks only in figures (comme il rend tous ses sentiments en images, son langage est toujours figuré)." [46] The metaphorical language which, in the fictional diachrony of the *Essai*, is called "premier" has no literal referent. Its only referent is "le néant des choses humaines."

Although—with regard to his own as well as to Derrida's main statement on the nature of language—Rousseau's theory of rhetoric is peripheral, it is not unimportant within the narrow context of our own question, which deals with the cognitive structure of the interpretative process. To extend the argument to other areas of assent and disagreement with Derrida, would be tedious and unnecessary. On the question of rhetoric, on the nature of figural language, Rousseau was not deluded and said what he meant to say. And it is equally significant that, precisely on this same point, his best modern interpreter had to go out of his way *not* to understand him. The *Discours sur l'origine de l'inégalité* and the *Essai sur l'origine des langues* are texts whose discursive assertions account for their rhetorical mode. What is being said about the nature of language makes it unavoidable that the texts should be written in the form of a fictionally diachronic narrative or, if one prefers to call it so, of an allegory.[47] The allegorical mode is accounted for in the description of all language as figural and in the necessarily diachronic structure of the reflection that reveals this insight.

46. Rousseau, *La Nouvelle Héloïse*, Pléiade edition, vol. II, p. 15.
47. For another preparatory statement on allegory in Rousseau, see Paul de Man, "The Rhetoric of Temporality" in *Interpretation: Theory and Practise*, Charles Singleton, ed. (Johns Hopkins Press, 1969), pp. 184–88.

The text goes beyond this, however, for as it accounts for its own mode of writing, it states at the same time the necessity of making this statement itself in an indirect, figural way that knows it will be misunderstood by being taken literally. Accounting for the "rhetoricity" of its own mode, the text also postulates the necessity of its own misreading. It knows and asserts that it will be misunderstood. It tells the story, the allegory of its misunderstanding: the necessary degradation of melody into harmony, of language into painting, of the language of passion into the language of need, of metaphor into literal meaning. In accordance with its own language, it can only tell this story as a fiction, knowing full well that the fiction will be taken for fact and the fact for fiction; such is the necessarily ambivalent nature of literary language. Rousseau's own language, however, is not blind to this ambivalence: proof of this lies in the entire organization of his discourse and more explicit in what it says about representation and metaphor as the cornerstone of a theory of rhetoric. The consistency of a rhetoric that can assert itself only in a manner that leaves open the possibility of misunderstanding, adds further proof. The rhetorical character of literary language opens up the possibility of the archetypal error: the recurrent confusion of sign and substance. That Rousseau was misunderstood confirms his own theory of misunderstanding. Derrida's version of this misunderstanding comes closer than any previous version to Rousseau's actual statement because it singles out as the point of maximum blindness the area of greatest lucidity: the theory of rhetoric and its inevitable consequences.

How then does Derrida's text differ from Rousseau's? We are entitled to generalize in working our way toward a definition by giving Rousseau exemplary value and calling "literary," in the full sense of the term, any text that implicitly or explicitly signifies its own rhetorical mode and prefigures its own misunderstanding as the correlative of its rhetorical nature; that is, of its "rhetoricity." It can do so by declarative statement or by poetic inference.[48] "To

48. A discursive, critical, or philosophical text that does this by means of statements is therefore not more or less literary than a poetic text that would avoid direct statement. In practice, the distinctions are often blurred: the logic of many philosophical texts relies heavily on narrative coherence and figures of speech,

account for" or "to signify," in the sentence above, does not designate a subjective process: it follows from the rhetorical nature of literary language that the cognitive function resides in the language and not in the subject. The question as to whether the author himself is or is not blinded is to some extent irrelevant; it can only be asked heuristically, as a means to accede to the true question: whether his language is or is not blind to its own statement. By asking this question of *De la Grammatologie*, a way back can be found to the starting-point of the inquiry: the interplay between critical and literary language in terms of blindness and insight.

It would seem to matter very little whether Derrida is right or wrong about Rousseau, since his own text resembles the *Essai* so closely, in its rhetoric as well as in its statement. It also tells a story: the repression of written language by what is here called the "logocentric" fallacy of favoring voice over writing is narrated as a consecutive, historical process. Throughout, Derrida uses Heidegger's and Nietzsche's fiction of metaphysics as a *period* in Western thought in order to dramatize, to give tension and suspense to the argument, exactly as Rousseau gave tension and suspense to the story of language and of society by making them pseudo-historical. Neither is Derrida taken in by the theatricality of his gesture or the fiction of his narrative: exactly as Rousseau tells us obliquely, but consistently, that we are reading a fiction and not a history. Derrida's Nietzschean theory of language as "play" warns us not to take him literally, especially when his statements seem to refer to concrete historical situations such as the present. The use of a philosophical terminology with the avowed purpose of discrediting this very terminology is an established philosophical procedure that has many antecedents besides Rousseau and is one that Derrida practices with exemplary skill. Finally, Derrida's theory of *écriture* corresponds closely to Rousseau's statement on the figural nature of the language of passion. Does it matter then whether we attribute the final statement to Rousseau or to Derrida since both are in fact saying the same

---

while poetry abounds in general statements. The criterion of literary specificity does not depend on the greater or lesser discursiveness of the mode but on the degree of consistent "rhetoricity" of the language.

thing? Of course, if Rousseau does not belong to the logocentric "period," then the scheme of periodization used by Derrida is avowedly arbitrary.[49] If we argue, moreover, that Rousseau escapes from the logocentric fallacy precisely to the extent that his language *is literary,* then we are saying by implication that the myth of the priority of oral language over written language has always already been demystified by literature, although literature remains persistently open to being misunderstood for doing the opposite. None of this seems to be inconsistent with Derrida's insight, but it might distress some of his more literal-minded followers: his historical scheme is merely a narrative convention and the brief passage on the nature of literary language in *De la Grammatologie* seems to tend in the direction suggested. Nevertheless, although Derrida can be "right" on the nature of literary language and consistent in the application of this insight to his own text, he remains unwilling or unable to read Rousseau as literature. Why does he have to reproach Rousseau for doing exactly what he legitimately does himself? According to Derrida, Rousseau's rejection of a logocentric theory of language, which the author of the *Essai* encounters in the guise of the aesthetic sensualism of the eighteenth century, "could not be a radical rejection, for it occurs within the framework inherited from this philosophy and of the 'metaphysical' conception of art."[50] I have tried to show instead that Rousseau's use of a traditional vocabulary is exactly similar, in its strategy and its implications, to the use Derrida consciously makes of the traditional vocabulary of Western philosophy. What happens in Rousseau is exactly what happens in Derrida: a vocabulary of substance and of presence is no longer used declaratively but rhetorically, for the very reasons that are being (metaphor-

49. It is an open question whether Derrida would be willing to accept all the consequences of such a change in historical periodization—such as, for example, the possibility of an entirely affirmative answer to the question asked with reference to Lévi-Strauss: "Accorder en soi Rousseau, Marx et Freud est une tâche difficile. Les accorder entre eux, dans la rigueur systématique du concept, est-ce possible?" (*Gr.,* p. 173).

50. *Gr.,* p. 297. "Metaphysical" here means, in Heidegger's post-Nietzschean terminology, the era during which the ontological difference between being and entity (*Sein und Seiendes*) remains implicit (*ungedacht*). Derrida radicalizes the ontological difference by locating the differential tension within language, between language as voice and language as sign.

ically) stated. Rousseau's text has no blind spots:[51] it accounts at all moments for its own rhetorical mode. Derrida misconstrues as blindness what is instead a transposition from the literal to the figural level of discourse.

There are two possible explanations for Derrida's blindness with regard to Rousseau: either he actually misreads Rousseau, possibly because he substitutes Rousseau's interpreters for the author himself—maybe whenever Derrida writes "Rousseau," we should read "Starobinski" or "Raymond" or "Poulet"—or he deliberately misreads Rousseau for the sake of his own exposition and rhetoric. In the first case, Derrida's blindness merely confirms Rousseau's foreknowledge of the misinterpretation of his work. It would be a classical case of critical blindness, somewhat different in aspect but not in essence from the pattern encountered in critics such as Lukács, Poulet, or Blanchot. Their blindness, it will be remembered, consisted in the affirmation of a methodology that could be "deconstructed" in terms of their own findings: Poulet's "self" turns out to be language, Blanchot's impersonality a metaphor for self-reading, etc.; in all these cases, the methodological dogma is being played off against the literary insight, and this interplay between methodology and literature develops in turn the highly literary rhetoric of what could be called systematic criticism. Derrida's case is somewhat different: his chapter on method, on literary interpretation as deconstruction, is flawless in itself but made to apply to the wrong object. There is no need to deconstruct Rousseau; the established tradition of Rousseau interpretation, however, stands in dire need of deconstruction. Derrida found himself in the most favorable of all critical positions: he was dealing with an author as clear-sighted as language lets him be who, for that very reason, is being systematically misread; the author's own works, newly interpreted, can then be played off against the most talented of his deluded interpreters or followers. Needless to say, this new interpretation will, in its turn, be caught in its own form of blindness, but not without having produced its own bright moment of literary insight. Derrida did not choose to adopt this pattern: instead of having Rousseau deconstruct his critics, we

51. The choice of the wrong example to illustrate metaphor (fear instead of pity) is a mistake, not a blind spot.

have Derrida deconstructing a pseudo-Rousseau by means of insights that could have been gained from the "real" Rousseau. The pattern is too interesting not to be deliberate.

At any rate, the pattern accounts very well for the slight thematic difference between Derrida's story and Rousseau's story. Whereas Rousseau tells the story of an inexorable regression, Derrida rectifies a recurrent error of judgment. His text, as he puts it so well, is the unmaking of a construct. However negative it may sound, deconstruction implies the possibility of rebuilding. Derrida's dialectical energy, especially in the first half of his book, which does not deal directly with Rousseau, clearly gains its momentum from the movement of deconstruction that takes place in the second part, using Rousseau as a sparring partner. Rousseau plays for Derrida somewhat the same part that Wagner plays for Nietzsche in *The Birth of Tragedy,* a text *De la Grammatologie* resembles even more closely than it resembles the *Essai sur l'origine des langues.* The fact that Wagner serves a presumptively positive function in Nietzsche, whereas Rousseau is an antithetical mask or shadow for Derrida, matters very little: the type of misreading is very similar in both cases. Rousseau needed no equivalent mediating figure in the *Essai;* he takes his energy entirely from the strength of his radical rejection of the present moment. The attacks on Rameau, on Condillac, on Du Bos or the tradition Du Bos represents, are contingent polemics not an essential part of the structure: what stands under indictment is language itself and not somebody's philosophical error. Neither does Rousseau hold up any hope that one could ever escape from the regressive process of misunderstanding that he describes; he cuts himself off once and forever from all future disciples. In this respect, Derrida's text is less radical, less mature than Rousseau's, though not less literary. Nor is it less important from a philosophical point of view than *The Birth of Tragedy.* As is well known, Nietzsche himself later criticized the use he had made of Wagner in the early book, not merely because he changed his mind about the latter's merits—he had, in fact, already lost most of his illusions about Wagner when he wrote *The Birth of Tragedy*—but because his presence in that text stood in the way of the musicality, the allegory of its mode: "Sie hätte singen sollen, diese 'neue Seele'— und nicht reden"—"it should have sung, this 'new soul,' and not have spoken." He went on to write *Zarathustra* and *Will to Power*, and one may wonder if he was ever able to free himself entirely from Wagner: it may be that an all too hopeful future was converted into an all too aberrant past. Rousseau went on to write a "pure" fiction, *La Nouvelle Héloïse*, and a treatise of constitutional law, *Le Contrat social*—but that is another story, as is the future of Jacques Derrida's own work.

The critical reading of Derrida's critical reading of Rousseau shows blindness to be the necessary correlative of the rhetorical nature of literary language. Within the structure of the system: text-reader-critic (in which the critic can be defined as the "second" reader or reading) the moment of blindness can be located differently. If the literary text itself has areas of blindness, the system can be binary; reader and critic coincide in their attempt to make the unseen visible. Our reading of some literary critics, in this volume, is a special, somewhat more complex case of this structure: the literary texts are themselves critical but blinded, and the critical reading of the critics tries to deconstruct the blindness. It should be clear by now that "blindness" implies no literary value-judgment: Lukács, Blanchot, Poulet, and Derrida can be called "literary," in the full sense of the term, because of their blindness, not in spite of it. In the more complicated case of the non-blinded author—as we have claimed Rousseau to be —the system has to be triadic: the blindness is transferred from the writer to his first readers, the "traditional" disciples or commentators. These blinded first readers—they could be replaced for the sake of exposition, by the fiction of a naïve reader, though the tradition is likely to provide ample material—then need, in turn, a critical reader who reverses the tradition and momentarily takes us closer to the original insight. The existence of a particularly rich aberrant tradition in the case of the writers who can legitimately be called the most enlightened, is therefore no accident, but a constitutive part of all literature, the basis, in fact, of literary history. And since interpretation is nothing but the possibility of error, by claiming that a certain degree of blindness is part of the specificity of all literature we also reaffirm the absolute dependence of the interpretation on the text and of the text on the interpretation.

VIII

Literary History and Literary Modernity

To write reflectively about modernity leads to problems that put the usefullness of the term into question, especially as it applies, or fails to apply, to literature. There may well be an inherent contradiction between modernity, which is a way of acting and behaving, and such terms as "reflection" or "ideas" that play an important part in literature and history. The spontaneity of being modern conflicts with the claim to think and write about modernity; it is not at all certain that literature and modernity are in any way compatible concepts. Yet we all speak readily about modern literature and even use this term as a device for historical periodization, with the same apparent unawareness that history and modernity may well be even more incompatible than literature and modernity. The innocuous-sounding title of this essay may therefore contain no less than two logical absurdities—a most inauspicious beginning.

The term "modernity" reappears with increasing frequency and seems again to have become an issue not only as an ideological weapon, but as a theoretical problem as well. It may even be one of the ways by means of which the link between literary theory and literary praxis is being partly restored. At other moments in history, the topic "modernity" might be used just as an attempt at self-definition, as a way of diagnosing one's own present. This can happen during periods of considerable inventiveness, periods that seem, looking back, to have been unusually productive. At such actual or imaginary times, modernity would not be a value in itself, but would designate a set of values that exist independently of their modernity: Renaissance art is not admired because it may have been, at a certain moment, a distinctively "modern" form of art. We do not feel this way about the present, perhaps because such self-assurance can exist only retrospectively. It would be a hopeless task to try to define descriptively the elusive pattern of our own literary modernity; we draw nearer to the problem, however, by asking how modernity can, in itself, become an issue and why this issue seems to be raised with particular urgency with regard to literature or, even more specifically, with regard to theoretical speculations about literature.

That this is indeed the case can be easily verified in Europe as well as in the United States. It is particularly conspicuous, for example, in Germany where, after being banned for political reasons, the term modernity now receives a strong positive value-emphasis and has of late been much in evidence as a battlecry as well as a serious topic of investigation. The same is true in France and in the United States, perhaps most clearly in the renewed interest shown in the transfer of methods derived from the social sciences to literary studies.

Not so long ago, a concern with modernity would in all likelihood have coincided with a commitment to avant-garde movements such as dada, surrealism, or expressionism. The term would have appeared in manifestoes and proclamations, not in learned articles or international colloquia. But this does not mean that we can divide the twentieth century into two parts: a "creative" part that was actually modern, and a "reflective" or "critical" part that feeds on this modernity in the manner of a parasite, with active modernity replaced by theorizing about the modern. Certain forces that could legitimately be called modern and that were at work in lyric poetry, in the novel, and the theater have also now become operative in the field of literary theory and criticism. The gap between the manifestoes and the learned articles has narrowed to the point where some manifestoes are quite learned and some articles—though by no means all—are quite provocative. This development has by itself complicated and changed the texture of our literary modernity a great deal and brought to the fore difficulties inherent in the term itself as soon as it is used historically or reflectively. It is perhaps somewhat disconcerting to learn that our usage of the word goes back to the late fifth century of our era and that there is nothing modern about the concept of modernity. It is even more disturbing to discover the host of complications that beset one as soon as a conceptual definition of the term is attempted, especially with regard to literature. One is soon forced to resort to paradoxical formulations, such as defining the modernity of a literary period as the manner in which it discovers the impossibility of being modern.

It is this complication I would like to explore with the help of some examples that are not necessarily taken from our immediate present. They should illuminate the problematic structure of a concept that, like all concepts that are in essence temporal, acquires a particularly rich complexity when it is made to refer to events that are in essence linguistic. I will be less concerned with a description of our own modernity than with the challenge to the methods or the possibility of literary history that the concept implies.

Among the various antonyms that come to mind as possible opposites for "modernity"—a variety which is itself symptomatic of the complexity of the term—none is more fruitful than "history." "Modern" can be used in opposition to "traditional" or even to "classical." For some French and American contemporaries, "modern" could even mean the opposite of "romantic," a usage that would be harder to conceive for some specialists of German literature. Antimodernists such as Emil Staiger do not hesitate to see the sources of a modernism they deplore in the Frühromantik of Friedrich Schlegel and Novalis, and the lively quarrel now taking place in Germany is still focused on the early nineteenth-century tensions between Weimar and Jena. But each of these antonyms—ancient, traditional, classical, and romantic—would embroil us in qualifications and discriminations that are, in fact, superficial matters of geographical and historical contingency. We will reach further if we try to think through the latent opposition between "modern" and "historical," and this will also bring us closest to the contemporary version of the problem.

The vested interest that academics have in the value of history makes it difficult to put the term seriously into question. Only an exceptionally talented and perhaps eccentric member of the profession could undertake this task with sufficient energy to make it effective, and even then it is likely to be accompanied by the violence that surrounds passion and rebellion. One of the most striking instances of such a rebellion occurred when Nietzsche, then a young philologist who had been treated quite generously by the academic establishment, turned violently against the traditional foundations of his own discipline in a polemical essay entitled "Of the Use and Misuse of History for Life" ("Vom Nutzen und Nachteil der Historie für das Leben"). The text is a good example of the complications that ensue when a genuine impulse toward modernity collides with the demands of a historical consciousness or a culture based on the disciplines of history. It can serve as an introduction to the more delicate problems that arise when modernity is applied more specifically to literature.

It is not at once clear that Nietzsche is concerned with a conflict between modernity and history in his Second *Unzeitgemässe Betrachtung*. That history is being challenged in a fundamental way is obvious from the start, but it is not obvious that this happens in the name of modernity. The term "modern" most frequently appears in the text with negative connotations as descriptive of the way in which Nietzsche considers his contemporaries to be corrupted and enfeebled by an excessive interest in the past. As opposed to the Greeks, Nietzsche's "moderns" escape from the issues of the present, which they are too weak and sterile to confront, into the sheltering inwardness that history can provide, but that bears no relation to actual existence.[1] History and moder-

---

1. Friedrich Nietzsche, "Vom Nutzen und Nachteil der Historie für das Leben," *Unzeitgemässe Betrachtung II* in Karl Schlechta, ed., *Werke I* (Munich, 1954), pp. 232–33, 243.

nity seem to go hand in hand and jointly fall prey to Nietzsche's
cultural criticism. Used in this sense, modernity is merely a descriptive term that designates a certain state of mind Nietzsche
considers prevalent among the Germans of his time. A much
more dynamic concept of modernity, far-reaching enough to
serve as a first definition, appears in what is here directly being
opposed to history, namely what Nietzsche calls "life."

"Life" is conceived not just in biological but in temporal terms
as the ability to *forget* whatever precedes a present situation. Like
most opponents of Rousseau in the nineteenth century, Nietzsche's
thought follows purely Rousseauistic patterns; the text starts
with a contrasting parallel between nature and culture that stems
directly from the *Second Discourse on the Origins of Inequality.*
The restlessness of human society, in contrast to the placid state
of nature of the animal herd, is diagnosed as man's inability to
forget the past.

> [Man] wonders about himself, about his inability [to learn]
> to forget, and about his tendency to remain tied to the past:
> No matter how far and how swiftly he runs, the chain runs
> with him . . . Man says "I remember," and envies the ani-
> mal that forgets at once, and watches each moment die, dis-
> appear in night and mist, and disappear forever. Thus the ani-
> mal lives unhistorically: It hides nothing and coincides at all
> moments exactly with that which it is; it is bound to be truth-
> ful at all times, unable to be anything else.[2]

This ability to forget and to live without historical awareness exists
not only on an animal level. Since "life" has an ontological as
well as a biological meaning, the condition of animality persists as
a constitutive part of man. Not only are there moments when it
governs his actions, but these are also the moments when he re-
establishes contact with his spontaneity and allows his truly human nature to assert itself.

> We saw that the animal, which is truly unhistorical and lives
> confined within a horizon almost without extension, exists in
> a relative state of happiness: We will therefore have to con-
> sider the ability to experience life in a nonhistorical way as

2. *Ibid.* p. 211.

the most important and most original of experiences, as the foundation on which right, health, greatness, and anything truly human can be erected.[3]

Moments of genuine humanity thus are moments at which all anteriority vanishes, annihilated by the power of an absolute forgetting. Although such a radical rejection of history may be illusory or unfair to the achievements of the past, it nevertheless remains justified as necessary to the fulfillment of our human destiny and as the condition for action.

> As the man who acts must, according to Goethe, be without a conscience, he must also be without knowledge; he forgets everything in order to be able to *do* something; he is unfair toward what lies behind and knows only one right, the right of what is now coming into being as the result of his own action.[4]

We are touching here upon the radical impulse that stands behind all genuine modernity when it is not merely a descriptive synonym for the contemporaneous or for a passing fashion. Fashion (mode) can sometimes be only what remains of modernity after the impulse has subsided, as soon—and this can be almost at once—as it has changed from being an incandescent point in time into a reproducible cliché, all that remains of an invention that has lost the desire that produced it. Fashion is like the ashes left behind by the uniquely shaped flames of the fire, the trace alone revealing that a fire actually took place. But Nietzsche's ruthless forgetting, the blindness with which he throws himself into an action lightened of all previous experience, captures the authentic spirit of modernity. It is the tone of Rimbaud when he declares that he has no antecedents whatever in the history of France, that all one has to expect from poets is "du nouveau" and that one must be "absolutely modern"; it is the tone of Antonin Artaud when he asserts that "written poetry has value for one single moment and should then be destroyed. Let the dead poets make room for the living . . . the time for masterpieces is

3. *Ibid.* p. 215.
4. *Ibid.* p. 216.

past." [5] Modernity exists in the form of a desire to wipe out whatever came earlier, in the hope of reaching at last a point that could be called a true present, a point of origin that marks a new departure. This combined interplay of deliberate forgetting with an action that is also a new origin reaches the full power of the idea of modernity. Thus defined, modernity and history are diametrically opposed to each other in Nietzsche's text. Nor is there any doubt as to his commitment to modernity, the only way to reach the meta-historical realm in which the rhythm of one's existence coincides with that of the eternal return. Yet the shrill grandiloquence of the tone may make one suspect that the issue is not as simple as it may at first appear.

Of course, within the polemical circumstances in which it was written, the essay has to overstate the case against history and to aim beyond its target in the hope of reaching it. This tactic is less interesting, however, than the question of whether Nietzsche can free his own thought from historical prerogatives, whether his own text can approach the condition of modernity it advocates. From the start, the intoxication with the history-transcending life-process is counterbalanced by a deeply pessimistic wisdom that remains rooted in a sense of historical causality, although it reverses the movement of history from one of development to one of regression. Human "existence," we are told near the beginning of the essay, "is an uninterrupted pastness that lives from its own denial and destruction, from its own contradictions." ("Das Dasein ist nur ein ununterbrochenes Gewesensein, ein Ding, das davon lebt, sich selbst zu verneinen and zu verzehren, sich selbst zu widersprechen.")[6] This description of life as a constant regression has nothing to do with cultural errors, such as the excess of historical disciplines in contemporary education against which the essay polemicizes, but lies much deeper in the nature of things, beyond the reach of culture. It is a temporal experience of human mutability, historical in the deepest sense of the term in that it implies the necessary experience of any present as a *passing* experience that makes the past irrevocable and unforgettable, because it is

5. Antonin Artaud, *Le Théâtre et son double,* vol. IV of *Oeuvres complètes* (Paris, 1956).
6. Nietzsche, *op. cit.* p. 212.

inseparable from any present or future. Keats gained access to the same awareness when, in *The Fall of Hyperion,* he contemplated in the fallen Saturn the past as a foreknowledge of his own mortal future:

> Without stay or prop
> But my own weak mortality, I bore
> The load of this eternal quietude,
> The unchanging gloom . . .

Modernity invests its trust in the power of the present moment as an origin, but discovers that, in severing itself from the past, it has at the same time severed itself from the present. Nietzsche's text leads him irrevocably to this discovery, perhaps most strikingly (because most implicitly) when he comes close to describing his own function as a *critical* historian and discovers that the rejection of the past is not so much an act of forgetting as an act of critical judgment directed against himself.

> [The critical student of the past] must possess the strength, and must at times apply this strength, to the destruction and dissolution of the past in order to be able to live. He achieves this by calling the past into court, putting it under indictment, and finally condemning it; any past, however, deserves to be condemned, for such is the condition of human affairs that they are ruled by violence and weakness. . . . "It takes a great deal of strength to be able to live and forget to what extent life and injustice go together." . . . But this very life that has to forget must also at times be able to stop forgetting; then it will become clear how illegitimate the existence of something, of a privilege, a caste or a dynasty actually is, and how much it deserves to be destroyed. Then the past is judged critically, attacked at its very roots with a sharp knife, and brutally cut down, regardless of established pieties. This is always a dangerous process, dangerous for life itself. Men and eras that serve life in this manner, by judging and destroying the past, are always dangerous and endangered. For we are inevitably the result of earlier generations and thus the result of their mistakes, their passions and aberrations, even of their crimes; it is not possible to loosen oneself entirely from this chain. . . . Afterwards, we try to give ourselves a new past

from which we should have liked to descend instead of the past from which we actually descended. But this is also danger- ous, because it is so difficult to trace the limit of one's denial of the past, and because the newly invented nature is likely to be weaker than the previous one. . . .[7]

The parricidal imagery of the passage, the weaker son condemning and killing the stronger father, reaches the inherent paradox of the denial of history implied in modernity.

As soon as modernism becomes conscious of its own strategies— and it cannot fail to do so if it is justified, as in this text, in the name of a concern for the future—it discovers itself to be a genera- tive power that not only engenders history, but is part of a genera- tive scheme that extends far back into the past. The image of the chain, to which Nietzsche instinctively resorts when he speaks of history, reveals this very clearly. Considered as a principle of life, modernity becomes a principle of origination and turns at once into a generative power that is itself historical. It becomes impos- sible to overcome history in the name of life or to forget the past in the name of modernity, because both are linked by a temporal chain that gives them a common destiny. Nietzsche finds it im- possible to escape from history, and he finally has to bring the two incompatibles, history and modernity (now using the term in the full sense of a radical renewal), together in a paradox that cannot be resolved, an aporia that comes very close to describing the predicament of our own present modernity:

> For the impulse that stands behind our history-oriented edu- cation—in radical inner contradiction to the spirit of a "new time" or a "modern spirit"—must in turn be understood histori- cally; history itself must resolve the problem of history, histori- cal knowledge must turn its weapon against itself—this three- fold "must" is the imperative of the "new times," if they are to achieve something truly new, powerful, life-giving, and original.[8]

Only through history is history conquered; modernity now ap- pears as the horizon of a historical process that has to remain a

7. *Ibid.* p. 230.
8. *Ibid.* p. 261.

gamble. Nietzsche sees no assurance that his own reflective and historical attempt achieves any genuine change; he realizes that his text itself can be nothing but another historical document,[9] and finally he has to delegate the power of renewal and modernity to a mythical entity called "youth" to which he can only recommend the effort of self-knowledge that has brought him to his own abdication.

The bad faith implied in advocating self-knowledge to a younger generation, while demanding from this generation that it act blindly, out of a self-forgetting that one is unwilling or unable to achieve oneself, forms a pattern all too familiar in our own experience to need comment. In this way Nietzsche, at this early point in his career, copes with a paradox that his thought has revealed with impressive clarity: Modernity and history relate to each other in a curiously contradictory way that goes beyond antithesis or opposition. If history is not to become sheer regression or paralysis, it depends on modernity for its duration and renewal; but modernity cannot assert itself without being at once swallowed up and reintegrated into a regressive historical process. Nietzsche offers no real escape out of a predicament in which we readily recognize the mood of our own modernity. Modernity and history seem condemned to being linked together in a self-destroying union that threatens the survival of both.

If we see in this paradoxical condition a diagnosis of our own modernity, then literature has always been essentially modern. Nietzsche was speaking of life and of culture in general, of modernity and history as they appear in all human enterprises in the most general sense possible. The problem becomes more intricate when it is restricted to literature. Here we are dealing with an activity that necessarily contains, within its own specificity, the very contradiction that Nietzsche discovered at the endpoint of his rebellion against a historically minded culture. Regardless of historical or cultural conditions, beyond the reach of educational or moral imperatives, the modernity of literature confronts us at all times with an unsolvable paradox. On the one hand, literature has a constitutive affinity with action, with the unmediated, free

9. *Ibid.* p. 277.

act that knows no past; some of the impatience of Rimbaud or Artaud echoes in all literary texts, no matter how serene and detached they may seem. The historian, in his function as historian, can remain quite remote from the collective acts he records; his language and the events that the language denotes are clearly distinct entities. But the writer's language is to some degree the product of his own action; he is both the historian and the agent of his own language. The ambivalence of writing is such that it can be considered both an act and an interpretative process that follows after an act with which it cannot coincide. As such, it both affirms and denies its own nature or specificity. Unlike the historian, the writer remains so closely involved with action that he can never free himself of the temptation to destroy whatever stands between him and his deed, especially the temporal distance that makes him dependent on an earlier past. The appeal of modernity haunts all literature. It is revealed in numberless images and emblems that appear at all periods—in the obsession with a *tabula rasa,* with new beginnings—that finds recurrent expression in all forms of writing. No true account of literary language can bypass this persistent temptation of literature to fulfill itself in a single moment. The temptation of immediacy is constitutive of a literary consciousness and has to be included in a definition of the specificity of literature.

The manner in which this specificity asserts itself, however, the form of its actual manifestation, is curiously oblique and confusing. Often in the course of literary history writers openly assert their commitment to modernity thus conceived. Yet whenever this happens, a curious logic that seems almost uncontrolled, a necessity inherent in the nature of the problem rather than in the will of the writer, directs their utterance away from their avowed purpose. Assertions of literary modernity often end up by putting the possibility of being modern seriously into question. But precisely because this discovery goes against an original commitment that cannot simply be dismissed as erroneous, it never gets stated outright, but hides instead behind rhetorical devices of language that disguise and distort what the writer is actually saying, perhaps in contrast to what he meant to say. Hence the need for the interpreter of such texts to respond to levels of meaning not immediately obvious. The very presence of such complexities indicates the existence of a special problem: How is it that a specific and important feature of a literary consciousness, its desire for modernity, seems to lead outside literature into something that no longer shares this specificity, thus forcing the writer to undermine his own assertions in order to remain faithful to his vocation?

It is time to clarify what we are trying to convey with some examples taken from texts that openly plead the cause of modernity. Many, but by no means all, of these texts are written by people who stand outside literature from the start, either because they instinctively tend toward the interpretative distance of the historian, or because they incline toward a form of action no longer linked to language. During the quarrel between the Ancients and the Moderns, the debate between a traditional conception of literature and modernity that took place in France near the end of the seventeenth century and that is still considered by some[10] as the starting point of a "modern" sense of history, it is striking that the modern camp not only contained men of slighter literary talent, but that their arguments against classical literature were often simply against literature as such. The nature of the debate forced the participants to make comparative critical evaluations of ancient versus contemporary writing; it obliged them to offer something resembling readings of passages in Homer, Pindar, or Theocritus. Although no one covered himself with critical glory in the performance of this task—mainly because the powerful imperative of decorum (*bienséance*) tends to become a particularly opaque screen that stands between the antique text and the classical reading[11]—the partisans of the Ancients still performed a great deal better than the pro-moderns. If one compares the remarks of a "moderne" such as Charles Perrault on Homer or his application in 1688 of seventeenth-century *bienséance* to Hellenic texts in

---

10. See, for example, Werner Krauss, "Cartaud de la Villate und die Entstehung des geschichtlichen Weltbildes in der Frühaufklärung," *Studien zur Deutschen und Französischen Aufklärung* (Berlin, 1963), and H. R. Jauss's substantial introduction to his facsimile edition of Charles Perrault, *Parallèle des anciens et des modernes* (Munich, 1964), pp. 12–13.

11. Critical utterances concerning the Homeric question are particularly revealing in this respect, in a partisan of the Moderns like Charles Perrault as well as in a partisan of the Ancients like Boileau.

Parallèle des anciens et des modernes with Boileau's reply in *Réflexions critiques sur quelques passages du rhéteur Longin* of 1694,[12] it then becomes clear that the "anciens" had a notion of decorum that remained in much closer contact with literature, including its constitutive impulse toward literary modernity, than the "modernes." This fact undoubtedly strengthens, in the long run, the cause of the moderns, despite their own critical shortcomings, but the point is precisely that a partisan and deliberately pro-modern stance is much more easily taken by someone devoid of literary sensitivity than by a genuine writer. Literature, which is inconceivable without a passion for modernity, also seems to oppose from the inside a subtle resistance to this passion.

Thus we find in the same period a detached and ironical mind like that of the early Fontenelle openly take the side of the moderns in asserting that "nothing stands so firmly in the way of progress, nothing restricts the mind so effectively as an excessive admiration for the Ancients." [13] Having to demystify the merit of invention and origin on which the superiority of the Ancients is founded—and which, in fact, roots their merit in their genuine modernity—Fontenelle becomes himself entertainingly inventive in his assertion that the prestige of so-called origins is merely an illusion created by the distance separating us from a remote past. At the same time he expresses the mock-anxious fear that our own progressing rationality will prevent us from benefiting, in the eyes of future generations, from the favorable prejudice we were silly enough to bestow on the Greeks and the Romans.

> By virtue of these compensations, we can hope to be excessively admired in future centuries, to make up for the little consideration we are given in our own. Critics will vie to discover in our works hidden beauties that we never thought of putting there; obvious weaknesses, that the author would be the first to acknowledge if they were pointed out to him to-day, will find staunch defenders. God knows with what contempt

12. H. R. Jauss, *op. cit.,* mentions as other convincing instances of critical insight among the defenders of the Ancients La Bruyère's *Discours sur Théophraste* (1699) and Saint-Evremont's *Sur les poèmes des anciens* (1685).
13. Fontenelle, "Digression sur les anciens et les modernes," *Oeuvres,* IV (Paris, 1767), pp. 170–200.

the fashionable writers of these future days—which may well
turn out to be Americans—will be treated in comparison with
us. The same prejudice that degrades us at one time enhances
our value at another; we are first the victims, then the gods of
the same error in judgment—an amusing play to observe with
detached eyes.

The same playful indifference prompts Fontenelle to add the remark:

> But, in all likelihood, reason will grow more perfect in time
> and the crude prejudice in favor of the Ancients is bound to
> vanish. It may well not be with us much longer. We may well
> be wasting our time admiring the Ancients in vain, without
> expectations of ever being admired in the same capacity. What
> a pity! [14]

Fontenelle's historical irony is far from being unliterary, but if
taken at face value it stands at the very opposite pole of the impulse toward action without which literature would not be what
it is. Nietzsche admired Fontenelle, but it must have been as an
Apollinian anti-self, for nothing is more remote from the spirit of
modernity than Fontenelle's *perfectibilité,* a kind of statistical,
quantitative balance between right and wrong, a process of trial-
by-chance that may perhaps lead to certain rules by means of
which aberrations could be prevented in the future. In the name
of *perfectibilité,* he can reduce critical norms to a set of mechanical
rules and assert, with only a trace of irony, that literature progressed
faster than science because the imagination obeys a smaller number of easier rules than does reason. He can easily dismiss poetry
and the arts as "unimportant," since he pretends to have moved
so far away from their concerns. His stance is that of the objective,
scientific historian. Even if taken seriously, this stance would
engage him in a task of interpretation closer to literature than
that of Charles Perrault, for example, who has to resort to the
military and imperial achievements of his age to find instances of
the superiority of the moderns. That such a type of modernism
leads outside literature is clear enough. The topos of the anti-
literary, technological man as an incarnation of modernity is re-

14. *Ibid.* pp. 195–96, 199.

current among the *idées reçues* of the nineteenth century and symptomatic of the alacrity with which modernity welcomes the opportunity to abandon literature altogether. The opposite temptation toward a purely detached interpretation, of which we find an ironic version in Fontenelle, also reveals the inherent trend to draw away from the literary. Perrault's committed, as well as Fontenelle's detached, modernism both lead away from literary understanding.

Our examples may have been one-sided, however, since we were dealing with nonliterary figures. More revealing is the case of writers whose proximity to literature is beyond dispute and who find themselves, in true accordance with their literary vocation, defenders of modernity—not just in the choice of their themes and settings, but as representative of a fundamental attitude of mind. The poetry of Baudelaire, as well as his plea for modernity in several critical texts, would be a good case in point.

As seen in the famous essay on Constantin Guys, "Le peintre de la vie moderne," Baudelaire's conception of modernity is very close to that of Nietzsche in his second *Unzeitgemässe Betrachtung*. It stems from an acute sense of the present as a constitutive element of all aesthetic experience:

> The pleasure we derive from the *representation of the present* (la représentation du présent) is not merely due to the beauty it may display, but also to the essential "present-ness" of the present.[15]

The paradox of the problem is potentially contained in the formula "représentation du présent," which combines a repetitive with an instantaneous pattern without apparent awareness of the incompatibility. Yet this latent tension governs the development of the entire essay. Baudelaire remains faithful throughout to the seduction of the present; any temporal awareness is so closely tied for him to the present moment that memory comes to apply more naturally to the present than it does to the past:

> Woe be to him who, in Antiquity, studies anything besides pure art, logic and general method! By plunging into the past

15. Charles Baudelaire, "Le peintre de la vie moderne" in F. F. Gautier, ed., *l'Art romantique, Oeuvres complètes, IV* (Paris, 1923), p. 208. Our italics.

he may well lose the *memory of the present* (la mémoire du présent). He abdicates the values and privileges provided by actual circumstance, for almost all our originality stems from the stamp that time prints on our sensations.[16]

The same temporal ambivalence prompts Baudelaire to couple any evocation of the present with terms such as "représentation," "mémoire," or even "temps," all opening perspectives of distance and difference within the apparent uniqueness of the instant. Yet his modernity too, like Nietzsche's, is a forgetting or a suppression of anteriority. The human figures that epitomize modernity are defined by experiences such as childhood or convalescence, a freshness of perception that results from a slate wiped clear, from the absence of a past that has not yet had time to tarnish the immediacy of perception (although what is thus freshly discovered prefigures the end of this very freshness), of a past that, in the case of convalescence, is so threatening that it has to be forgotten.

All these experiences of immediacy coupled with their implicit negation, strive to combine the openness and freedom of a present severed from all other temporal dimensions, the weight of the past as well as the concern with a future, with a sense of totality and completeness that could not be achieved if a more extended awareness of time were not also involved. Thus we find Constantin Guys, who is made to serve as a kind of emblem for the poetic mind, to be a curious synthesis of a man of action (that is, a man of the moment, severed from past and future) with an observer and recorder of moments that are necessarily combined within a larger totality. Like the photographer or reporter of today, he has to be present at the battles and the murders of the world not to inform, but to freeze what is most transient and ephemeral into a recorded image. Constantin Guys, before being an artist, has to be "homme du monde," driven by curiosity and "always, spiritually, in the state of mind of the convalescent." The description of his technique offers perhaps the best formulation of this ideal combination of the instantaneous with a completed whole, of pure fluid movement with form—a combination that would achieve a reconciliation between the impulse toward modernity and the demand

16. *Ibid.* pp. 224–25. Our italics.

of the work of art to achieve duration. The painting remains steadily in motion and exists in the open, improvised manner of a sketch that is like a constant new beginning. The final closing of the form, constantly postponed, occurs so swiftly and suddenly that it hides its dependence on previous moments in its own precipitous instantaneity. The entire process tries to outrun time, to achieve a swiftness that would transcend the latent opposition between action and form.

> In M[onsieur] G[uys]'s manner, two features can be observed; in the first place, the contention of a highly suggestive, resurrecting power of memory, a memory that addresses all things with: "Lazarus, arise!"; on the other hand, a fiery, intoxicating vigor of pencil and brushstroke that almost resembles fury. He seems to be in anguish of not going fast enough, of letting the phantom escape before the synthesis has been extracted from it and recorded. . . . M. G. begins by slight pencil-marks that merely designate the place assigned to various objects in space. Then he indicates the main surfaces. . . . At the last moment, the definitive contour of the objects is sealed with ink. . . . This simple, almost elementary method . . . has the incomparable advantage that, at each point in the process of its elaboration, each drawing seems sufficiently completed; you may call this a sketch, if you like, but it is a perfect sketch.[17]

That Baudelaire has to refer to this synthesis as a "fantôme" is another instance of the rigor that forces him to double any assertion by a qualifying use of language that puts it at once into question. The Constantin Guys of the essay is himself a phantom, bearing some resemblance to the actual painter, but differing from him in being the fictional achievement of what existed only potentially in the "real" man. Even if we consider the character in the essay to be a mediator used to formulate the prospective vision of Baudelaire's own work, we can still witness in this vision a similar disincarnation and reduction of meaning. At first, in the enumeration of the themes that the painter (or writer) will select, we again find the temptation of modernity to move outside art, its nostalgia for the immediacy, the facticity of entities that are in contact with

17. *Ibid.* p. 228.

the present and illustrate the heroic ability to ignore or to forget that this present contains the prospective self-knowledge of its end. The figure chosen can be more or less close to being aware of this: it can be the mere surface, the outer garment of the present, the unwitting defiance of death in the soldier's colorful coat, or it can be the philosophically conscious sense of time of the dandy. In each case, however, the "subject" Baudelaire chose for a theme is preferred because it exists in the facticity, in the modernity, of a present that is ruled by experiences that lie outside language and escape from the successive temporality, the duration involved in writing. Baudelaire states clearly that the attraction of a writer toward his theme—which is also the attraction toward an action, a modernity, and an autonomous *meaning* that would exist outside the realm of language—is primarily an attraction to what is not art. The statement occurs with reference to the most anonymous and shapeless "theme" of all, that of the crowd: "C'est un moi insatiable de non-moi. (It is a self insatiable for non-selfhood). . . ."[18] If one remembers that this "moi" designates, in the metaphor of a subject, the specificity of literature, then this specificity is defined by its inability to remain constant to its own specificity.

This, at least, corresponds to the first moment of a certain mode of being, called literature. It soon appears that literature is an entity that exists not as a single moment of self-denial, but as a plurality of moments that can, if one wishes, be represented—but this is a mere representation—as a succession of moments or a duration. In other words, literature can be represented as a movement and is, in essence, the fictional narration of this movement. After the initial moment of flight away from its own specificity, a moment of return follows that leads literature back to what it is —but we must bear in mind that terms such as "after" and "follows" do not designate actual moments in a diachrony, but are used purely as *metaphors* of duration. Baudelaire's text illustrates this return, this *reprise,* with striking clarity. The "moi insatiable de non-moi . . ." has been moving toward a series of "themes" that reveal the impatience with which it tries to move away from its own center. These themes become less and less concrete and

18. *Ibid.* p. 219.

substantial, however, although they are being evoked with increasing realism and mimetic rigor in the description of their surfaces. The more realistic and pictorial they become, the more abstract they are, the slighter the residue of meaning that would exist outside their specificity as mere language and mere *signifiant*. The last theme that Baudelaire evokes, that of the carriages, has nothing whatever to do with the facticity of the carriage—although Baudelaire insists that in the paintings by Constantin Guys "the entire structure of the carriage-body is perfectly orthodox: every part is in its place and nothing needs to be corrected." [19] The substantial, thematic *meaning* of the carriage as such, however, has disappeared:

> Regardless of attitude and position, regardless of the speed at which it is launched, a carriage, like a ship, receives from its motion a mysteriously complex graceful air, very hard to capture in short-hand (très difficile à sténographier). The pleasure that the artist's eye derives from it is drawn, or so it seems, from the sequence of geometrical figures that this already so complicated object engenders successively and swiftly in space. [20]

What is here being stenographed is the movement by which, in apparent and metaphorical succession, literature first moves away from itself and then returns. All that remains of the theme is a mere outline, less than a sketch, a time-arabesque rather than a figure. The carriage has been allegorized into nothingness and exists as the purely temporal vibration of a successive movement that has only linguistic existence—for nothing is more radically metaphorical than the expression "figures géométriques" that Baudelaire is compelled to use to make himself understood. But that he wants to be understood, and not misunderstood in the belief that this geometry would have recourse to anything that is not language, is clear from its implied identification with a mode of writing. The *stenos* in the word stenography, meaning narrow, could be used to designate the confinement of literature within its own boundaries, its dependence on duration and repetition that

19. *Ibid*. p. 259.
20. *Ibid*.

Baudelaire experienced as a curse. But the fact that the word designates a form of writing indicates the compulsion to return to a literary mode of being, as a form of language that knows itself to be mere repetition, mere fiction and allegory, forever unable to participate in the spontaneity of action or modernity.

The movement of this text—that could be shown to parallel the development of Baudelaire's poetry as it moves from the sensory richness of the earlier poems to their gradual allegorization in the prose versions of the *Spleen de Paris*—recurs with various degrees of explicitness in all writers and measures the legitimacy of their claim to be called writers. Modernity turns out to be indeed one of the concepts by means of which the distinctive nature of literature can be revealed in all its intricacy. No wonder it had to become a central issue in critical discussions and a source of torment to writers who have to confront it as a challenge to their vocation. They can neither accept nor reject it with good conscience. When they assert their own modernity, they are bound to discover their dependence on similar assertions made by their literary predecessors; their claim to being a new beginning turns out to be the repetition of a claim that has always already been made. As soon as Baudelaire has to replace the single instant of invention, conceived as an act, by a successive movement that involves at least two distinct moments, he enters into a world that assumes the depths and complications of an articulated time, an interdependence between past and future that prevents any present from ever coming into being.

The more radical the rejection of anything that came before, the greater the dependence on the past. Antonin Artaud can go to the extreme of rejecting all forms of theatrical art prior to his own; in his own work, he can demand the destruction of any form of written text—he nevertheless finally has to ground his own vision in examples such as the Balinese theater, the least modern, the most text-frozen type of theater conceivable. And he has to do so with full knowledge that he thus destroys his own project, with the hatred of the traitor for the camp that he has chosen to join. Quoting the lines in which Artaud attacks the very concept of the theater on which he has waged his entire undertaking ("Rien de plus impie que le système des Balinais . . ."), Jacques Derrida can rightly comment: "[Artaud] was unable to resign himself to a theater based on repetition, unable to renounce a theater that would do away with all forms of repetition." [21] The same fatal interplay governs the writer's attitude toward modernity: he cannot renounce the claim to being modern but also cannot resign himself to his dependence on predecessors—who, for that matter, were caught in the same situation. Never is Baudelaire as close to his predecessor Rousseau as in the extreme modernity of his latest prose poems, and never is Rousseau as tied to his literary ancestors as when he pretends to have nothing more to do with literature.

The distinctive character of literature thus becomes manifest as an inability to escape from a condition that is felt to be unbearable. It seems that there can be no end, no respite in the ceaseless pressure of this contradiction, at least as long as we consider it from the point of view of the writer as subject. The discovery of his inability to be modern leads him back to the fold, within the autonomous domain of literature, but never with genuine appeasement. As soon as he can feel appeased in this situation he ceases to be a writer. His language may be capable of a certain degree of tranquillity; it is, after all, the product of a renunciation that has allowed for the metaphorical thematization of the predicament. But this renunciation does not involve the subject. The continuous appeal of modernity, the desire to break out of literature toward the reality of the moment, prevails and, in its turn, folding back upon itself, engenders the repetition and the continuation of literature. Thus modernity, which is fundamentally a falling away from literature and a rejection of history, also acts as the principle that gives literature duration and historical existence.

The manner in which this inherent conflict determines the structure of literary language cannot be treated within the limits of this essay. We are more concerned, at this point, with the question of whether a history of an entity as self-contradictory as literature is conceivable. In the present state of literary studies this possibility is far from being clearly established. It is generally admitted that a positivistic history of literature, treating it as if it

21. Jacques Derrida, "Le théâtre de la cruauté et la clôture de la représentation," *L'Écriture et la différence* (Édition du Seuil: Paris, 1967), p. 367.

were a collection of empirical data, can only be a history of what literature is not. At best, it would be a preliminary classification opening the way for actual literary study, and at worst, an obstacle in the way of literary understanding. On the other hand, the intrinsic interpretation of literature claims to be anti- or a-historical, but often presupposes a notion of history of which the critic is not himself aware.

In describing literature, from the standpoint of the concept of modernity, as the steady fluctuation of an entity away from and toward its own mode of being, we have constantly stressed that this movement does not take place as an actual sequence in time; to represent it as such is merely a metaphor making a sequence out of what occurs in fact as a synchronic juxtaposition. The sequential, diachronic structure of the process stems from the nature of literary language as an entity, not as an event. Things do not happen as if a literary text (or a literary vocation) moved for a certain period of time away from its center, then turned around, folding back upon itself at one specific moment to travel back to its genuine point of origin. These imaginary motions between fictional points cannot be located, dated, and represented as if they were places in a geography or events in a genetic history. Even in the discursive texts we have used—in Baudelaire, in Nietzsche, or even in Fontenelle—the three moments of flight, return, and the turning point at which flight changes into return or vice-versa, exist simultaneously on levels of meaning that are so intimately intertwined that they cannot be separated. When Baudelaire, for example, speaks of "représentation du présent," of "mémoire du présent," of "synthèse du fantôme," or of "ébauche finie," his language names, at the same time, the flight, the turning point, and the return. Our entire argument lies compressed in such formulations. This would even be more obvious if we had used poetic instead of discursive texts. It follows that it would be a mistake to think of literary history as the diachronic narrative of the fluctuating motion we have tried to describe. Such a narrative can be only metaphorical, and history is not fiction.

With respect to its own specificity (that is, as an existing entity susceptible to historical description), literature exists at the same time in the modes of error and truth; it both betrays and obeys its own mode of being. A positivistic history that sees literature only as what it is not (as an objective fact, an empirical psyche, or a communication that transcends the literary text as text) is, therefore, necessarily inadequate. The same is true of approaches to literature that take for granted the specificity of literature (what the French structuralists, echoing the Russian formalists, call literarity [*littérarité*] of literature). If literature rested at ease within its own self-definition, it could be studied according to methods that are scientific rather than historical. We are obliged to confine ourselves to history when this is no longer the case, when the entity steadily puts its own ontological status into question. The structuralist goal of a science of literary forms assumes this stability and treats literature as if the fluctuating movement of aborted self-definition were not a constitutive part of its language. Structuralist formalism, therefore, systematically bypasses the necessary component of literature for which the term "modernity" is not such a bad name after all, despite its ideological and polemical overtones. It is a very revealing paradox, confirming again that anything touching upon literature becomes at once a Pandora's box, that the critical method which denies literary modernity would appear —and even, in certain respects, would be—the most modern of critical movements.

Could we conceive of a literary history that would not truncate literature by putting us misleadingly *into* or *outside* it, that would be able to maintain the literary aporia throughout, account at the same time for the truth and the falsehood of the knowledge literature conveys about itself, distinguish rigorously between metaphorical and historical language, and account for literary modernity as well as for its historicity? Clearly, such a conception would imply a revision of the notion of history and, beyond that, of the notion of time on which our idea of history is based. It would imply, for instance, abandoning the pre-assumed concept of history as a generative process that we found operative in Nietzsche's text—although this text also began to rebel against it—of history as a temporal hierarchy that resembles a parental structure in which the past is like an ancestor begetting, in a moment of unmediated presence, a future capable of repeating in its turn the same generative process. The relationship between truth and error that prevails in literature cannot be represented genetically, since truth and error exist simultaneously, thus preventing the favoring of the one over the other. The need to revise the foundations of literary history may seem like a desperately vast undertaking; the task appears even more disquieting if we contend that literary history could in fact be paradigmatic for history in general, since man himself, like literature, can be defined as an entity capable of putting his own mode of being into question. The task may well be less sizable, however, than it seems at first. All the directives we have formulated as guidelines for a literary history are more or less taken for granted when we are engaged in the much more humble task of reading and understanding a literary text. To become good literary historians, we must remember that what we usually call literary history has little or nothing to do with literature and that what we call literary interpretation—provided only *—or reading* it is good interpretation—is in fact literary history. If we extend this notion beyond literature, it merely confirms that the bases for historical knowledge are not empirical facts but written texts, even if these texts masquerade in the guise of wars or revolutions.

IX

Lyric and Modernity

My essay title and procedure call for some preliminary clarification before I get involved in the technicalities of detailed exegesis. I am not concerned, in this paper, with a descriptive characterization of contemporary poetry but with the problem of literary modernity in general. The term "modernity" is not used in a simple chronological sense as an approximate synonym for "recent" or "contemporary" with a positive or negative value-emphasis added. It designates more generally the problematical possibility of all literature's existing in the present, of being considered, or read, from a point of view that claims to share with it its own sense of a temporal present. In theory, the question of modernity could therefore be asked of any literature at any time, contemporaneous or not. In practice, however, the question has to be put somewhat more pragmatically from a point of view that postulates a roughly contemporaneous perspective and that favors recent over older literature. This necessity is inherent in the ambivalent status of the term "modernity," which is itself partly pragmatic and descriptive, partly conceptual and normative. In the common usage of the word the pragmatic implications usually overshadow theoretical possibilities that remain unexplored. My emphasis tries to restore this balance to some degree: hence the stress on literary categories and dimensions that exist independently of historical contingencies, the main concession being that the examples are chosen from so-called modern literature and criticism. The conclusions, however, could, with some minor modifications, be transferred to other historical periods and be applicable whenever or wherever literature as such occurs.

What is thus assumed to be possible in time—and it is a mere assumption, since the compromise or theorizing about examples chosen on pragmatic grounds does in fact beg the question and postpones the issue—can much more easily be justified in geographical, spatial terms. My examples are taken primarily from French and German literature. The polemical aspects of the argument are directed against a trend prevalent among a relatively small group of German scholars, a group that is representative but by no means predominant in Continental criticism. But it should not be difficult to find equivalent texts and critical attitudes in English or American literature; the indirect route by way of France and Germany should allow for a clearer view of the local scene, once the necessary transitions have been made. The natural expansion of the essay would lie in this direction.

With modernity thus conceived of as a general and theoretical rather than as a historical theme, it is not a priori certain that it should be treated differently when discussing lyric poetry than it should, for example, when discussing narrative prose or the drama. Can the factual distinction between prose, poetry, and the drama relevantly be extended to modernity, a notion that is not inherently bound to any particular genre? Can we find out something about the nature of modernity by relating it to lyric poetry that we could not find out in dealing with novels or plays? Here again, the point of departure has to be chosen for reasons of expediency rather than for theoretical reasons, in the hope that the expediency may eventually receive theoretical confirmation. It is an established fact that, in contemporary criticism, the question of modernity is asked in a somewhat different manner with regard to lyric poetry than with regard to prose. Genre concepts seem somehow to be sensitive to the idea of modernity, thus suggesting a possible differentiation between them in terms of their temporal structures —since modernity is, in essence, a temporal notion. Yet the link between modernity and the basic genres is far from clear. On the one hand, lyric poetry is often seen not as an evolved but as an early and spontaneous form of language, in open contrast to more self-conscious and reflective forms of literary discourse in prose. In eighteenth-century speculations about the origins of language, the assertion that the archaic language is that of poetry, the contemporary or modern language that of prose is a commonplace. Vico, Rousseau, and Herder, to mention only the most famous names, all assert the priority of poetry over prose, often with a value-emphasis that seems to interpret the loss of spontaneity as a decline—although this particular aspect of eighteenth-century primitivism is in fact a great deal less single-minded and uniform in the authors themselves than in their later interpreters. Be this as it may, it remains that, regardless of value judgments, the definition of poetry as the first language gives it an archaic, ancient quality that is the opposite of modern, whereas the deliberate, cold, and rational character of discursive prose, which can only imitate or represent the original impulse if it does not ignore it altogether, would be the true language of modernity. The same assumption appears during the eighteenth century, with "music" substituting for "poetry" and opposed to language or literature as an equivalent of prose. This becomes, as is well known, a commonplace of post-symbolist aesthetics, still present in writers such as Valéry or Proust, though here perhaps in an ironic context that has not always been recognized as such. Music is seen, as Proust puts it, as a unified, preanalytical "communication of the soul," a "possibility that remained without sequel [because] mankind chose other ways, those of spoken and written language." [1] In this nostalgic primitivism—which Proust is demystifying rather than sharing— the music of poetry and the rationality of prose are opposed as ancient is opposed to modern. Within this perspective, it would be an absurdity to speak of the modernity of lyric poetry, since the lyric is precisely the antithesis of modernity.

1. Marcel Proust, *A la recherche du temps perdu*, Pierre Clarac and André Ferré, eds., Pléiade edition (Paris, 1954), vol. III, "La Prisonnière," p. 258.

Yet, in our own twentieth century, the social projection of modernity known as the avant-garde consisted predominantly of poets rather than of prose writers. The most aggressively modern literary movements of the century, surrealism and expressionism, in no way value prose over poetry, the dramatic or the narrative over the lyric. In the recent past, this trend may have changed. One speaks readily, in contemporary French literature, of a *nouveau roman*, but not of a *nouvelle poésie*. French structuralist "new criticism" is much more concerned with narrative prose than with poetry and sometimes rationalizes this preference into an overtly anti-poetic aesthetics. But this is in part a local phenomenon, a reaction against a traditional bias in French criticism in favor of poetry, perhaps also an innocent rejoicing like that of a child that has been given a new toy. The discovery that there are critical devices suitable for the analysis of prose is by no means such a sensational novelty for English and American critics, in whom these new French studies of narrative modes may awaken a more sedate feeling of *déjà vu*. In Germany, however, among critics that are by no means adverse or ideologically opposed to the contemporary French schools, lyric poetry remains the preferred topic of investigation for a definition of modernity. The editors of a recent symposium on the subject "The Lyric as Paradigm of Modernity" assert as a matter of course that "the lyric was chosen as paradigmatic for the evolution toward modern literature, because the breakdown of literary forms occurred earlier and can be better documented in this genre than in any other." [2] Here then, far from being judged absurd, the question of modernity in the lyric is considered as the best means of access to a discussion of literary modernity in general. In purely historical terms, this position is certainly sensible: it would be impossible to speak relevantly about modern literature without giving a prominent place to lyric poetry; some of the most suggestive theoretical writing on modernity is to be found in essays dealing with poetry. Nevertheless, the tension that develops between poetry and prose when they are considered within the perspective of modernity is far from meaningless; the question is

2. *Immanente Ästhetik, Ästhetische Reflexion: Lyrik als Paradigma der Moderne,* W. Iser, ed., Poetik und Hermeneutik, Arbeitsergebnisse einer Forschungsgruppe, II (Munich, 1966), p. 4.

complex enough to have to be postponed until well beyond the point we can hope to reach in this essay.

When Yeats, in 1936, had to write the introduction to his anthology of modern English poetry, in a text that otherwise shows more traces of fatigue than of inspiration, he largely used the opportunity to set himself apart from Eliot and Pound as more modern than they, using Walter James Turner and Dorothy Wellesley as props to represent a truly modern tendency of which he considered himself to be the main representative. That he also had the courage of his convictions is made clear by the fact that he allotted to himself, in the body of the anthology, twice as much space as to anyone else—with the sole exception of Oliver St. John Gogarty, hardly a dangerous rival. The theoretical justification given for this claim is slight but, in the light of later developments, quite astute. The opposition between "good" and modern poetry —his own—and not so good and not so modern poetry—mainly Eliot's and Pound's—is made in terms of a contrast between poetry of representation and a poetry that would no longer be mimetic. The mimetic poetry has for its emblem the mirror, somewhat incongruously associated with Stendhal, though it is revealing that the reference is to a writer of prose and that the prosaic element in Eliot's precision and in Pound's chaos is under attack. This is a poetry depending on an outside world, regardless of whether this world is seen in neat, objective contours or as shapeless flux. Much less easy to characterize is the other kind of poetry, said to be of the "private soul . . . always behind our knowledge, though always hidden . . . the sole source of pain, stupefaction, evil." [3] Its emblem, as we all know from M. H. Abrams, if not necessarily from Yeats, is the lamp, though here Abrams's stroke of genius in singling out this emblematic pair for the title of his book on romantic literary theory is perhaps slightly misleading, not in terms of the poetics of romanticism but with regard to Yeats's own meaning. In Abrams's book, the lamp becomes the symbol of the constitutive, autonomous self, the creative subjectivity that certainty looms large in romantic theory, as an analogous microcosm of the

3. *Oxford Book of Modern Verse, 1892–1935*, W. B. Yeats, ed. (New York, 1936), Introduction, p. XXXI.

world of nature. The light of that lamp is the self-knowledge of a consciousness, an internalized metaphor of daylight vision; mirror and lamp are both symbols of light, whatever their further differences and oppositions may be. But Yeats's lamp is not that of the self, but of what he calls the "soul," and self and soul, as we know from his poetry, are antithetical. Soul does not, at any rate, belong to the realm of natural or artificial (i.e., represented or imitated) light, but to that of sleep and darkness. It does not dwell in real or copied nature, but rather in the kind of wisdom that lies hidden away in books. To the extent that it is private and inward, the soul resembles the self, and only by ways of the self (and not by ways of nature) can one find access to it. But one has to move through the self and beyond the self; truly modern poetry is a poetry that has become aware of the incessant conflict that opposes a self, still engaged in the daylight world of reality, of representation, and of life, to what Yeats calls the soul. Translated into terms of poetic diction, this implies that modern poetry uses an imagery that is both symbol and allegory, that represents objects in nature but is actually taken from purely literary sources. The tension between these two modes of language also puts in question the autonomy of the self. Modern poetry is described by Yeats as the conscious expression of a conflict within the function of language as representation and within the conception of language as the act of an autonomous self.

Some literary historians, who necessarily approached the problem of modern poetry in a less personal way, have written about modern lyric poetry in strikingly similar terms. Hugo Friedrich, one of the last representatives of an outstanding group of Romanic scholars of German origin that includes Vossler, Curtius, Auerbach, and Leo Spitzer, has exercised a great deal of influence through his short book *The Structure of the Modern Lyric*.[4] Friedrich uses the traditional historical pattern, also present in Marcel Raymond's *From Baudelaire to Surrealism*, making French poetry of the nineteenth century and especially Baudelaire the starting point of a movement that spread to the whole body of Western lyric poetry. His main concern, understandably enough in an

4. Hugo Friedrich, *Die Struktur der Modernen Lyrik*, expanded edition (Hamburg, 1967). By May, 1967, 111,000 copies of this book had been printed.

explicator of texts, is the particular difficulty and obscurity of
modern poetry, an obscurity not unrelated to the light-symbolism
of Yeats's mirror and lamp. The cause of the specifically modern
kind of obscurity—which Friedrich to some extent deplores—resides for him, as for Yeats, in a loss of the representational function of poetry that goes parallel with the loss of a sense of selfhood.
Loss of representational reality (*Entrealisierung*) and loss of self
(*Entpersönlichung*) go hand in hand: "With Baudelaire, the depersonalization of the modern lyric starts, at least in the sense
that the lyrical voice is no longer the expression of a unity between the work and the empirical person, a unity that the romantics, contrary to several centuries of earlier lyrical poetry, had
tried to achieve." [5] And in Baudelaire "idealization no longer, as
in the older aesthetic, strives toward an embellishment of reality
but strives for loss of reality." Modern poetry—this is said with
reference to Rimbaud—"is no longer concerned with a reader.
It does not want to be understood. It is a hallucinatory storm,
flashes of lightning hoping at most to create the fear before danger
that stems from an attraction toward danger. They are texts without self, without 'I.' For the self that appears from time to time
is the artificial, alien self projected in the *lettre du voyant*." Ultimately, the function of representation is entirely taken over by
sound effects without reference to any meaning whatever.

Friedrich offers no theoretical reasons to explain why the loss of
representation (it would be more accurate to speak of a putting
into question or an ambivalence of representation) and the loss of
self—with the same qualification—are thus linked. He gives instead the crudest extraneous and pseudo-historical explanation of
this tendency as a mere escape from a reality that is said to have
become gradually more unpleasant ever since the middle of the
nineteenth century. Gratuitous fantasies, ". . . the absurd," he
writes, "become aspects of irreality into which Baudelaire and his
followers want to penetrate, *in order to* avoid an increasingly confining reality." Critical overtones of morbidity and decadence are
unmistakable, and the possibility of reading Friedrich's book as an
indictment of modern poetry—a thesis nowhere explicitly stated

5. Quotations in this paragraph and the next are (in order) from *ibid.* pp. 36,
56, 84, 53, and 44. All italics are my own.

by the author—is certainly not entirely foreign to the considerable popular success of the book. Here again, it is preferable for the sake of clarity to put the value judgment temporarily between brackets. Friedrich's historicist background, however crude, and his suggestion that the evolution of modern literature follows a line that is part of a wider historical pattern allow him to give his essay a genetic historical coherence. A continuous genetic chain links the work of Baudelaire to that of his successors Mallarmé, Rimbaud, Valéry, and their counterparts in the other European literatures. The chain extends in both directions, for Friedrich finds antecedents of the modern trend as far back as Rousseau and Diderot, and makes romanticism a link in the same chain. Symbolist and post-symbolist poetry appear therefore as a later, more self-conscious but also more morbid version of certain romantic insights; both form a historical continuum in which distinctions can be made only in terms of degree, not of kind, or in terms of extrinsic considerations, ethical, psychological, sociological, or purely formal. A similar view is represented in this country by M. H. Abrams, for example, in a paper entitled "Coleridge, Baudelaire and Modernist Poetics" published in 1964.

This scheme is so satisfying to our inherent sense of historical order that it has rarely been challenged, even by some who would not in the least agree with its potential ideological implications. We find, for instance, a group of younger German scholars, whose evaluation of modernity would be strongly opposed to what is implied by Friedrich, still adhering to exactly the same historical scheme. Hans Robert Jauss and some of his colleagues have considerably refined the diagnosis of obscurity that Friedrich had made the center of his analysis. Their understanding of medieval and baroque literature—which Friedrich chose to use merely in a contrasting way when writing on the modern lyric—influenced by the kind of fundamental reinterpretations that made it possible for a critic such as Walter Benjamin to speak about sixteenth-century literature and about Baudelaire in closely similar terms, allows them to describe Friedrich's *Entrealisierung* and *Entpersönlichung* with new stylistic rigor. The traditional term of allegory that Benjamin, perhaps more than anyone else in Germany, helped to restore to some of its full implications is frequently used by them to describe a tension within the language that can no longer be modeled on the subject-object relationships derived from experiences of perception, or from theories of the imagination derived from perception. In an earlier essay, Benjamin had suggested that "the intensity of the interrelationship between the perceptual and the intellectual element" [6] be made the main concern of the interpreter of poetry. This indicates that the assumed correspondence between meaning and object is put into question. From this point on, the very presence of any outward object can become superfluous, and, in an important article published in 1960, H. R. Jauss characterizes an allegorical style as "beauté inutile," the absence of any reference to an exterior reality of which it would be the sign. The "disappearance of the object" has become the main theme.[7] This development is seen as a historical process that can be more or less accurately dated: in the field of lyric poetry, Baudelaire is still named as the originator of a modern allegorical style. Friedrich's historical pattern survives, though now based on linguistic and rhetorical rather than on superficially sociological considerations. A student of Jauss, Karlheinz Stierle, tries to document this scheme in a consecutive reading of three poems by Nerval, Mallarmé, and Rimbaud, showing the gradual process of irrealization dialectically at work in these three texts.[8]

Stierle's detailed reading of a late and difficult sonnet by Mallarmé can serve as a model for the discussion of the *idées reçues* that this group of scholars still shares with Friedrich, all political appearances to the contrary. His interpretation of the *Tombeau de Verlaine*—chronologically though not stylistically perhaps Mal-

6. ". . . die Intensität der Verbundenheit der anschaulichen und der geistigen Elemente." Walter Benjamin, "Zwei Gedichte von Hölderlin," in *Schriften*, II (Frankfurt a. M., 1955), p. 377.
7. Hans Robert Jauss, "Zur Frage der Struktureinheit älterer und moderner Lyrik," *GRM*, XLI (1960), p. 266.
8. Karlheinz Stierle, "Möglichkeiten des dunklen Stils in den Anfängen moderner Lyrik in Frankreich," in *Lyrik als Paradigma der Moderne*, pp. 157–94. My argument is more polemical in tone than in substance. Some of the doubts expressed about the possibilty of a nonrepresentational poetry are conceded by K. Stierle himself in a later addition to his original paper (*ibid*. pp. 193–94). The possibility of complete "irrealization" asserted in the analysis of the Mallarmé text is thus put into question. Rather than by the contrast between literature and painting suggested by Stierle, I approach the problem in terms of a contrast between a genetic concept of literary history and modernity.

larmé's last text—following Benjamin's dictum, consciously ana-
lyzes the obscurity of the poem and the resistance of its diction
to a definitive meaning or set of meanings, as the interpenetration
between intellectual and perceptual elements. And Stierle comes
to the conclusion that, at least in certain lines of the poem, the
sensory elements have entirely vanished. At the beginning of the
sonnet, an actual object—a tombstone—is introduced:

Le noir roc courroucé que la bise le roule

but this actual object, according to Stierle, is "at once transcended
into irreality by a movement that cannot be represented." As for
the second stanza, "it can no longer be referred to an exterior reality." Although Mallarmé's poetry, more than any other (including
Baudelaire's or Nerval's), uses objects rather than subjective feelings or inward emotions, this apparent return to objects (*Vergegen-
ständlichung*), far from augmenting our sense of reality, of language adequately representing the object, is in fact a subtle and
successful strategy to achieve complete irreality. The logic of the
relationships that exist between the various objects in the poem
is no longer based on the logic of nature or of representation, but
on a purely intellectual and allegorical logic decreed and maintained by the poet in total defiance of natural events. "The situation of the poem," writes Stierle, referring to the dramatic action
that takes place between the various "things" that appear in it,

> can no longer be represented in sensory terms. . . . If we
> consider, not the object but that which makes it unreal, then
> this is a poetry of allegorical reification (*Vergegenständ-
> lichung*). One is struck most of all by the nonrepresentability
> of what is assumedly being shown: the stone rolling by its own
> will. . . . In traditonal allegory, the function of the concrete
> image was to make the meaning stand out more vividly. The
> *sensus allegoricus*, as a concrete representation, acquired a
> new clarity. But for Mallarmé the concrete image no longer
> leads to a clearer vision. The unity reached on the level of
> the object can no longer be represented. And it is precisely
> this unreal constellation that is intended as the product of
> the poetic activity.

This particular Mallarméan strategy is seen as a development leading beyond Baudelaire, whose allegory is still centered on a subject and is psychologically motivated. Mallarmé's modernity stems from the impersonality of an allegorical (i.e., nonrepresentational) diction entirely freed from a subject. The historical continuity from Baudelaire to Mallarmé follows a genetic movement of gradual allegorization and depersonalization.

The test of such a theory has to be found in the quality of the exegetic work performed by it proponent. Returning to the text, we can confine ourselves to one or two of the key words that play an important part in Stierle's argument. First of all, the word "roc" in the first line:

> Le noir roc courroucé que la bise le roule

The movement of this rock, driven by the cold north wind, is said by Stierle to be "at once" beyond representation. As we know from the actual occasion for which the poem was written and which is alluded to in the title, as well as from the other *Tombeaux* poems of Mallarmé on Poe, Gautier, and Baudelaire, this rock indeed represents the monument of Verlaine's grave around which a group of writers gathered to celebrate the first anniversary of his death. The thought that such a stone could be made to move by the sheer force of the wind, and that it could then be halted (or an attempt be made to halt it) by applying hands to it ("Ne s'arrêtera ni sous de pieuses mains/Tâtant sa ressemblance avec les maux humains"), is indeed absurd from a representational point of view. Equally absurd is the pseudo-representational phrase that combines a literal action ("tâter") with an abstraction ("la ressemblance"), made more unreal yet because the resemblance is in its turn to something general and abstract ("la ressemblance avec les maux humains"). We are supposed to touch not a stone but the resemblance of a stone, wandering about driven by the wind, to a human emotion. Stierle certainly seems to have a point when he characterizes this dramatic "situation" as beyond representation.

But why should the significance of "roc" be restricted to one single meaning? At the furthest remove from the literal reading, we can think of the rock in purely emblematic terms as the stone miraculously removed from the grave of a sacrificial figure and allowing for the metamorphosis of Christ from an earthly into a heavenly body; such a miracle could easily be accomplished by an allegorical, divine wind. There is nothing farfetched in such a reference. The circumstance of the poem is precisely the "empty tomb" (to quote Yeats) that honors the spiritual entity of Verlaine's work and not his bodily remains. Verlaine himself, in *Sagesse,* singled out by Mallarmé as his most important work,[9] constantly sees his own destiny as an *Imitatio Christi* and, at his death, much was made of the redeeming virtue of suffering for the repenting sinner. In Mallarmé's short prose texts on Verlaine, one senses his irritation with a facile Christianization of the poet, left to die in poverty and scorned as the alchoholic tramp that he was during his lifetime, but whose destiny becomes overnight a lesson in Christian redemption. This sentimental rehabilitation of Verlaine as a Christ figure, alluded to in the reference to the miracle of the Ascension, making his death exemplary for the suffering of all mankind, goes directly against Mallarmé's own conception of poetic immortality. The real movement of the work, its future destiny and correct understanding, will not be halted ("ne s'arrêtera pas") by such hypocritical piety. The opposition against a conventional Christian notion of death as redemption, a theme that recurs constantly in all the *Tombeaux* poems with their undeniable Masonic overtones, is introduced from the start by an emblematic reading of "roc" as an allusion to Scripture.[10]

What concerns us must for our argument is that the word "roc" thus can have several meanings and that, within the system of meanings so set up, a different representational logic can be expected to function; within the scriptural context of miraculous events we can no longer expect naturalistic consistency. But between the literal rock of the gravestone and the emblematic rock of Christ's tomb, many intermediary readings are possible. In another prose text of Mallarmé's on Verlaine (that Stierle never mentions) Verlaine, later called tramp (vagabond) in the poem,

9. Mallarmé, *Oeuvres complètes,* Henri Modor and G. Jean-Aubry, eds., Pléiade edition (Paris, 1945), p. 873.
10. The same polemical tone is apparent in a brief prose text written for the same occasion, the first anniversary of Verlaine's death (January 15, 1897) (Pléiade edition, p. 865). The sonnet, which appeared in *La Revue blanche* of January 1, 1897, actually precedes this text.

is seen as a victim of cold, solitude, and poverty.[11] On another
level, "roc" can then designate Verlaine himself, whose dark and
hulking shape can without too much visual effort be seen as a
"noir roc." And the black object driven by a cold wind in the
month of January suggests still another meaning: that of a dark
cloud. In Mallarmé's poems of this period (one thinks of *Un Coup
de Dés,* of "A la nue accablante tu," etc.) the cloud symbolism
plays a prominent part and would almost have to enter into the
symbolic paraphernalia of any poem—since Mallarmé strives for
the inclusion of his entire symbolic apparatus in each text, however
brief it may be. The hidden cloud imagery in this sonnet, first
perceived by the intuitive but astute Mallarmé reader Thibaudet
in a commentary on the poem, which Stierle mentions,[12] reappears
in the second stanza and completes the cosmic symbolic system
that starts out "here" ("ici," in line 5), on this pastoral earth, and
ascends, by way of the cloud, to the highest hierarchy of the star
in line 7: ". . . l'astre mûri des lendemains/Dont un scintillement
argentera les foules." With a little ingenuity, more meanings still
could be added, always bearing in mind the auto-exegetic symbolic
vocabulary that Mallarmé has developed by this time: thus the
word "roulé," written in 1897, suggests a cross-reference to the
rolling of the dice in *Un Coup de Dés,* making the "roc" into a
symbolical equivalent of the dice. And so on: the more relevant
symbolic meanings one can discover, the closer one comes to the
spirit of Mallarmé's metaphorical play in his later vocabulary.

"Noir roc" for a cloud may seem visually farfetched and forced,
but it is not visually absurd. The process that takes us from the
literal rock to Verlaine, to a cloud and the tomb of Christ, in an

11. "La solitude, le froid, l'inélégance et la pénurie d'ordinaire composent le
sort qu'encourt l'enfant . . . marchant en l'existence selon sa divinité . . ."
(Pléiade edition, p. 511). This text was written at the time of Verlaine's death
(January 9, 1896) and predates the sonnet by one year. Gardner Davies (*Les
Poèmes commémoratifs de Mallarmé, essai d'exégèse raisonné* [Paris, 1950], p.
191) quotes the passage as a gloss on "maux humains" in line 3 but states, without further evidence, that the tombstone unambiguously represents Verlaine (p.
189).
12. Stierle, p. 174. The reference is to A. Thibaudet, *La Poésie de Stéphane
Mallarmé* (Paris, 1926), pp. 307–8. The same passage from Thibaudet is
quoted by Emilie Noulet, *Vingt poèmes de Stéphane Mallarmé* (Paris, 1967),
p. 259, whose commentary on this poem generally follows Davies.

ascending curve from earth to heaven, has a certain representational, naturalistic consistency. We easily recognize it for the traditional poetic *topos* that it is, a metamorphosis, with exactly the
degree of naturalistic verisimilitude that one would have to expect
in this case. The entire poem is in fact a poem about a metamorphosis, the change brought about by death that transformed the
actual person Verlaine into the intellectual abstraction of his work,
"tel qu'en lui-même enfin l'éternité le change," with emphasis on
the metamorphosis implied in "change." Confining himself to
the single literal meaning of "roc," Stierle can rightly say that no
representational element is at play in the text, but he also has
to lose the main part of the meaning. A considerable extension of
meaning, consistent with the thematic concerns of Mallarmé's
other works of the same period, is brought about by allowing for
the metamorphosis of one object into a number of other symbolic
referents. Regardless of the final importance or value of Mallarmé's
poetry as *statement,* the semantic plurality has to be taken into
account at all stages, even and especially if the ultimate "message"
is held to be a mere play of meanings that cancel each other out.
But this polysemic process can only be perceived by a reader willing to remain with a natural logic of representation—the wind
driving a cloud, Verlaine suffering physically from the cold—for
a longer span of time than is allowed for by Stierle, who wants us
to give up any representational reference from the start, without
trying out some of the possibilities of a representational reading.

In the second stanza of the sonnet, Stierle is certainly right
when he asserts that a *summum* of incomprehensibility is reached
in the lines

> Ici . . .
> Cet immatériel deuil opprime de maints
> Nubiles plis l'astre mûri des lendemains . . .

What on earth (or, for that matter, in heaven) could be these
nubile folds that oppress a star or, if one follows Stierle's tempting,
because syntactically very Mallarméan suggestion that "maints
nubiles plis" by inversion modifies "astre" and not "opprime," what
then is this mourning that oppresses a star made up of many nubile
folds? The word "pli" is one of the key-symbols of Mallarmé's

later vocabulary, too rich to even begin to summarize the series of related meanings it implies. Stierle rightly suggests that one of the meanings refers to the book, the fold being the uncut page that distinguishes the self-reflective volume from the mere information contained in the unfolded, unreflective newspaper. The "nubility" of the book, echoed in the "astre *mûri* des lendemains," helps to identify the star as being the timeless project of the universal Book, the literary paradigm that Mallarmé, half-ironically, half-prophetically, keeps announcing as the *telos* of his and of all literary enterprise. The permanence, the immortality of this Book is the true poetic glory bequeathed to future generations. But "nubile," aside from erotic associations (that can be sacrificed to the economy of our exposition), also suggests the bad etymological but very Mallarméan pun on *nubere* (to marry) and *nubes* (cloud). "Nubiles plis," in a visual synecdoche that is bolder than it is felicitous, underscored by an etymological pun, sees the clouds as folds of vapor about to discharge their rain. The cloud imagery already present in "roc" is thus carried further in the second stanza of the sonnet. This reading, which nowise cancels out the reading of "pli" as book—the syntactical ambivalence of giving "maints nubiles plis" both adjectival and adverbial status is a controlled grammatical device entirely in the spirit of Mallarmé's later style— opens up access to the main theme of the poem: the difference between the false kind of transcendence that bases poetic immortality on the exemplary destiny of the poet considered as a person (in the case of Verlaine, the redeeming sacrifice of the suffering sinner) and authentic poetic immortality that is entirely devoid of any personal circumstances. Mallarmé's prose statements on Verlaine show that this is indeed one of his main concerns with regard to this particular poet, an illustration of his own reflections on the theme of poetic impersonality. The actual person Verlaine, as the first tercet unambiguously states, is now part of the material earth— ". . . il est caché parmi l'herbe, Verlaine"—and far removed from the heavenly constellation of which his work has become a part. The symbol of the false transcendence that tries to rise from the person to the work, from the earthly Verlaine to the poetic text, is the cloud. The misdirected mourning of the contemporaries, the superficial judgments of the journalists, all prevent the true significance of the work from manifesting itself. In the straightforward representational logic of the line, the cloud ("maints nubiles plis") covers up the star ("opprime . . . l'astre") and hides it from sight. In the dramatic action performed by the various symbolic objects, the set of meanings associated with clouds ("roc," "nubiles plis" . . .) denounces the psychological fallacy of confusing the impersonal self of the poetry with the empirical self of the life. Verlaine himself did not share in this mystification, or rather, the correct critical reading of his work shows that his poetry is in fact not a poetry of redemption, sacrifice, or personal transcendence. The *Tombeaux* poems always also contain Mallarmé's own critical interpretation of the other poet's work and he sees Verlaine very much the way Yeats saw William Morris, as a naïvely pagan poet unaware of the tragic, Christian sense of death, a fundamentally happy pastoral poet of earth despite the misery of his existence. In the second part of the sonnet, the imagery shifts from Christian to pagan sources, from the Ascension to the river Styx, with the suggestion that he, Mallarmé, might repeat consciously the experience Verlaine went through in naïve ignorance. Verlaine's death and poetic transfiguration prefigure in a naïve tonality the highly self-conscious repetition of the same experience by Mallarmé himself. Like all true poets, Verlaine is a poet of death, but death for Mallarmé means precisely the discontinuity between the personal self and the voice that speaks in the poetry from the other bank of the river, beyond death.

These brief indications do not begin to do justice to the complexity of this poem or to the depth of the Mallarméan theme linking impersonality with death. They merely confirm that, as one would expect, the sonnet on Verlaine shares the thematic concerns that are present in the poetry and in the prose texts of the same period, including *Un Coup de Dés* with its insistence on the necessary transposition of the sacrificial death from the life into the work. It is important for our argument that these themes can only be reached if one admits the persistent presence, in the poetry, of levels of meaning that remain representational. The natural image of the cloud covering a star is an indispensable element in the development of the dramatic action that takes place in the poem. The image of the poetic work as a star implies that poetic understanding is still, for Mallarmé, analogous to an act of seeing and therefore best represented by a natural metaphor of light, like the lamp in Abrams's title. The poem uses a representational poetics that remains fundamentally mimetic throughout.

It can be argued that this representational moment is not the ultimate horizon of Mallarmé's poetry and that, in certain texts that would probably not include the *Tombeau de Verlaine,* we move beyond any thematic meaning whatsoever.[13] Even in this poem, the "ideas" that allow for direct statement, however subtle and profound, however philosophically valid in their own right they may be, are not the ultimate *raison d'être* of the text, but mere pre-text. To say this, however—and the statement would require many developments and qualifications—is to say something quite different from Stierle's assertion that a language of representation is immediately transcended and replaced by an allegorical, figural language. Only after all possible representational meanings have been exhausted can one begin to ask if and by what these meanings have been replaced, and chances are that this will be nothing as harmless as Stierle's entirely formal notions of allegory. Up to a very advanced point, not reached in this poem and perhaps never reached at all, Mallarmé remains a representational poet as he remains in fact a poet of the self, however impersonal, disincarnated, and ironical this self may become in a figure like the "Maître" of *Un Coup de Dés.* Poetry does not give up its mimetic function and its dependence on the fiction of a self that easily and at such little cost.

The implications of this conclusion for the problem of modernity in the lyric reach further than their apparent scholasticism may at first suggest. For Stierle, following Jauss who himself followed Friedrich, it goes without saying that the crisis of the self and of representation in lyric poetry of the nineteenth and twentieth centuries should be interpreted as a gradual process. Baudelaire continues trends implicitly present in Diderot; Mallarmé (as he himself stated) felt he had to begin where Baudelaire had ended; Rimbaud takes an even further step in opening up the experimentation of the surrealists—in short, the modernity of po-

13. See also footnote 9 in Chapter V.

etry occurs as a continuous historical movement. This reconciliation of modernity with history in a common genetic process is highly satisfying, because it allows one to be both origin and offspring at the same time. The son understands the father and takes his work a step further, becoming in turn the father, the source of future offspring, "l'astre *mûri* des lendemains," as Mallarmé puts it in a properly genetic imagery of ripening. The process by no means has to be as easy and spontaneous at is appears in nature: its closest mythological version, the War of the Titans, is far from idyllic. Yet, as far as the idea of modernity is concerned, it remains an optimistic story. Jupiter and his kin may have their share of guilt and sorrow about the fate of Saturn, but they nevertheless are modern men as well as historical figures, linked to a past that they carry within themselves. Their sorrow is a life-giving form of understanding and it integrates the past as an active presence within the future. The literary historian gets a similar satisfaction from a rigorous historical method that remembers the past while he takes part in the excitement of a youthful new present, in the activism of modernity. Such a reconciliation of memory with action is the dream of all historians. In the field of literary studies, the documented modernism of Hans Robert Jauss and his group, who seem to have no qualms about dating the origins of modernism with historical accuracy, is a good contemporary example of this dream. In their case, it rests on the assumption that the movement of lyric poetry away from representation is a historical process that dates back to Baudelaire as well as being the very movement of modernity. Mallarmé might in all likelihood have agreed with this, since he himself resorts frequently, and especially in his later works, to images of filial descent, images of projected futurity which, although no longer founded on organic continuity, nevertheless remain genetic.

There is one curious and puzzling exception, however. Many critics have pointed out that among the various *Tombeaux* poems paying tribute to his predecessors, the sonnet on Baudelaire is oddly unsatisfying. The subtle critical understanding that allows Mallarmé to state his kinship as well as his differences with other artists such as Poe, Gautier, Verlaine, or even Wagner seems to be lacking in the Baudelaire poem. Contrary to the controlled obscurity of the others, this text may well contain genuine areas of blindness. In fact, Mallarmé's relationship to Baudelaire is so complex that little of real insight has yet been said on the bond that united them. The question is not helped by such lapidary pronouncements as Stierle's assertion that "Mallarmé began as a pupil of Baudelaire with pastiches of the *Fleurs du Mal*. His latest poems show how far he went beyond his starting point." In the early poems, most of all in *Hérodiade,* Mallarmé is in fact systematically opposing a certain conception of Baudelaire as a sensuous and subjective poet—which might well be the limit of his own explicit understanding of Baudelaire at that time—while simultaneously responding, especially in his prose poems, to another, darker aspect of the later Baudelaire. The two strains remain operative till the end, the first developing into the main body of his poetic production, the latter remaining more subterranean but never disappearing altogether. The truly allegorical, later Baudelaire of the *Petits Poèmes en Prose* never stopped haunting Mallarmé, though he may have tried to exorcize his presence. Here was, in fact, the example of a poetry that came close to being no longer representational but that remained for him entirely enigmatic. The darkness of this hidden center obscures later allusions to Baudelaire, including the *Tombeau* poem devoted to the author of the *Fleurs du Mal.* Far from being an older kinsman who sent him on his way, Baudelaire, or, at least, the most significant aspect of Baudelaire, was for him a dark zone into which he could never penetrate. The same is true, in different ways, of the view of Baudelaire held by Rimbaud and the surrealists. The understanding of the nonrepresentational, allegorical element in Baudelaire —and, for that matter, in Baudelaire's predecessors in romanticism —is very recent and owes little to Mallarmé or Rimbaud. In terms of the poetics of representation, the relationship from Baudelaire to so-called modern poetry is by no means genetic. He is not the father of modern poetry but an enigmatic stranger that later poets tried to ignore by taking from him only the superficial themes and devices which they could rather easily "go beyond." In authentic poets such as Mallarmé, this betrayal caused the slightly obsessive bad conscience that shines through in his later allusions to Baudelaire. Such a relationship is not the genetic movement of a historical process but is more like the uneasy and shifting border line that separates poetic truth from poetic falsehood.

It could not have been otherwise, for if one takes the allegorization of poetry seriously and calls it the distinctive characteristic of modernity in the lyric, then all remnants of a genetic historicism have to be abandoned. When one of the most significant of modern lyricists, the German poet Paul Celan, writes a poem about his main predecessor Hölderlin, he does not write a poem about light but about blindness.[14] The blindness here is not caused by an absence of natural light but by the absolute ambivalence of a language. It is a self-willed rather than a natural blindness, not the blindness of the soothsayer but rather that of Oedipus at Colonus, who has learned that it is not in his power to solve the enigma of language. One of the ways in which lyrical poetry encounters this enigma is in the ambivalence of a language that is representational and nonrepresentational at the same time. All representational poetry is always also allegorical, whether it be aware of it or not, and the allegorical power of the language undermines and obscures the specific literal meaning of a representation open to understanding. But all allegorical poetry must contain a representational element that invites and allows for understanding, only to discover that the understanding it reaches is necessarily in error. The Mallarmé-Baudelaire relationship is exemplary for all intrapoetic relationships in that it illustrates the impossibility for a representational and an allegorical poetics to engage in a mutually clarifying dialectic. Both are necessarily closed to each other, blind to each other's wisdom. Always again, the allegorical is made representational, as we saw Jauss and his disciples do when they tried to understand the relationship between mimesis and allegory as

14. Paul Celan, "Tübingen, Jänner," in *Die Niemandsrose* (Frankfurt a. M., 1963), p. 24. The first stanza of the poem goes as follows:

Zur Blindheit über—
redete Augen.
Ihre—"ein
Rätsel ist Rein-
entsprungenes"—, ihre
Erinnerung an
schwimmende Hölderlintürme, möwen-
umschwirrt.

a genetic process, forcing into a pattern of continuity that which is, by definition, the negation of all continuity. Or we see ultimate truth being read back into a representation by forcing literal meaning into an allegorical mold, the way Stierle prematurely allegorized a Mallarmé who knew himself to be forever trapped in the deluding appearance of natural images. The question of modernity reveals the paradoxical nature of a structure that makes lyric poetry into an enigma which never stops asking for the unreachable answer to its own riddle. To claim, with Friedrich, that modernity is a form of obscurity is to call the oldest, most ingrained characteristics of poetry modern. To claim that the loss of representation is modern is to make us again aware of an allegorical element in the lyric that had never ceased to be present, but that is itself necessarily dependent on the existence of an earlier allegory and so is the negation of modernity. The worst mystification is to believe that one can move from representation to allegory, or vice versa, as one moves from the old to the new, from father to son, from history to modernity. Allegory can only blindly repeat its earlier model, without final understanding, the way Celan repeats quotations from Hölderlin that assert their own incomprehensibility. The less we understand a poet, the more he is compulsively misinterpreted and oversimplified and made to say the opposite of what he actually said, the better the chances are that he is truly modern; that is, different from what we—mistakenly—think we are ourselves. This would make Baudelaire into a truly modern French poet, Hölderlin into a truly modern German poet and Wordsworth and Yeats into truly modern English poets.

X

The Rhetoric
of Temporality

I. Allegory and Symbol

Since the advent, in the course of the nineteenth century,
of a subjectivistic critical vocabulary, the traditional forms of rhetoric
have fallen into disrepute. It is becoming increasingly clear, however,
that this was only a temporary eclipse: recent developments in
criticism[1] reveal the possibility of a rhetoric that would no longer

1. The trend is apparent in various critical movements that develop independently of one
another in several countries. Thus, for example, in the attempt of some French critics to
fuse the conceptual terminology of structural linguistics with traditional terms of rhetoric
(see, among others, Roland Barthes, "Éléments de sémiologie," in *Communications* 4 [1964],
trans. Annette Lavers and Colin Smith, *Elements of Semiology* [New York: Hill and Wang,
1967]; Gérard Genette, *Figures* [Paris: Seuil, 1966]; Michel Foucault, *Les Mots et les choses*
[Paris: Gallimard, 1966], trans. *The Order of Things* [New York: Random House, Inc., 1970]).
In Germany a similar trend often takes the form of a rediscovery and reinterpretation of
the allegorical and emblematic style of the baroque (see, among others, Walter Benjamin,
Ursprung des deutschen Trauerspiels [Berlin: 1928; reissued in Frankfurt: Suhrkamp, 1963],
trans. John Osborne, *The Origin of German Tragic Drama* [London: NLB, 1977]; Albrecht
Schöne, *Emblematik und Drama im Zeitalter des Barock* [Munich: Beck, 1964]). The evolution from the New Criticism to the criticism of Northrop Frye in North America tends in
the same direction.

187

be normative or descriptive but that would more or less openly raise the question of the intentionality of rhetorical figures. Such concerns are implicitly present in many works in which the terms "mimesis," "metaphor," "allegory," or "irony" play a prominent part. One of the main difficulties that still hamper these investigations stems from the association of rhetorical terms with value judgments that blur distinctions and hide the real structures. In most cases, their use is governed by assumptions that go back at least as far as the romantic period; hence the need for historical clarification as a preliminary to a more systematic treatment of an intentional rhetoric. One has to return, in the history of European literature, to the moment when the rhetorical key-terms undergo significant changes and are at the center of important tensions. A first and obvious example would be the change that takes place in the latter half of the eighteenth century, when the word "symbol" tends to supplant other denominations for figural language, including that of "allegory."

Although the problem is perhaps most in evidence in the history of German literature, we do not intend to retrace the itinerary that led the German writers of the age of Goethe to consider symbol and allegory as antithetical, when they were still synonymous for Winckelmann. The itinerary is too complex for cursory treatment. In *Wahrheit und Methode*, Hans-Georg Gadamer makes the valorization of symbol at the expense of allegory coincide with the growth of an aesthetics that refuses to distinguish between experience and the representation of this experience. The poetic language of genius is capable of transcending this distinction and can thus transform all individual experience directly into general truth. The subjectivity of experience is preserved when it is translated into language; the world is then no longer seen as a configuration of entities that designate a plurality of distinct and isolated meanings, but as a configuration of symbols ultimately leading to a total, single, and universal meaning. This appeal to the infinity of a totality constitutes the main attraction of the symbol as opposed to allegory, a sign that refers to one specific meaning and thus exhausts its suggestive potentialities once it has been deciphered. "Symbol and allegory," writes Gadamer, "are opposed as art is opposed to non-art, in that the former seems endlessly suggestive in the indefiniteness of its meaning, whereas the latter, as soon as its meaning is reached, has run its full course.''[2] Allegory appears as dryly rational and dogmatic in its reference to a meaning that it does not itself constitute, whereas the symbol is founded on an intimate unity between the image that rises up before the senses and the supersensory totality that the image suggests. In this historical perspective, the names of Goethe, Schiller, and Schelling stand out from the background of the classical idea of a unity between incarnate and ideal beauty.

Even within the area of German thought other currents complicate this historical scheme. In the perspective of traditional German classicism, allegory appears as the product of the age of Enlightenment and is vulnerable to the reproach of excessive rationality. Other trends, however, consider allegory as the very place where the contact with a superhuman origin of language has been preserved. Thus the polemical utterances of Hamann against Herder on the problem of the origin of language are closely related to Hamann's considerations on the allegorical nature of all language,[3] as well as with his literary praxis that mingles allegory with irony. It is certainly not in the name of an enlightened rationalism that the idea of a transcendental distance between the incarnate world of man and the divine origin of the word is here being defended. Herder's humanism encounters in Hamann a resistance that reveals the complexity of the intellectual climate in which the debate between symbol and allegory will take place.

These questions have been treated at length in the historiography of the period. We do not have to return to them here, except to indicate how contradictory the origins of the debate appear to be. It is therefore not at all surprising that, even in the case of Goethe, the choice in favor of the symbol is accompanied by all kinds of reservations and qualification. But, as one progresses into the nineteenth century, these qualifications tend to disappear. The supremacy of the symbol, conceived as an expression of unity between the representative and the semantic function of language, becomes a commonplace that underlies literary taste, literary criticism, and literary history. The

2. Hans-George Gadamer, *Wahrheit und Methode* (Tübingen: J. C. B. Mohr, 1960; 4th ed., 1975), p. 70; trans. G. Barden and J. Cumming, *Truth and Method* (New York: Seabury Press, 1975), p. 67.

3. Johann Georg Hamann, "Die Rezension der Herderschen Preisschrift," in *J. G. Hamann's Hauptschriften erklärt, vol. 4 (Über den Ursprung der Sprache)*, Elfriede Büchsel (Gütersloh: Gerd Mohn, 1963).

supremacy of the symbol still functions as the basis of recent French and English studies of the romantic and post-romantic eras, to such an extent that allegory is frequently considered an anachronism and dismissed as non-poetic.

Yet certain questions remain unsolved. At the very moment when properly symbolic modes, in the full strength of their development, are supplanting allegory, we can witness the growth of metaphorical styles in no way related to the decorative allegorism of the rococo, but that cannot be called "symbolic" in the Goethian sense. Thus it would be difficult to assert that in the poems of Hölderlin, the island Patmos, the river Rhine, or, more generally, the landscapes and places that are often described at the beginning of the poems would be symbolic landscapes or entities that represent, as by analogy, the spiritual truths that appear in the more abstract parts of the text. To state this would be to misjudge the literality of these passages, to ignore that they derive their considerable poetic authority from the fact that they are not synecdoches designating a totality of which they are a part, but are themselves already this totality. They are not the sensorial equivalence of a more general, ideal meaning; they are themselves this idea, just as much as the abstract expression that will appear in philosophical or historical form in the later parts of the poem. A metaphorical style such as Hölderlin's can at any rate not be described in terms of the antimony between allegory and symbol—and the same could be said, albeit in a very different way, of Goethe's late style. Also, when the term "allegory" continues to appear in the writers of the period, such as Friedrich Schlegel, or later in Solger or E. T. A. Hoffmann, one should not assume that its use is merely a matter of habit, devoid of deeper meaning. Between 1800 and 1832, under the influence of Creuzer and Schelling, Friedrich Schlegel substitutes the word "symbolic" for "allegorical" in the oft-quoted passage of the "Gespräch über die Poesie": " . . . alle Schönheit ist Allegorie. Das Höchste kann man eben weil es unaussprechlich ist, nur allegorisch sagen."[4] But can we deduce from this, with Schlegel's editor Hans Eichner, that Schlegel "simply uses allegory where we would nowadays say symbol"?[5] It could

---

4. Friedrich Schlegel, "Gespräch über die Poesie," in *Kritische Ausgabe*, Band 2, *Charakteristiken und Kritiken I, (1796-1801)*, Hans Eichner, ed. (Paderborn: Ferdinand Schöningh, 1967), pp. 324ff.
5. *Ibid.*, p. xci, n. 2.

be shown that, precisely because it suggests a disjunction between the way in which the world appears in reality and the way it appears in language, the word "allegory" fits the general problematic of the "Gespräch," whereas the word "symbol" becomes an alien presence in the later version.

We must go even further than this. Ever since the study of *topoi* has made us more aware of the importance of tradition in the choice of images, the symbol, in the post-romantic sense of the term, appears more and more as a special case of figural language in general, a special case that can lay no claim to historical or philosophical priority over other figures. After such otherwise divergent studies as those of E. R. Curtius, of Erich Auerbach, of Walter Benjamin,[6] and of H. -G. Gadamer, we can no longer consider the supremacy of the symbol as a "solution" to the problem of metaphorical diction. "The basis of aesthetics during the nineteenth century," writes Gadamer, "was the freedom of the symbolizing power of the mind. But is this still a firm basis? Is the symbolizing activity not actually still bound today by the survival of a mythological and allegorical tradition?"[7]

To make some headway in this difficult question, it may be useful to leave the field of German literature and see how the same problem appears in English and French writers of the same period. Some help may be gained from a broader perspective.

The English contemporary of Goethe who has expressed himself most explicitly in the relationship between allegory and symbol is, of course, Coleridge. We find in Coleridge what appears to be, at first sight, an unqualified assertion of the superiority of the symbol over allegory. The symbol is the product of the organic growth of form; in the world of the symbol, life and form are identical: "such as the life is, such is the form."[8] Its structure is that of the synecdoche, for the symbol is always a part of the totality that it represents. Consequently, in the symbolic imagination, no disjunction of the constitutive faculties takes place, since the material perception and the symbolical imagination are continuous, as the part is continuous with the whole. In contrast, the allegorical form appears purely mechanical, an abstraction whose

---

6. See note 1 above.
7. Gadamer, p. 76; Eng., p. 72.
8. S. T. Coleridge, *Essays and Lectures on Shakespeare and Some Other Old Poets and Dramatists* (London: Everyman, 1907), p. 46.

original meaning is even more devoid of substance than its "phantom proxy," the allegorical representative; it is an immaterial shape that represents a sheer phantom devoid of shape and substance.[9]

But even in the passage from *The Statesman's Manual*, from which this quotation is taken, a certain degree of ambiguity is manifest. After associating the essential thinness of allegory with a lack of substantiality, Coleridge wants to stress, by contrast, the worth of the symbol. One would expect the latter to be valued for its organic or material richness, but instead the notion of "translucence" is suddenly put in evidence: "The symbol is characterized by the translucence of the special in the individual, or of the general in the special, or of the universal in the general; above all by the translucence of the eternal through and in the temporal."[10]

The material substantiality dissolves and becomes a mere reflection of a more original unity that does not exist in the material world. It is all the more surprising to see Coleridge, in the final part of the passage, characterize allegory negatively as being *merely* a reflection. In truth, the spiritualization of the symbol has been carried so far that the moment of material existence by which it was originally defined has now become altogether unimportant; symbol and allegory alike now have a common origin beyond the world of matter. The reference, in both cases, to a transcendental source, is now more important than the kind of relationship that exists between the reflection and its source. It becomes of secondary importance whether this relationship is based, as in the case of the symbol, on the organic coherence of the synecdoche, or whether, as in the case of allegory, it is a pure decision of the mind. Both figures designate, in fact, the transcendental source, albeit in an oblique and ambiguous way. Coleridge stresses the ambiguity in a definition of allegory in which it is said that allegory " . . . convey[s], while in disguise, either moral qualities or conceptions of the mind that are not in themselves objects of the senses . . . ," but then goes on to state that, on the level of language, allegory can "combine the parts to form a consistent whole."[11] Starting out from the as-

9. S. T. Coleridge, *The Statesman's Manual*, W. G. T. Shedd, ed. (New York: Harper and Brothers, 1875), pp. 437-38, quoted in Angus Fletcher, *Allegory: The Theory of a Symbolic Mode* (Ithaca, N. Y.: Cornell University Press, 1964), p. 16, n. 29.
10. *Ibid.*
11. S. T. Coleridge, *Miscellaneous Criticism*, T. M. Raysor, ed. (London: Constable and Co., Ltd., 1936), p. 30; also quoted by Fletcher, p. 19.

sumed superiority of the symbol in terms of organic substantiality, we end up with a description of figural language as translucence, a description in which the distinction between allegory and symbol has become of secondary importance.

It is not, however, in this direction that Coleridge's considerable influence on later English and American criticism has been most manifest. The very prominent place given in this criticism to the study of metaphor and imagery, often considered as more important than problems of metrics or thematic considerations, is well enough known. But the conception of metaphor that is being assumed, often with explicit reference to Coleridge, is that of a dialectic between object and subject, in which the experience of the object takes on the form of a perception or a sensation. The ultimate intent of the image is not, however, as in Coleridge, translucence, but synthesis, and the mode of this synthesis is defined as "symbolic" by the priority conferred on the initial moment of sensory perception.

The main interpretative effort of English and American historians of romanticism has focused on the transition that leads from eighteenth-century to romantic nature poetry. Among American interpreters of romanticism, there is general agreement about the importance of eighteenth-century antecedents for Wordsworth and Coleridge, but when it comes to describing just in what way romantic nature poetry differs from the earlier forms, certain difficulties arise. They center on the tendency shared by all commentators to define the romantic image as a relationship between mind and nature, between subject and object. The fluent transition in romantic diction, from descriptive to inward, meditative passages, bears out the notion that this relationship is indeed of fundamental importance. The same applies to a large extent to eighteenth-century landscape poets who constantly mix descriptions of nature with abstract moralizings; commentators tend to agree, however, that the relationship between mind and nature becomes much more intimate toward the end of the century. Wimsatt was the first to show convincingly, by the juxtaposition of a sonnet of Coleridge and a sonnet of Bowles that, for all external similitudes, a fundamental change in substance and in tone separated the two texts.[12] He points to a greater specificity in Coleridge's details, thus

12. William Wimsatt, "The Structure of Romantic Nature Imagery," *The Verbal Icon* (Lexington, Ky.: University of Kentucky Press, 1954) pp. 106-10.

romantic shift inward.

revealing a closer, more faithful observation of the outside object. But this finer attention given to the natural surfaces is accompanied, paradoxically enough, by a greater inwardness, by experiences of memory and of reverie that stem from deeper regions of subjectivity than in the earlier writer. How this closer attention to surfaces engenders greater depth remains problematic. Wimsatt writes: "The common feat of the romantic nature poets was to read meanings into the landscape. The meaning might be such as we have seen in Coleridge's sonnet, but it might more characteristically be more profound, concerning the spirit or soul of things—'the one life within us and abroad.' And that meaning especially was summoned out of the very surface of nature itself."[13] The synthesis of surface and depth would then be the manifestation, in language, of a fundamental unity that encompasses both mind and object, "the one life within us and abroad." It appears, however, that this unity can be hidden from a subject, who then has to look outside, in nature, for the confirmation of its existence. For Wimsatt, the unifying principle seems to reside primarily within nature, hence the necessity for the poets to start out from natural landscapes, the sources of the unifying, "symbolic" power.

moral landscape

The point receives more development and ampler documentation in recent articles by Meyer Abrams and Earl Wasserman that make use of very similar, at times even identical material.[14] The two interpreters agree on many issues, to the point of overlapping. Both name, for instance, the principle of analogy between mind and nature as the basis for the eighteenth-century habit of treating a moral issue in terms of a descriptive landscape. Abrams refers to Renaissance concepts of theology and philosophy as a main source for the later *paysage moralisé*: ". . . the divine Architect has designed the universe analogically, relating the physical, moral, and spiritual realms by an elaborate system of correspondences. . . . The metaphysics of a symbolic and analogical universe underlay the figurative tactics of the seventeenth-century metaphysical poets."[15] A "tamed and ordered" version of this cosmology, "smoothed

---

13. *Ibid.*, p. 110.
14. Meyer Abrams, "Structure and Style in the Greater Romantic Lyric," in *From Sensibility to Romanticism: Essays Presented to F. A. Pottle,* F. W. Hillis and H. Bloom, eds. (New York: Oxford University Press, 1965). Earl Wasserman, "The English Romantics, The Grounds of Knowledge," *Essays in Romanticism,* 4 (Autumn, 1964).
15. Abrams, p. 536.

to a neo-classic decency" and decorum, then becomes the origin of the eighteenth-century loco-descriptive poem, in which "sensuous phenomena are coupled with moral statements." And Wasserman points to eighteenth-century theoreticians of the imagination, such as Aken-side, who "can find [the most intimate relation] between subject and object is that of associative analogy, so that man beholds 'in lifeless things / The Inexpressive semblance of himself, / Of thought and passion.'"[16]

The key concept here is, in Wasserman's correct phrasing, that of an *associative* analogy, as contrasted with a more vital form of analogy in the romantics. Abrams makes it seem, at times, as if the romantic theory of imagination did away with analogy altogether and that Coleridge in particular replaced it by a genuine and working monism. "Nature is made thought and thought nature," he writes, "both by their sustained interaction and by their seamless metaphoric continuity."[17] But he does not really claim that this degree of fusion is achieved and sustained—at most that it corresponds to Coleridge's desire for a unity toward which his thought and poetic strategy strive. Analogy as such is certainly never abandoned as an epistemological pattern for natural images; even within the esoteric vocabulary of as late a version of a monistic universe as Baudelaire's correspondences, the expression "*analogie universelle*" is still being used.[18] Nevertheless, the relationship between mind and nature becomes indeed a lot less formal, less purely associative and external than it is in the eighteenth century. As a result, the critical—and even, at times, the poetic—vocabulary attempts to find terms better suited to express this relationship than is the somewhat formal concept of analogy. Words such as "affinity," or "sympathy," appear instead of the more abstract "analogy." This does not change the fundamental pattern of the structure, which remains that of a formal resemblance between entities that, in other respects, can be antithetical. But the new terminology indicates a gliding away from the formal problem of a congruence between the

16. Wasserman, p. 19.
17. Abrams, p. 551.
18. Charles Baudelaire, "Réflexions sur quelques-uns de mes contemporains, Victor Hugo," in *Curiosités esthétiques: L'Art romantique et autres Oeuvres critiques*, H. Lemaître, ed. (Paris: Garnier, 1962), p. 735.

two poles to that of the ontological priority of the one over the other.
For terms such as "affinity" or "sympathy" apply to the relationships between subjects rather than to relationships between a subject
and an object. The relationship with nature has been superseded by
an intersubjective, interpersonal relationship that, in the last analysis,
is a relationship of the subject toward itself. Thus the priority has passed
from the outside world entirely within the subject, and we end up with
something that resembles a radical idealism. Both Abrams and Wasserman offer quotations from Wordsworth and Coleridge, as well as sum-
marizing comments of their own, that seem to suggest that romanticism is, in fact, such an idealism. Both quote Wordsworth: "I was
often unable to think of external things as having external existence,
and I communed with all that I saw as something not apart from, but
inherent in, my own immaterial nature"—and Wasserman comments
that "Wordsworth's poetic experience seeks to recapture that condition."[19]

Since the assertion of a radical priority of the subject over objective
nature is not easily compatible with the poetic praxis of the romantic
poets, who all gave a great deal of importance to the presence of nature,
a certain degree of confusion ensues. One can find numerous quotations and examples that plead for the predominance, in romantic poetry,
of an analogical imagination that is founded on the priority of natural
substances over the consciousness of the self. Coleridge can speak, in
nearly Fichtean terms, of the infinite self in opposition to the "necessarily finite" character of natural objects, and insist on the need for the
self to give life to the dead forms of nature.[20] But the finite nature
of the objective world is seen, at that moment, in spatial terms, and
the substitution of vital (i.e., in Coleridge, intersubjective) relationships
that are dynamic, for the physical relationships that exist between entities in the natural world is not necessarily convincing. It could very
well be argued that Coleridge's own concept of organic unity as a
dynamic principle is derived from the movements of nature, not from
those of the self. Wordsworth is more clearly conscious of what is involved here when he sees the same dialectic between the self and nature
in temporal terms. The movements of nature are for him instances of

19. Wasserman, p. 26.
20. *Ibid.*, p. 29.

what Goethe calls *Dauer im Wechsel*, endurance within a pattern of
change, the assertion of a metatemporal, stationary state beyond the
apparent decay of a mutability that attacks certain outward aspects
of nature but leaves the core intact. Hence we have famous passages
such as the description of the mountain scenes in *The Prelude* in which
a striking temporal paradox is evoked:

> . . . these majestic floods—these shining cliffs
> The untransmuted shapes of many worlds,
> Cerulian ether's pure inhabitants,
> These forests unapproachable by death,
> That shall endure as long as man endures . . .;

or

> The immeasurable height
> Of woods decaying, never to be decayed
> The stationary blast of waterfalls. . . .

Such paradoxical assertions of eternity in motion can be applied
to nature but not to a self caught up entirely within mutability. The
temptation exists, then, for the self to borrow, so to speak, the temporal stability that it lacks from nature, and to devise strategies by
means of which nature is brought down to a human level while still
escaping from "the unimaginable touch of time." This strategy is
certainly present in Coleridge. And it is present, though perhaps
not consciously, in critics such as Abrams and Wasserman, who see
Coleridge as the great synthesizer and who take his dialectic of subject and object to be the authentic pattern of romantic imagery.
But this forces them, in fact, into a persistent contradiction. They
are obliged, on the one hand, to assert the priority of object over
subject that is implicit in an organic conception of language. So
Abrams states: "The best Romantic meditations on a landscape,
following Coleridge's example, all manifest a transaction between
subject and object in which the thought incorporates and makes
explicit what was already implicit in the outer scene."[21] This puts
the priority unquestionably in the natural world, limiting the task
of the mind to interpreting what is given in nature. Yet this statement is taken from the same paragraph in which Abrams quotes the

21. Abrams, p. 551.

passages from Wordsworth and Coleridge that confer an equally absolute priority to the self over nature. The contradiction reaches a genuine impasse. For what are to believe? Is romanticism a subjective
idealism, open to all the attacks of solipsism that, from Hazlitt to the
French structuralists, a succession of de-mystifiers of the self have
directed against it? Or is it instead a return to a certain form of
naturalism after the forced abstraction of the Enlightenment, but a
return which our urban and alienated world can conceive of only as
a nostalgic and unreachable past? Wasserman is caught in the same
impasse: for him, Wordsworth represents the extreme form of subjec-
tivism whereas Keats, as a quasi-Shakespearean poet of negative
capability, exemplifies a sympathetic and objective form of material
imagination. Coleridge acts as the synthesis of this antithetical polarity. But Wasserman's claim for Coleridge as the reconciler of what he
calls "the phenomenal world of understanding with the noumenal world
of reason"[22] is based on a quotation in which Coleridge simply
substitutes another self for the category of the object and thus removes
the problem from nature altogether, reducing it to a purely intersubjective pattern. "To make the object one with us, we must become one
with the object—ergo, an object. Ergo, the object must be itself a
subject—partially a favorite dog, principally a friend, wholly God, *the
Friend.*"[23] Wordsworth was never guilty of thus reducing a theocentric to an interpersonal relationship.

Does the confusion originate with the critics, or does it reside in
the romantic poets themselves? Were they really unable to move beyond
the analogism that they inherited from the eighteenth century and were
they trapped in the contradiction of a pseudo dialectic between subject and object? Certain commentators believe this to be the case;[24]
before following them, we should make certain that we have indeed
been dealing with the main romantic problem when we interpret the
romantic image in terms of a subject-object tension. For this dialectic
originates, it must be remembered, in the assumed predominance of
the symbol as the outstanding characteristic of romantic diction, and
this predominance must, in its turn, be put into question.

22. Wasserman, p. 30.
23. *Ibid.*, pp. 29-30.
24. As one instance among others, see E. E. Bostetter, *The Romantic Ventriloquists* (Seat-
tle: University of Washington Press, 1963).

It might be helpful, at this point, to shift attention from English to French literary history. Because French pre-romanticism occurs, with Rousseau, so early in the eighteenth century, and because the Lockian heritage in France never reached, not even with Condillac, the degree of automaticism against which Coleridge and Wordsworth had to rebel in Hartley, the entire problem of analogy, as connected with the use of nature imagery, is somewhat clearer there than in England. Some of the writers of the period were at least as aware as their later commentators of what was involved in a development of the general taste that felt attracted toward a new kind of landscape. To take one example: in his *De la composition des paysages sur le terrain*, which dates from 1777, the Marquis de Girardin describes a landscape explicitly as "romantic," made up of dark woods, snow-capped mountains, and a crystalline lake with an island on which an idyllic "*ménage rustique*" enjoys a happy combination of sociability and solitude among cascades and rushing brooks. And he comments on the scene as follows: "It is in situations like this that one feels all the strength of this analogy between natural beauty and moral sentiment."[25] One could establish a long list of similar quotations dating from the same general period, all expressing the intimate proximity between nature and its beholder in a language that evokes the material shape of the landscape as well as the mood of its inhabitants.

Later historians and critics have stressed this close unity between mind and nature as a fundamental characteristic of romantic diction. "Often the outer and the inner world are so deeply intermingled," writes Daniel Mornet, "that nothing distinguishes the images perceived by the senses from the chimera of the imagination."[26] The same emphasis, still present in the more recent writings on the period,[27] closely resembles the opinion expressed in Anglo-American criticism. There is the same stress on the analogical unity of nature and consciousness, the same priority given to the symbol as the unit of language in which the subject-object synthesis can take place, the same tendency to transfer

25. Quoted by Daniel Mornet, *Le Sentiment de la Nature en France au XVIIIe siècle de Jean-Jacques Rousseau à Bernardin de Saint-Pierre* (Paris, 1932), p. 248.
26. *Ibid.*, p. 187.
27. See, for example, Herbert Dieckmann, "Zur Theorie der Lyrik im 18. Jahrhundert in Frankreich, mit gelegentlicher Berücksichtigung der Englischen Kritik," in *Poetik und Hermeneutik*, vol. 2, W. Iser, ed. (Munich: Wilhelm Fink, 1966), p. 108.

into nature attributes of consciousness and to unify it organically with respect to a center that acts, for natural objects, as the identity of the self functions for a consciousness. In French literary history dealing with the period of Rousseau to the present, ambivalences closely akin to those found in the American historians of romanticism could be pointed out, ambivalences derived from an illusionary priority of a subject that had, in fact, to borrow from the outside world a temporal stability which it lacked within itself.

In the case of French romanticism, it is perhaps easier than it is in English literature to designate the historical origin of this tendency. One can point to a certain number of specific texts in which a symbolic language, based on the close interpenetration between observation and passion, begins to acquire a priority that it will never relinquish during the nineteenth and twentieth centuries. Among these texts none is more often singled out than Rousseau's novel *La Nouvelle Héloïse*. It forms the basis of Daniel Mornet's study on the sentiment of nature in the eighteenth century.[28] In more recent works, such as Robert Mauzi's *Idée du bonheur dans la littérature française du 18ème siècle*,[29] the same predominant importance is given to Rousseau's novel. "When one knows *Cleveland* and *La Nouvelle Héloïse*, there is little left to discover about the 18th century," Mauzi asserts in his preface.[30] There is certainly no better reference to be found than *La Nouvelle Héloïse* for putting to the test the nearly unanimous conviction that the origins of romanticism coincide with the beginnings of a predominantly symbolical diction.

Interpreters of Rousseau's epistolary novel have had no difficulty in pointing out the close correspondence between inner states of the soul and the outward aspect of nature, especially in passages such as the Meillerie episode in the fourth part of the novel.[31] In this letter, St. Preux revisits, in the company of the now-married Julie, the deserted region on the northern bank of the lake from which he had, in earlier days, written the letter that sealed their destiny. Rousseau stresses that

28. See note 25 above.
29. Robert Mauzi, *L'Idée du bonheur dans la littérature et la pensée française du XVIIIe siècle* (Paris: A. Colin, 1960).
30. *Ibid.*, p. 10.
31. J. J. Rousseau, *Julie ou la Nouvelle Héloïse*, pt. 4, letter 17, in *Oeuvres complètes*, B. Gagnebin and Marcel Raymond, eds. (Paris: Gallimard [Bibliotèque de la Pléiade], 1961), 2: 514ff.

the *lieu solitaire* he describes is like a wild desert *"sauvage et désert; mais plein de ces sortes de beautés qui ne plaisent qu'aux âmes sensibles et paraissent horribles aux autres."*[32] A polemical reference to current taste is certainly present here, and such passages can be cited to illustrate the transition from the eighteenth-century, idyllic landscape that we still find in Girardin to the somber, tormented scenes that are soon to predominate in Macpherson. But this polemic of taste is superficial, for Rousseau's concerns are clearly entirely different. It is true that the intimate analogy between scenery and emotion serves as a basis for some of the dramatic and poetic effects of the passage: the sensuous passion, reawakened by memory and threatening to disturb a precarious tranquillity, is conveyed by the contrasting effects of light and setting which give the passage its dramatic power. The analogism of the style and the sensuous intensity of the passion are closely related. But this should not blind us to the explicit thematic function of the letter, which is one of temptation and near-fatal relapse into former error, openly and explicitly condemned, without any trace of ambiguity, in the larger context of Rousseau's novel.

In this respect, the reference to the Meillerie landscape as a wilderness is particularly revealing, especially when contrasted with other landscapes in the novel that are not emblematic of error, but of the virtue associated with the figure of Julie. This is the case for the central emblem of the novel, the garden that Julie has created on the Wolmar estate as a place of refuge. On the allegorical level the garden functions as the landscape representative of the "beautiful soul." Our question is whether this garden, the Elysium described at length in the eleventh letter of the fourth part of the novel, is based on the same kind of subject/object relationship that was thematically and stylistically present in the Meillerie episode.

A brief consideration of Rousseau's sources for the passage is enlightening. The main non-literary source has been all too strongly emphasized by Mornet in his critical edition of the novel:[33] Rousseau derives several of the exterior aspects of his garden from the so-called *jardins anglais*, which, well before him, were being preferred to the

32. *Ibid.*, p. 518.
33. *La Nouvelle Héloïse*, Daniel Mornet, ed. (Paris: 1925), Introduction, 1: 67-74, and notes, 3: 223-47.

geometrical abstraction of the classical French gardens. The excessive symmetry of Le Nôtre, writes Rousseau, echoing a commonplace of sophisticated taste at the time, is *"ennemie de la nature et de la variété."*[34] But this "natural" look of the garden is by no means the main theme of the passage. From the beginning we are told that the natural aspect of the site is in fact the result of extreme artifice, that in this bower of bliss, contrary to the tradition of the *topos*, we are entirely in the realm of art and not that of nature. "Il est vrai," Rousseau has Julie say, "que la nature a tout fait [dans ce jardin] mais sous ma direction, et il n'y a rien là que je n'aie ordonné."[35] The statement should at least alert us to the literary sources of the gardens of the passage that Mornet, preoccupied as he was with the outward history of taste, was led to neglect.

Confining ourselves to the explicit literary allusions that can be found in the text, the reference to *"une Ile déserte . . . (où) je n'aperçois aucuns pas d'hommes"*[36] points directly toward Rousseau's favorite contemporary novel, the only one considered suitable for Emile's education, Defoe's *Robinson Crusoe*, whereas the allusion to the *Roman de la rose* in the pages immediately preceding the letter on Julie's Elysium[37] is equally revealing. The combination of *Robinson Crusoe* with the *Roman de la rose* may not look very promising at first sight, but it has, in fact, considerable hidden possiblities. The fact that the medieval romance, re-issued in 1735 and widely read in Rousseau's time,[38] had given the novel its subtitle of *"La Nouvelle Héloïse"* is well known, but its influence is manifest in many other ways as well. The close similarity between Julie's garden and the love garden of Deduit, which appears in the first part of Guillaume de Lorris' poem, is obvious. There is hardly a detail of Rousseau's description that does not find its counterpart in the medieval text: the self-enclosed, isolated space of the *"asile"*; the special privilege reserved to the happy few who possess a key that unlocks the gate; the traditional enumeration of natural attributes—a catalogue of the various flowers, trees, fruits, perfumes, and, above

34. Rousseau, p. 483.
35. *Ibid.*, p. 472.
36. *Ibid.*, p. 479.
37. "Richesse ne fait pas riche, dit le Roman de la Rose," quoted in letter 10 of pt. 4, *ibid.*, p. 466 and n.
38. *Ibid.*, p. 1606, n. 2. I have consulted a copy of the Lenglet du Fresnoy edition which, at first sight, offers no variants that are immediately relevant to our question.

all, of the birds, culminating in the description of their song.[39] Most revealing of all is the emphasis on water, on fountains and pools that, in *Julie* as in the *Roman de la rose*, are controlled not by nature but by the ingenuity of the inhabitants.[40] Far from being an observed scene or the expression of a personal *état d'âme*, it is clear that Rousseau has deliberately taken all the details of his setting from the medieval literary source, one of the best-known versions of the traditional *topos* of the erotic garden.

In linguistic terms, we have something very different, then, from the descriptive and metaphorical language that, from Chateaubriand on, will predominate in French romantic diction. Rousseau does not even pretend to be observing. The language is purely figural, not based on perception, less still on an experienced dialectic between nature and consciousness. Julie's claim of domination and control over nature (*"il n'y a rien là que je n'aie ordonné"*) may well be considered as the fitting emblem for a language that submits the outside world entirely to its own purposes, contrary to what happens in the Meillerie episode, where the language fuses together the parallel movements of nature and of passion.

In the first part of the *Roman de la rose*, however, the use of figural language in no way conflicts with the exalted treatment of erotic themes; quite to the contrary, the erotic aspects of the allegory hardly need to be stressed. But in *La Nouvelle Héloïse* the emphasis on an ethic of renunciation conveys a moral climate that differs entirely from the moralizing sections of the medieval romance. Rousseau's theme of renunciation is far from being one-sided and is certainly not to be equated with a puritanical denial of the world of the senses. Nevertheless, it is in the use of allegorical diction rather than of the language of correspondences that the medieval and eighteenth-century sources converge. Recent studies of Defoe, such as G. A. Starr's *Defoe and Spiritual Autobiography*[41] and Paul Hunter's *The Reluctant Pilgrim*,[42] have reversed the trend to see in Defoe one of the inventors of a modern

39. Guillaume de Lorris and Jean de Meun, *Le Roman de la rose*, Félix Lecoy, ed. (Paris: Champion, 1965), vol. 1, esp. ll. 499ff., 629ff., 1345ff.
40. *Ibid.*, ll. 1385ff.
41. G. A. Starr, *Defoe and Spiritual Autobiography* (Princeton, N.J.: Princeton University Press, 1965).
42. J. Paul Hunter, *The Reluctant Pilgrim: Defoe's Emblematic Method and Quest in Robinson Crusoe* (Baltimore: Johns Hopkins University Press, 1966).

"realistic" idiom and have rediscovered the importance of the puritanical, religious element to which Rousseau responded. Paul Hunter has strongly emphasized the stylistic importance of this element, which led Defoe to make an allegorical rather than a metaphorical and descriptive use of nature. Thus Defoe's gardens, far from being realistic natural settings, are stylized emblems, quite similar in structure and detail to the gardens of the *Roman de la rose*. But they serve primarily a redemptive, ethical function. Defoe's garden, writes Paul Hunter, "is not . . . a prelapsarian paradise but rather an earthly paradise *in posse*, for Crusoe is postlapsarian man who has to toil to cultivate his land into full abundance."[43] The same stress on hardship, toil, and virtue is present in Julie's garden, relating the scene closely to the Protestant allegorical tradition of which the English version, culminating in Bunyan, reached Rousseau through a variety of sources, including Defoe. The stylistic likeness of the sources supersedes all further differences between them; the tension arises not between the two distant literary sources, the one erotic, the other puritanical, but between the allegorical language of a scene such as Julie's Elysium and the symbolic language of passages such as the Meillerie episode. The moral contrast between these two worlds epitomizes the dramatic conflict of the novel. This conflict is ultimately resolved in the triumph of a controlled and lucid renunciation of the values associated with a cult of the moment, and this renunciation establishes the priority of an allegorical over a symbolic diction. The novel could not exist without the simultaneous presence of both metaphorical modes, nor could it reach its conclusion without the implied choice in favor of allegory over symbol.

Subsequent interpreters of *La Nouvelle Héloïse* have, in general, ignored the presence of allegorical elements in shaping the diction of the novel, and it is only recently that one begins to realize how false the image of Rousseau as a primitivist or as a naturalist actually is. These false interpretations, very revealing in their own right, resist correction with a remarkable tenacity, thereby indicating how deeply this correction conflicts with the widespread *"idées reçues"* on the nature and the origins of European romanticism.

For, if the dialectic between subject and object does not designate the main romantic experience, but only one passing moment in a dia-

43. *Ibid.*, p. 172.

lectic, and a negative moment at that, since it represents a temptation that has to be overcome, then the entire historical and philosophical pattern changes a great deal. Similar allegorizing tendencies, though often in a very different form, are present not only in Rousseau but in all European literature between 1760 and 1800. Far from being a mannerism inherited from the exterior aspects of the baroque and the rococo, they appear at the most original and profound moments in the works, when an authentic voice becomes audible. The historians of English romanticism have been forced, by the nature of things, to mention allegory, although it is often a problem of secondary importance. Wimsatt has to encounter it in dealing with Blake; he quotes two brief poems by Blake, entitled "To Spring" and "To Summer," and comments: "Blake's starting point . . . is the opposite of Wordsworth's and Byron's, not the landscape but a spirit personified or allegorized. Nevertheless, this spirit as it approaches the 'western isle' takes on certain distinctly terrestrial hues. . . . These early romantic poets are examples of the Biblical, classical, and Renaissance tradition of allegory as it approaches the romantic condition of landscape naturalism—as Spring and Summer descend into the landscape and are fused with it."[44] Rather than such a continuous development from allegory to romantic naturalism, the example of Rousseau shows that we are dealing instead with the rediscovery of an allegorical tradition beyond the sensualistic analogism of the eighteenth century. This rediscovery, far from being spontaneous and easy, implies instead the discontinuity of a renunciation, even of a sacrifice. Taking for his starting point the descriptive poem of the eighteenth century, Abrams can speak with more historical precision. After having stressed the thematic resemblance between the romantic lyric and the metaphysical poem of the seventeenth century, he writes: "There is a very conspicuous and significant difference between the Romantic lyric and the seventeenth-century meditation on created nature. . . . [In the seventeenth century] the 'composition of place' was not a specific locality, nor did it need to be present to the eyes of the speaker, but was a typical scene or object, usually called up . . . before 'the eyes of the imagination' in order to set off and guide the thought by means of correspondences whose interpretation was firmly controlled by an inherited typology."[45] The distinction between

44. Wimsatt, p. 113.
45. Abrams, p. 556.

seventeenth- and late eighteenth-century poetry is made in terms of
the determining role played by the geographical *place* as establishing
the link between the language of the poem and the empirical experience
of the reader. However, in observing the development of even as geographically concrete a poet as Wordsworth, the significance of the locale
can extend so far as to include a meaning that is no longer circumscribed
by the literal horizon of a given place. The meaning of the site is often
made problematic by a sequence of spatial ambiguities, to such an extent that one ends up no longer at a specific place but with a mere
name whose geographical significance has become almost meaningless.
Raising the question of the geographical locale of a given metaphorical
object (in this case, a river), Wordsworth writes: "The spirit of the answer
[as to the whereabouts of the river] through the word might be a certain stream, accompanied perhaps with an image gathered from a Map,
or from a real object in nature—these might have been the latter, but
the spirit of the answer must have been, as inevitably—a receptacle
without bounds or dimensions;—nothing less than infinity."[46] Passages
in Wordsworth such as the crossing of the Alps or the ascent of Mount
Snowden, or texts less sublime in character, such as the sequence of
poems on the river Duddon, can no longer be classified with the
locodescriptive poem of the eighteenth century. In the terminology proposed by Abrams, passages of this kind no longer depend on the choice
of a specific locale, but are controlled by "a traditional and inherited
typology," exactly as in the case of the poems from the sixteenth and
seventeenth centuries—with this distinction, however, that the typology
is no longer the same and that the poet, sometimes after long and difficult inner struggle, had to renounce the seductiveness and the poetic
resources of a symbolical diction.

Whether it occurs in the form of an ethical conflict, as in *La Nouvelle
Héloïse*, or as an allegorization of the geographical site, as in Wordsworth, the prevalence of allegory always corresponds to the unveiling
of an authentically temporal destiny. This unveiling takes place in a
subject that has sought refuge against the impact of time in a natural
world to which, in truth, it bears no resemblance. The secularized
thought of the pre-romantic period no longer allows a transcendance
of the antinomies between the created world and the act of creation

---

46. W. Wordsworth, "Essay upon Epitaphs," in *The Poetical Works* (Oxford, 1949), 4:446.

by means of a positive recourse to the notion of divine will; the failure of the attempt to conceive of a language that would be symbolical as well as allegorical, the suppression, in the allegory, of the analogical and anagogical levels, is one of the ways in which this impossibility becomes manifest. In the world of the symbol it would be possible for the image to coincide with the substance, since the substance and its representation do not differ in their being but only in their extension: they are part and whole of the same set of categories. Their relationship is one of simultaneity, which, in truth, is spatial in kind, and in which the intervention of time is merely a matter of contingency, whereas, in the world of allegory, time is the originary constitutive category. The relationship between the allegorical sign and its meaning (*signifié*) is not decreed by dogma; in the instances we have seen in Rousseau and in Wordsworth, this is not at all the case. We have, instead, a relationship between signs in which the reference to their respective meanings has become of secondary importance. But this relationship between signs necessarily contains a constitutive temporal element; it remains necessary, if there is to be allegory, that the allegorical sign refer to another sign that precedes it. The meaning constituted by the allegorical sign can then consist only in the *repetition* (in the Kierkegaardian sense of the term) of a previous sign with which it can never coincide, since it is of the essence of this previous sign to be pure anteriority. The secularized allegory of the early romantics thus necessarily contains the negative moment which in Rousseau is that of renunciation, in Wordsworth that of the loss of self in death or in error.

Whereas the symbol postulates the possibility of an identity or identification, allegory designates primarily a distance in relation to its own origin, and, renouncing the nostalgia and the desire to coincide, it establishes its language in the void of this temporal difference. In so doing, it prevents the self from an illusory identification with the non-self, which is now fully, though painfully, recognized as a non-self. It is this painful knowledge that we perceive at the moments when early romantic literature finds its true voice. It is ironically revealing that this voice is so rarely recognized for what it really is and that the literary movement in which it appears has repeatedly been called a primitive naturalism or a mystified solipsism. The authors with whom we are dealing had often gone out of their way to designate their theological

and philosophical sources: too little attention has been paid to the complex and controlled set of literary allusions which, in *La Nouvelle
Héloïse*, established the link between Rousseau and his Augustinian
sources, mostly by way of Petrarch.

We are led, in conclusion, to a historical scheme that differs entirely from the customary picture. The dialectical relationship between
subject and object is no longer the central statement of romantic
thought, but this dialectic is now located entirely in the temporal relationships that exist within a system of allegorical signs. It becomes
a conflict between a conception of the self seen in its authentically
temporal predicament and a defensive strategy that tries to hide from
this negative self-knowledge. On the level of language the asserted
superiority of the symbol over allegory, so frequent during the nineteenth century, is one of the forms taken by this tenacious self-
mystification. Wide areas of European literature of the nineteenth and
twentieth centuries appear as regressive with regards to the truths that
come to light in the last quarter of the eighteenth century. For the
lucidity of the pre-romantic writers does not persist. It does not take
long for a symbolic conception of metaphorical language to establish
itself everywhere, despite the ambiguities that persist in aesthetic theory
and poetic practice. But this symbolical style will never be allowed
to exist in serenity; since it is a veil thrown over a light one no longer
wishes to perceive, it will never be able to gain an entirely good poetic
conscience.

II. Irony

Around the same time that the tension between symbol and allegory
finds expression in the works and the theoretical speculations of the
early romantics, the problem of irony also receives more and more
self-conscious attention. At times, a concern with the figural aspects
of language and, more specifically, an awareness of the persistence
of allegorical modes go hand in hand with a theoretical concern for
the trope "irony" as such. This is by no means always the case. We
cited Rousseau and Wordsworth, and alluded to Hölderlin, as possible
instances of romantic allegorism; the use of irony is conspicuously
absent from all these poets. In others, however, the implicit and
rather enigmatic link between allegory and irony which runs
through the history of rhetoric seems to prevail. We mentioned

Hamann;[47] in Germany alone, the names of Friedrich Schlegel, Friedrich Solger, E. T. A. Hoffmann, and Kierkegaard would be obvious additions to the list. In all these instances a more-or-less systematic theory of figural language, with explicit stress on allegory, runs parallel with an equally prevalent stress on irony. Friedrich Schlegel, of course, is well known as the main theoretician of romantic irony. That he was also affected, as well as somewhat puzzled, by the problem of metaphorical diction is clear from many of the *Fragmenten*, as well as from the revisions he made between the 1800 and 1823 editions of his works.[48] A similar parallelism between the problem of allegory and that of irony is certainly present in Solger, who elevates irony to the constitutive mode of all literature and suggestively distinguishes between symbol and allegory in terms of a dialectic of identity and difference.[49]

Nevertheless, the connection and the distinction between allegory and irony never become, at that time, independent subjects for reflection. The terms are rarely used as a means to reach a sharper definition, which, especially in the case of irony, is greatly needed. It obviously does not suffice to refer back to the descriptive rhetorical tradition which, from Aristotle to the eighteenth century, defines irony as "saying one thing and meaning another" or, in an even more restrictive context, as "blame-by-praise and praise-by-blame."[50] This definition points to a structure shared by irony and allegory in that, in both cases, the relationship between sign and meaning is discontinuous, involving an extraneous principle that determines the point and the manner at and in which the relationship is articulated. In both cases, the sign points to something that differs from its literal meaning and has for its function the thematization of this difference. But this important structural aspect may well be a description of figural language in general; it clearly lacks discriminatory precision. The relationship between allegory and irony appears in history as a casual and apparently contingent fact, in the form of a common concern of some writers with

47. See note 3 above.
48. Schlegel, Band 2, p. xci.
49. Friedrich Solger, *Erwin: Vier Gespräche über das Schöne und die Kunst* (Leipzig, 1829).
50. Norman Knox, *The Word Irony and its Context, 1500-1755* (Durham, N.C.: Duke University Press, 1961).

both modes. It is this empirical event that has to receive a more general and theoretical interpretation.

The question is made more complex, but also somewhat more concrete, by an additional connection between a concern with irony and the development of the modern novel. The link is made in many critical texts: in Goethe, in Friedrich Schlegel, more recently in Lukács and in structuralist studies of narrative form. The tie between irony and the novel seems to be so strong that one feels tempted to follow Lukács in making the novel into the equivalent, in the history of literary genres, of irony itself. From the very beginning, the possibility of extending the trope to make it encompass lengthy narratives existed; in the *Institutio*, Quintilian described irony as capable of coloring an entire discourse pronounced in a tone of voice that did not correspond to the true situation, or even, with reference to Socrates, as pervading an entire life.[51] The passage from the localized trope to the extended novel is tempting, although the correlation between irony and the novel is far from simple. Even the superficial and empirical observation of literary history reveals this complexity. The growth of theoretical insight into irony around 1800 bears a by no means obvious relationship to the growth of the nineteenth-century novel. In Germany, for instance, the advent of a full-fledged ironic consciousness, which will persist from Friedrich Schlegel to Kierkegaard and to Nietzsche, certainly does not coincide with a parallel blossoming of the novel. Friedrich Schlegel, writing on the novel, has to take his recent examples from Sterne and Diderot and has to strain to find a comparable level of ironic insight in *Wilhelm Meisters Lehrjahre* and in Jean Paul Richter.[52] The opposite is true in France and England, where the spectacular development of the novel is not necessarily accompanied by a parallel interest in the theory of irony; one has to wait until Baudelaire to find a French equivalent of Schlegel's penetration. It could be argued that the greatest ironists of the nineteenth century generally are not novelists: they often tend toward novelistic forms and devices—one thinks of Kierkegaard, Hoffmann, Baudelaire, Mallarmé, or Nietzsche—but they show a prevalent tendency toward aphoristic, rapid, and brief texts (which are incom-

51. Quintilian *Institutio* 9. 2. 44-53, quoted in Knox.
52. Schlegel, 'Brief über den Roman,' in "Gespräch über die Poesie," pp. 331ff.

patible with the duration that is the basis of the novel), as if there were something in the nature of irony that did not allow for sustained movements. The great and all-important exception is, of course, Stendhal. But it should be clear by now that, aside from having to give insight into the relationship between irony and allegory, an intentional theory of irony should also deal with the relationship between irony and the novel.

In the case of irony one cannot so easily take refuge in the need for a historical de-mystification of the term, as when we tried to show that the term "symbol" had in fact been substituted for that of "allegory" in an act of ontological bad faith. The tension between allegory and symbol justified this procedure: the mystification is a fact of history and must therefore be dealt with in a historical manner before actual theorization can start. But in the case of irony one has to start out from the structure of the trope itself, taking one's cue from texts that are de-mystified and, to a large extent, themselves ironical. For that manner, the target of their irony is very often the claim to speak about human matters as if they were facts of history. It is a historical fact that irony becomes increasingly conscious of itself in the course of demonstrating the impossibility of our being historical. In speaking of irony we are dealing not with the history of an error but with a problem that exists within the self. We cannot escape, therefore, the need for a definition toward which this essay is oriented. On the other hand, a great deal of assistance can be gained from existing texts on irony. Curiously enough, it seems to be only in describing a mode of language which does not mean what it says that one can actually say what one means.

Thus freed from the necessity of respecting historical chronology, we can take Baudelaire's text, "De l'essence du rire," as a starting point. Among the various examples of ridicule cited and analyzed, it is the simplest situation of all that best reveals the predominant traits of an ironic consciousness: the spectacle of a man tripping and falling into the street. "Le comique," writes Baudelaire, "la puissance du rire est dans le rieur et nullement dans l'objet du rire. Ce n'est point l'homme qui tombe qui rit de sa propre chute, à moins qu'il ne soit un philosophe, un homme qui ait acquis, par habitude, la force de se dédoubler rapidement et d'assister comme spectateur désintéressé aux phénomènes de son *moi*."[53] In this simple observation several key concepts are already present. In the first place, the accent falls on the notion of *dédoublement* as the characteristic that sets apart a reflective activity, such as that of the philosopher, from the activity of the ordinary self caught in everyday concerns. Hidden away at first in side-remarks such as this one, or masked behind a vocabulary of superiority and inferiority, of master and slave, the notion of self-duplication or self-multiplication emerges at the end of the essay as the key concept of the article, the concept for the sake of which the essay has in fact been written.

> ... pour qu'il y ait comique, c'est-à-dire émanation, explosion, dégagement de comique, il faut qu'il y ait deux êtres en présence;—que c'est spécialement dans le rieur, dans le spectateur, que gît le comique;—que cependant, relativement à cette loi d'ignorance, il faut faire une exception pour les hommes qui ont fait métier de développer en eux le sentiment du comique et de le tirer d'eux-mêmes pour le divertissement de leurs semblables, lequel phénomène rentre dans la classe de tous les phénomènes artistiques qui dénotent dans l'être humain l'existence d'une dualité permanente, la puissance d'être à la fois soi et un autre.[54]

The nature of this duplication is essential for an understanding of irony. It is a relationship, within consciousness, between two selves, yet it is not an intersubjective relationship. Baudelaire spends several pages of his essay distinguishing between a simple sense of comedy that is oriented toward others, and thus exists on the necessarily empirical level of interpersonal relationships, and what he calls "*le comique absolu*" (by which he designates that which, at other moments in his work, he calls irony), where the relationship is not between man and man, two entities that are in essence similar, but between man and what he calls nature, that is, two entities that are in essence different. Within the realm of intersubjectivity one would indeed speak of difference in terms of the superiority of one subject over another, with all the implications of will to power, of violence, and possession which come into play when a person is laughing at someone else—including the will to educate and to improve. But, when the concept of "superior-

53. Charles Baudelaire, "De l'essence du rire," in *Curiosités esthétiques: L'Art romantique et autres Oeuvres critiques*, H. Lemaître, ed. (Paris: Garnier, 1962), pp. 215ff.
54. *Ibid.*, p. 262.

ity" is still being used when the self is engaged in a relationship not to other subjects, but to what is precisely not a self, then the so-called superiority merely designates the *distance* constitutive of all acts of reflection. Superiority and inferiority then become merely spatial metaphors to indicate a discontinuity and a plurality of levels within a subject that comes to know itself by an increasing differentiation from what is not. Baudelaire insists that irony, as *"comique absolu,"* is an infinitely higher form of comedy than is the intersubjective kind of humor he finds so frequently among the French; hence his preference for Italian *commedia dell' arte*, English pantomime, or the tales of E. T. A. Hoffmann over Molière, the typical example of a certain French comic spirit that is unable to rise above the level of intersubjectivity. Daumier is dismissed in the same terms in favor of Hogarth and Goya in the essays on caricature.[55]

The *dédoublement* thus designates the activity of a consciousness by which a man differentiates himself from the non-human world. The capacity for such duplication is rare, says Baudelaire, but belongs specifically to those who, like artists or philosophers, deal in language. His emphasis on a professional vocabulary, on *"se faire un métier,"* stresses the technicality of their action, the fact that language is their material, just as leather is the material of the cobbler or wood is that of the carpenter. In everyday, common existence, this is not how language usually operates; there it functions much more as does the cobbler's or the carpenter's hammer, not as the material itself, but as a tool by means of which the heterogeneous material of experience is more-or-less adequately made to fit. The reflective disjunction not only occurs *by means of* language as a privileged category, but it transfers the self out of the empirical world into a world constituted out of, and in, language—a language that it finds in the world like one entity among others, but that remains unique in being the only entity by means of which it can differentiate itself from the world. Language thus conceived divides the subject into an empirical self, immersed in the world, and a self that becomes like a sign in its attempt at differentiation and self-definition.

More important still, in Baudelaire's description the division of the subject into a multiple consciousness takes place in immediate connection with a fall. The element of falling introduces the specifically

55. Baudelaire, "Quelques caricaturistes français," *ibid.*, p. 281.

comical and ultimately ironical ingredient. At the moment that the artistic or philosophical, that is, the language-determined, man laughs
at himself falling, he is laughing at a mistaken, mystified assumption
he was making about himself. In a false feeling of pride the self has
substituted, in its relationship to nature, an intersubjective feeling (of
superiority) for the knowledge of a difference. As a being that stands
upright (as in the passage at the beginning of Ovid's *Metamorphoses*
to which Baudelaire alludes elsewhere[56]), man comes to believe that
he dominates nature, just as he can, at times, dominate others or watch
others dominate him. This is, of course, a major mystification. The
Fall, in the literal as well as the theological sense, reminds him of the
purely instrumental, reified character of his relationship to nature.
Nature can at all times treat him as if he were a thing and remind
him of his factitiousness, whereas he is quite powerless to convert even
the smallest particle of nature into something human. In the idea of
fall thus conceived, a progression in self-knowledge is certainly implicit:
the man who has fallen is somewhat wiser than the fool who walks around
oblivious of the crack in the pavement about to trip him up. And the
fallen philosopher reflecting on the discrepancy between the two successive stages is wiser still, but this does not in the least prevent him
from stumbling in his turn. It seems instead that his wisdom can be
gained only at the cost of such a fall. The mere falling of others does
not suffice; he has to go down himself. The ironic, twofold self that
the writer or philosopher constitutes by his language seems able to
come into being only at the expense of his empirical self, falling (or
rising) from a stage of mystified adjustment into the knowledge of his
mystification. The ironic language splits the subject into an empirical
self that exists in a state of inauthenticity and a self that exists only
in the form of a language that asserts the knowledge of this inauthenticity. This does not, however, make it into an authentic language, for
to know inauthenticity is not the same as to be authentic.

It becomes evident that the disjunction is by no means a reassuring
and serene process, despite the fact that it involves laughter. When
the contemporary French philosopher V. Jankélévitch entitled a book

56. For example, in the poem "Le Cygne":
Je vois ce malheureux, mythe étrange et fatal,
Vers le ciel quelquefois, comme l'homme d'Ovide. . . .
The allusion is to *Metamorphoses* 1. 84-86.

on irony *L'Ironie ou la bonne conscience*, he certainly was far removed
from Baudelaire's conception of irony—unless, of course, the choice
of the title itself was ironic. For Baudelaire, at any rate, the movement
of the ironic consciousness is anything but reassuring. The moment
the innocence or authenticity of our sense of being in the world is put
into question, a far from harmless process gets underway. It may start
as a casual bit of play with a stray loose end of the fabric, but before
long the entire texture of the self is unraveled and comes apart. The
whole process happens at an unsettling speed. Irony possesses an inherent tendency to gain momentum and not to stop until it has run
its full course; from the small and apparently innocuous exposure of
a small self-deception it soon reaches the dimensions of the absolute.
Often starting as litotes or understatement, it contains within itself the
power to become hyperbole. Baudelaire refers to this unsettling power
as "*vertige de l'hyperbole*" and conveys the feeling of its effect in
his description of the English pantomime he saw at the Théâtre des
Variétés:

> Une des choses les plus remarquables comme comique absolu, et, pour
> ainsi dire, comme métaphysique du comique absolu, était certainement
> le début de cette belle pièce, un prologue plein d'une haute esthétique.
> Les principaux personnages de la pièce, Pierrot, Cassandre, Harlequin,
> Colombine ... sont [d'abord] à peu près raisonnables et ne diffèrent pas
> beaucoup des braves gens qui sont dans la salle. Le souffle merveilleux
> qui va les faire se mouvoir extraordinairement n'a pas encore soufflé
> sur leurs cervelles. ... Une fée s'intéresse à Harlequin ... elle lui pro-
> met sa protection et, pour lui en donner une preuve immédiate, elle pro-
> mène avec un geste mystérieux et plein d'autorité sa baguette dans les
> airs. Aussitôt le vertige est entré, le vertige circule dans l'air; on respire
> le vertige; c'est le vertige qui remplit les poumons et renouvelle le sang
> dans le ventricule. Qu'est-ce que ce vertige? C'est le comique absolu;
> il s'est emparé de chaque être. Ils font des gestes extraordinaires, qui
> démontrent clairement qu'ils se sentent introduits de force dans une ex-
> istence nouvelle. ... Et ils s'élancent à travers l'oeuvre fantastique qui,
> à proprement parler, ne commence que là, c'est-à-dire sur la frontière
> du merveilleux.[57]

Irony is unrelieved *vertige*, dizziness to the point of madness. Sani-
ty can exist only because we are willing to function within the conven-

57. Baudelaire, "De l'essence du rire," pp. 259-60.

*cf.
Pirandello*

tions of duplicity and dissimulation, just as social language dissimulates the inherent violence of the actual relationships between human beings. Once this mask is shown to be a mask, the authentic being underneath appears necessarily as on the verge of madness. "Le rire est généralement l'apanage des fous," writes Baudelaire, and the term *"folie"* remains associated throughout with that of *"comique absolu."* "Il est notoire que tous les fous des hôpitaux ont l'idée de leur supériorité dévloppée outre mesure. Je ne connais guère de fous d'humilité. Remarquez que le rire est une des expressions les plus fréquentes et les plus nombreuses de la folie. . . . [Le rire] sorti des conditions fondamentales de la vie . . . est un rire qui ne dort jamais, comme une maladie qui va toujours son chemin et exécute un ordre providentiel."[58] And, most clearly of all, in the essay on caricature he states, in reference to Brueghel: "Je défie qu'on explique le capharnaüm diabolique et drôlatique de Breughel le Drôle autrement que par une espèce de grâce spéciale et satanique. Au mot grâce spéciale substituez, si vous voulez, le mot folie, ou hallucination; mais le mystère restera presque aussi noir."[59]

When we speak, then, of irony originating at the cost of the empirical self, the statement has to be taken seriously enough to be carried to the extreme: absolute irony is a consciousness of madness, itself the end of all consciousness; it is a consciousness of a non-consciousness, a reflection on madness from the inside of madness itself. But this reflection is made possible only by the double structure of ironic language: the ironist invents a form of himself that is "mad" but that does not know its own madness; he then proceeds to reflect on his madness thus objectified.

This might be construed to mean that irony, as a *"folie lucide"* which allows language to prevail even in extreme stages of self-alienation, could be a kind of therapy, a cure of madness by means of the spoken or written word. Baudelaire himself speaks of Hoffmann, whom he rightly considers to be an instance of absolute irony, as *"un physiologiste ou un médecin de fous des plus profonds, et qui s'amuserait à revêtir cette profonde science de formes poétiques."* Jean Starobinski, who has written very well on the subject, allows that irony can be considered

58. *Ibid.*, pp. 248-50.
59. Baudelaire, "Quelques caricaturistes étrangers," *ibid.*, p. 303.

a cure for a self lost in the alienation of its melancholy. He writes:

> Nothing prevents the ironist from conferring an expansive value to the
> freedom he has conquered for himself: he is then led to dream of a recon-
> ciliation of the spirit and the world, all things being reunited in the realm
> of the spirit. Then the great, eternal Return can take place, the univer-
> sal reparation of what evil had temporarily disrupted. This general
> recovery is accomplished through the mediation of art. More than any
> other romantic, Hoffmann longed for such a return to the world. The
> symbol of this return could be the "bourgeois" happiness that the young
> comedian couple finds at the end of the *Prinzessin Brambilla*—the Hoff-
> mann text to which Baudelaire had alluded in the essay on laughter as
> a *"haut bréviaire d'esthétique"* and which is also cited by Kierkegaard
> in his journals.[60]

Yet the effect of irony seems to be the opposite of what Starobinski
here proposes. Almost simultaneously with the first duplication of the
self, by means of which a purely "linguistic" subject replaces the
original self, a new disjunction has to take place. The temptation at
once arises for the ironic subject to construe its function as one of
assistance to the original self and to act as if it existed for the sake
of this world-bound person. This results in an immediate degradation
to an intersubjective level, away from the *"comique absolu"* into what
Baudelaire calls *"comique significatif,"* into a betrayal of the ironic
mode. Instead, the ironic subject at once has to ironize its own predicament and observe in turn, with the detachment and disinterestedness
that Baudelaire demands of this kind of spectator, the temptation to
which it is about to succumb. It does so precisely by avoiding the return
to the world mentioned by Starobinski, by reasserting the purely fictional nature of its own universe and by carefully maintaining the radical
difference that separates fiction from the world of empirical reality.
Hoffmann's *Prinzessin Brambilla* is a good case in point. It tells the
story of a young comedian couple thoroughly mystified into believing
that the fine and moving parts they are made to play on the stage give
them an equally exalted station in life. They are finally "cured" of
this delusion by the discovery of irony, manifest in their shift from
a tragic to a comical repertory, from the tearful tragedies of the Ab-
bato Chiari to a Gozzi-like type of *commedia dell' arte*. Near the end

---

60. Jean Starobinski, "Ironie et mélancolie: Gozzi, Hoffman, Kierkegaard," in *Estratto da
Sensibilità e Razionalità nel Settecento* (Florence, 1967), p. 459.

of the story, they exist indeed in a state of domestic bliss that might give credence to Starobinski's belief that art and the world have been reconciled by the right kind of art. But it takes no particular viciousness of character to notice that the bourgeois idyl of the end is treated by Hoffmann as pure parody, that the hero and the heroine, far from having returned to their natural selves, are more than ever playing the artificial parts of the happy couple. Their diction is more stilted, their minds more mystified, than ever before. Never have art and life been farther apart than at the moment they seem to be reconciled. Hoffmann has made the point clear enough throughout: at the very moment that irony is thought of as a knowledge able to order and to cure the world, the source of its invention immediately runs dry. The instant it construes the fall of the self as an event that could somehow benefit the self, it discovers that it has in fact substituted death for madness. "Der Moment, in dem der Mensch umfällt, ist der erste, in dem sein wahrhaftes Ich sich aufrichtet,"[61] Hoffman has his mythical king, initiated into the mysteries of irony, proclaim—and, lest we imagine that this is the assertion of a positive, hopeful future for prince and country, he immediately drops dead on the spot. Similarly, in the last paragraph of the text, when the prince pompously proclaims that the magical source of irony has given humanity eternal happiness in its ascent to self-knowledge, Hoffmann pursues: "Hier, versiegt plötzlich die Quelle, aus der . . . der Herausgeber dieser Blätter geschöpft hat"— and the story breaks off with the evocation of the painter Callot, whose drawings have indeed been the "source" of the story. These drawings represent figures from the *commedia dell' arte* floating against a background that is precisely *not* the world, adrift in an empty sky.

Far from being a return to the world, the irony to the second power or "irony of irony" that all true irony at once has to engender asserts and maintains its fictional character by stating the continued impossibility of reconciling the world of fiction with the actual world. Well before Baudelaire and Hoffmann, Friedrich Schlegel knew this very well when he defined *irony*, in a note from 1797, as *"eine permanente Parekbase."*[62] Parabasis is understood here as what is called in English criticism the "self-conscious narrator," the author's intrusion that

---

61. E. T. A. Hoffmann, *Prinzessin Brambilla*, chap. 5.
62. Schlegel, "Fragment 668," in *Kritische Ausgabe*, Band 18, *Philosphische Lehrjahre, (1796-1806)*, Ernst Behler, ed. (Paderborn: Ferdinand Schöningh, 1962), p. 85.

disrupts the fictional illusion. Schlegel makes clear, however, that the effect of this intrusion is not a heightened realism, an affirmation of the priority of a historical over a fictional act, but that it has the very opposite aim and effect: it serves to prevent the all too readily mystified reader from confusing fact and fiction and from forgetting the essential negativity of the fiction. The problem is familiar to students of point of view in a fictional narrative, in the distinction they have learned to make between the persona of the author and the persona of the fictional narrator. The moment when this difference is asserted is precisely the moment when the author does not return to the world. He asserts instead the ironic necessity of not becoming the dupe of his own irony and discovers that there is no way back from his fictional self to his actual self.

It is also at this point that the link between irony and the novel becomes apparent. For it is at this same point that the temporal structure of irony begins to emerge. Starobinski's error in seeing irony as a preliminary movement toward a recovered unity, as a reconciliation of the self with the world by means of art, is a common (and morally admirable) mistake. In temporal terms it makes irony into the prefiguration of a future recovery, fiction into the promise of a future happiness that, for the time being, exists only ideally. Commentators of Friedrich Schlegel have read him in the same way. To quote one of the best among them, this is how Peter Szondi describes the function of the ironic consciousness in Schlegel:

> The subject of romantic irony is the isolated, alienated man who has become the object of his own reflection and whose consciousness has deprived him of his ability to act. He nostalgically aspires toward unity and infinity; the world appears to him divided and finite. What he calls irony is his attempt to bear up under his critical predicament, to change his situation by achieving distance toward it. In an ever-expanding act of reflection[63] he tries to establish a point of view beyond himself and to resolve the tension between himself and the world on the level of fiction [*des Scheins*]. He cannot overcome the negativity of his situation by means of an act in which the reconciliation of finite achievement with infinite longing could take place; through prefiguration of a future unity, *in which he believes*, the negative is described as temporary [*vorläufig*]

63. *"In immer wieder potenzierter Reflexion . . ."* is a quotation from Schlegel, "Athenäum Fragment 116," Band 2, p. 182.

and, by the same token, it is kept in check and reversed. This reversal makes it appear tolerable and allows the subject to dwell in the subjective region of fiction. Because irony designates and checks the power of negativity, it becomes itself, although originally conceived as the overcoming of negativity, the power of the negative. Irony allows for fulfillment only in the past and in the future; it measures whatever it encounters in the present by the yardstick of infinity and thus destroys it. The knowledge of his own impotence prevents the ironist from respecting his achievements: therein resides his danger. Making this assumption about himself, he closes off the way to his fulfillment. Each achievement becomes in turn inadequate and finally leads into a void: therein resides his tragedy.[64]

Every word in this admirable quotation is right from the point of view of the mystified self, but wrong from the point of view of the ironist. Szondi has to posit the belief in a reconciliation between the ideal and the real as the result of an action or the activity of the mind. But it is precisely this assumption that the ironist denies. Friedrich Schlegel is altogether clear on this. The dialectic of the self-destruction and self-invention which for him, as for Baudelaire, characterizes the ironic mind is an endless process that leads to no synthesis. The positive name he gives to the infinity of this process is freedom, the unwillingness of the mind to accept any stage in its progression as definitive, since this would stop what he calls its "infinite agility." In temporal terms it designates the fact that irony engenders a temporal sequence of acts of consciousness which is endless. Contrary to Szondi's assertion, irony is not temporary (*vorläufig*) but repetitive, the recurrence of a self-escalating act of consciousness. Schlegel at times speaks of this endless process in exhilarating terms, understandably enough, since he is describing the freedom of a self-engendering invention. "(Die romantische Poesie)," he writes—and by this term he specifically designates a poetry of irony—

> kann . . . am meisten zwischen dem Dargestellten und dem Darstellenden, frei von allem realen und idealen Interesse, auf den Flügeln der poetischen Reflexion in der Mitte schweben, diese Reflexion immer wieder potenzieren und wie in einer endlosen Reihe von Spiegeln vervielfachen. . . . Die romantische Dichtart ist noch im Werden; ja das ist ihr eigentliches

64. Peter Szondi, "Friedrich Schlegel und die Romantische Ironie," *Satz und Gegensatz* (Frankfurt: Insel-Verlag, 1964), pp. 17-18; the italics are ours.

Wesen, daß sie ewig nur werden, nie vollendet sein kann. . . . Nur eine divinatorische Kritik dürfte es wagen, ihr Ideal charakterisieren zu wollen. Sie allein ist unendlich, wie sie allein frei ist, und das als ihr erstes Gesetz anerkennt, daß die Willkür des Dichters kein Gesetz über sich leide.[65]

But this same endless process, here stated from the positive viewpoint of the poetic self engaged in its own development, appears as something very close to Baudelaire's lucid madness when a slightly older Friedrich Schlegel describes it from a more personal point of view. The passage is from the curious essay in which he took leave from the readers of the *Athenäum*; written in 1798 and revised for the 1800 publication, it is entitled, ironically enough, "Über die Unverständlichkeit." It evokes, in the language of criticism, the same experience of *"vertige de l'hyperbole"* that the spectacle of the pantomime awakened in Baudelaire. Schlegel has described various kinds of irony and finally comes to what he calls "the irony of irony."

> . . . Im allgemeinen ist das wohl die gründlichste Ironie der Ironie, daß man sie doch eben auch überdrüssig wird, wenn sie uns überall und immer wieder geboten wird. Was wir aber hier zunächst unter Ironie der Ironie verstanden wissen wollen, das entsteht auf mehr als einem Wege. Wenn man ohne Ironie von der Ironie redet, wie es soeben der Fall war; wenn man mit Ironie von einer Ironie redet, ohne zu merken, daß man sich zu eben der Zeit in einer andren viel auffallenderen Ironie befindet; wenn man nicht wieder aus der Ironie herauskommen kann, wie es in diesem Versuch über die Unverständlichkeit zu sein scheint; wenn die Ironie Manier wird, und so den Dichter gleichsam wieder ironiert; wenn man Ironie zu einem überflüssigen Taschenbuche versprochen hat, ohne seinen Vorrat vorher zu überschlagen und nun wider Willen Ironie machen muß, wie ein Schauspielkünstler, der Leibschmerzen hat; wenn die Ironie wild wird, und sich gar nicht mehr regieren läßt.
>
> Welche Götter werden uns von allen diesen Ironien erretten können? Das einzige wäre, wenn sich eine Ironie fände, welche die Eigenschaft hätte, alle jene großen und kleinen Ironien zu verschlucken und zu verschlingen, daß nichts mehr davon zu sehen wäre, und ich muß gestehen, daß ich eben dazu in der meinigen eine merkliche Disposition fühle. Aber auch das würde nur auf kurze Zeit helfen können. Ich fürchte . . . es würde bald eine neue Generation von kleinen Ironien entstehn: denn wahrlich die Gestirne deuten auf phantastisch. Und gesetzt

65. Schlegel, "Athenäum Fragment 116," pp. 182-83.

es blieb auch während eines langen Zeitraums alles ruhig, so wäre doch nicht zu trauen. Mit der Ironie ist durchaus nicht zu scherzen. Sie kann unglaublich lange nachwirken. . . .[66]

Our description seems to have reached a provisional conclusion. The act of irony, as we know understand it, reveals the existence of a temporality that is definitely not organic, in that it relates to its source only in terms of distance and difference and allows for no end, for no totality. Irony divides the flow of temporal experience into a past that is pure mystification and a future that remains harassed forever by a relapse within the inauthentic. It can know this inauthenticity but can never overcome it. It can only restate and repeat it on an increasingly conscious level, but it remains endlessly caught in the impossibility of making this knowledge applicable to the empirical world. It dissolves in the narrowing spiral of a linguistic sign that becomes more and more remote from its meaning, and it can find no escape from this spiral. The temporal void that it reveals is the same void we encountered when we found allegory always implying an unreachable anteriority. Allegory and irony are thus linked in their common discovery of a truly temporal predicament. They are also linked in their common demystification of an organic world postulated in a symbolic mode of analogical correspondences or in a mimetic mode of representation in which fiction and reality could coincide. It is especially against the latter mystification that irony is directed: the regression in critical insight found in the transition from an allegorical to a symbolic theory of poetry would find its historical equivalent in the regression from the eighteenth-century ironic novel, based on what Friedrich Schlegel called *"Parekbase,"* to nineteenth-century realism.

This conclusion is dangerously satisfying and highly vulnerable to irony in that it rescues a coherent historical picture at the expense of stated human incoherence. Things cannot be left to rest at the point we have reached. More clearly even than allegory, the rhetorical mode of irony takes us back to the predicament of the conscious subject; this consciousness is clearly an unhappy one that strives to move beyond and outside itself. Schlegel's rhetorical question "What gods will be able to rescue us from all these ironies?" can also be taken quite literally. For the later Friedrich Schlegel, as for Kierkegaard, the solution could

66. Schlegel, "Uber die Unverständlichkeit," Band 2, p. 369.

only be a leap out of language into faith. Yet a question remains: certain poets, who were Schlegel's actual, and Baudelaire's spiritual, contemporaries, remained housed within language, refused to escape out
of time into apocalyptic conceptions of human temporality, but nevertheless were not ironic. In his essay on laughter Baudelaire speaks,
without apparent irony, of a semimythical poetic figure that would exist beyond the realm of irony: "si dans ces mêmes nations ultra-civilisées,
une intelligence, poussée par une ambition supérieure, veut franchir
les limites de l'orgeuil mondain et s'élancer hardiment vers la poésie
pure, dans cette poésie, limpide et profonde comme la nature, le rire
fera défaut comme dans l'âme du Sage."[67] Could we think of certain
texts of that period—and it is better to speak here of texts than of
individual names—as being truly meta-ironical, as having transcended irony without falling into the myth of an organic totality or bypass-
ing the temporality of all language? And, if we call these texts
"allegorical," would the language of allegory then be the overcoming
of irony? Would some of the definitely non-ironic, but, in our sense
of the term, allegorical, texts of the late Hölderlin, of Wordsworth, or
of Baudelaire himself be this "pure poetry from which laughter is absent as from the soul of the Sage"? It would be very tempting to think
so, but, since the implications are far-reaching, it might be better to
approach the question in a less exalted mood, by making a brief comparison of the temporal structure of allegory and irony.

   The text we can use for our demonstration has the advantage of being exceedingly brief and very well known. It would take some time
to show that it falls under the definition of what is here being referred
to as "allegorical" poetry; suffice it to say that it has the fundamentally profigurative pattern that is one of the characteristics of allegory.
The text clearly is not ironic, either in its tonality or in its meaning.
We are using one of Wordsworth's Lucy Gray poems:

> A slumber did my spirit seal;
> I had no human fears:
> She seemed a thing that could not feel
> The touch of earthly years.
>
> No motion has she now, no force;
> She neither hears nor sees;

67. Baudelaire, "De l'essence du rire," p. 251.

> Rolled round in earth's diurnal course,
> With rocks, and stones, and trees.

Examining the temporal structure of this text, we can point to the successive description of two stages of consciousness, one belonging to the past and mystified, the other to the *now* of the poem, the stage that has recovered from the mystification of a past now presented as being in error; the "slumber" is a condition of non-awareness. The event that separates the two states is the radical discontinuity of a death that remains quite impersonal; the identity of the unnamed "she" is not divulged. Lines 3 and 4 are particularly important for our purpose:

> She seemed a thing that could not feel
> The touch of earthly years.

These lines are curiously ambiguous, with the full weight of the am-biguity concentrated in the word "thing." Within the mystified world of the past, when the temporal reality of death was repressed or forgot-ten, the word "thing" could be used quite innocently, perhaps even in a playfully amorous way (since the deceased entity is a "she"). The line could almost be a gallant compliment to the well-preserved youth of the lady, in spite of the somewhat ominous "seemed." The curious shock of the poem, the very Wordsworthian "shock of mild surprise," is that this innocuous statement becomes literally true in the retrospec-tive perspective of the eternal "now" of the second part. She now has become a *thing* in the full sense of the word, not unlike Baudelaire's falling man who became a thing in the grip of gravity, and, indeed, she exists beyond the touch of earthly years. But the light-hearted com-pliment has turned into a grim awareness of the de-mystifying power of death, which makes all the past appear as a flight into the inauthen-ticity of a forgetting. It could be said that, read within the perspective of the entire poem, these two lines are ironic, though they are not ironic in themselves or within the context of the first stanza. Nor is the poem, as a whole, ironic. The stance of the speaker, who exists in the "now," is that of a subject whose insight is no longer in doubt and who is no longer vulnerable to irony. It could be called, if one so wished, a stance of wisdom. There is no real disjunction of the subject; the poem is written from the point of view of a unified self that fully recognizes a past condition as one of error and stands in a present that, however pain-ful, sees things as they actually are. This stance has been made possible by two things: first, the death alluded to is not the death of the speaker but apparently that of someone else; second, the poem is in the third person and uses the feminine gender throughout. If this were truly relevant, the question would remain whether Wordsworth could have written in the same manner about his own death. For the informed reader of Wordsworth the answer to this question is affirmative; Wordsworth is one of the few poets who can write proleptically about their own death and speak, as it were, from beyond their own graves. The "she" in the poem is in fact large enough to encompass Wordsworth as well. More important than the otherness of the dead person is the seemingly obvious fact that the poem describes the demystification as a temporal sequence: first there was error, then the death occurred, and now an eternal insight into the rocky barrenness of the human predicament prevails. The *difference* does not exist within the subject, which remains unique throughout and therefore can resolve the tragic irony of lines 3 and 4 in the wisdom of the concluding lines. The difference has been spread out over a temporality which is exclusively that of the poem and in which the conditions of error and of wisdom have become successive. This is possible within the ideal, self-created temporality engendered by the language of the poem, but it is not possible within the actual temporality of experience. The "now" of the poem is not an actual now, which is that of the moment of death, lies hidden in the blank space between the two stanzas. The fundamental structure of allegory reappears here in the tendency of the language toward narrative, the spreading out along the axis of an imaginary time in order to give duration to what is, in fact, simultaneous within the subject.

The structure of irony, however, is the reversed mirror-image of this form. In practically all the quotations from Baudelaire and Schlegel, irony appears as an instantaneous process that takes place rapidly, suddenly, in one single moment: Baudelaire speaks of *"la force de se dédoubler* rapidement," *"la puissance d'être* à la fois *soi-même et un autre"*; irony is instantaneous like an "explosion" and the fall is sudden. In describing the pantomime, he complains that his pen cannot possibly convey the simultaneity of the visual spectacle: *"avec une plume tout cela est pâle et glacé."*[68] His later, most ironic works, the prose poems of the *Tableaux parisiens*, grow

68. *Ibid.*, p. 259.

shorter and shorter and always climax in the single brief moment of a final *pointe*. This is the instant at which the two selves, the empirical as well as the ironic, are simultaneously present, juxtaposed within the same moment but as two irreconcilable and disjointed beings. The structure is precisely the opposite from that of the Wordsworth poem: the difference now resides in the subject, whereas time is reduced to one single moment. In this respect, irony comes closer to the pattern of factual experience and recaptures some of the factitiousness of human existence as a succession of isolated moments lived by a divided self. Essentially the mode of the present, it knows neither memory nor prefigurative duration, whereas allegory exists entirely within an ideal time that is never here and now but always a past or an endless future. Irony is a synchronic structure, while allegory appears as a successive mode capable of engendering duration as the illusion of a continuity that it knows to be illusionary. Yet the two modes, for all their profound distinctions in mood and structure, are the two faces of the same fundamental experience of time. One is tempted to play them off against each other and to attach value judgments to each, as if one were intrinsically superior to the other. We mentioned the temptation to confer on allegorical writers a wisdom superior to that of ironic writers; an equivalent temptation exists to consider ironists as more enlightened than their assumedly naïve counterparts, the allegorists. Both attitudes are in error. The knowledge derived from both modes is essentially the same; Hölderlin's or Wordsworth's wisdom could be stated ironically, and the rapidity of Schlegel or Baudelaire could be preserved in terms of general wisdom. Both modes are fully de-mystified when they remain within the realm of their respective languages but are totally vulnerable to renewed blindness as soon as they leave it for the empirical world. Both are determined by an authentic experience of temporality which, seen from the point of view of the self engaged in the world, is a negative one. The dialectical play between the two modes, as well as their common interplay with mystified forms of language (such as symbolic or mimetic representation), which it is not in their power to eradicate, make up what is called literary history.

We can conclude with a brief remark on the novel, which is caught with the truly perverse assignment of using both the narrative duration of the diachronic allegory and the instantaneity of the narrative present; to try for less than a combination of the two is to betray the inherent *gageure* of the genre. Things seem very simple for the novel when author and narrator are considered to be one and the same subject and when the time of the narrative is also assumed to be the natural time of days and years. They get somewhat more complex when, as in the scheme proposed by René Girard, the novel begins in error but works itself almost unwittingly into the knowledge of this error; this allows for a mystified structure that falls apart at the end and makes the novel into a pre-ironic mode. The real difficulty starts when we allow for the existence of a novelist who has all these preliminary stages behind him, who is a full-fledged ironist as well as an allegorist and has to seal, so to speak, the ironic moments within the allegorical duration.

Stendhal, in the *Chartreuse de Parme*, is a good example. We readily grant him irony, as in the famous Stendhalian speed that allows him to dispose of a seduction or a murder in the span of two brief sentences. All perceptive critics have noticed the emphasis on the moment with the resulting discontinuity. Georges Poulet, among others, describes it very well:

> In none of [Stendhal's truly happy moments] is the moment connected with other moments to form a continuous totality of fulfilled existence, as we almost always find it, for instance, in the characters of Flaubert, of Tolstoi, of Thomas Hardy, of Roger Martin du Gard. They all seem, at all times, to carry the full weight of their past (and even in their future destiny) on their shoulders. But the opposite is true of Stendhal's characters. Always living exclusively in their moments, they are entirely free of what does not belong to these moments. Would this mean that they lack an essential dimension, a certain consistency which is the consistency of duration? It could be. . . .[69]

This is true of Stendhal the ironist, whose reflective patterns are very thoroughly described in the rest of the article, although Poulet never uses the term "irony." But, especially in the *Chartreuse de Parme*, there clearly occur slow, meditative movements full of reverie, anticipation, and recollection: one thinks of Fabrice's return to his native town and the night he spends there in the church tower,[70] as well as of the famous courtship episodes in the high tower of the prison. Stephen

69. Georges Poulet, *Mesure de l'instant* (Paris: Plon, 1968), p. 250.
70. Stendhal, *La Chartreuse de Parme* (1839), chap. 8.

Gilman[71] has very convincingly shown how these episodes, with their numerous antecedents in previous works of literature, are allegorical and emblematic, just as Julie's garden in *La Nouvelle Héloïse* was found to be. And he has also shown very well how these allegorical episodes act prefiguratively and give the novel a duration that the *staccato* of irony would never be able, by definition, to achieve. It remains to be said that this successful combination of allegory and irony also determines the thematic substance of the novel as a whole, the underlying *mythos* of the allegory. The novel tells the story of two lovers who, like Eros and Psyche, are never allowed to come into full contact with each other. When they can see each other they are separated by an unbreachable distance; when they can touch, it has to be in a darkness imposed by a totally arbitrary and irrational decision, an act of the gods. The myth is that of the unovercomable distance which must always prevail between the selves, and it thematizes the ironic distance that Stendhal the writer always believed prevailed between his pseudonymous and nominal identities. As such, it reaffirms Schlegel's definition of irony as a "permanent parabasis" and singles out this novel as one of the few novels of novels, as the allegory of irony.

71. Stephen Gilman, *The Tower as Emblem*, Analecta Romanica, vol. 22 (Frankfurt: Vittorio Klostermann, 1967).

XI

The Dead-End
of Formalist Criticism

As a new generation enters the scene, a certain unease manifests itself in French literary criticism. This uncertainty prevails at once in the concern over fundamental methodological issues, and in the experimental, or polemical, character of several recent works. Roland Barthes's book-length essay, *Writing Degree Zero*,[1] for example, asserts its own *terrorism;* and Jean-Pierre Richard's two books, *Littérature et Sensation* and *Poésie et Profondeur*,[2] have recourse to a method whose systematic and exclusive use takes on the dimensions of a manifesto, an impression further reinforced by the author's own preface and that provided by Georges Poulet, both of which stress their opposition to other critical idioms. Explicitly, Poulet and Richard are opposed to Blanchot in the name of a criticism whose initiators would have been Marcel Raymond and Albert Beguin, and whose philosophical

Translator's note: This article was written for the express purpose of introducing the New Criticism to French readers at the moment that there were some stirrings in French Criticism, but before the advent of Structuralism on the literary scene.
1. Roland Barthes, *Le Degré Zéro de l'Écriture* (Paris: Seuil, 1953); trans. Annette Lavers and Colin Smith, *Writing Degree Zero* (New York: Hill and Wang, 1967).
2. Paris: Editions de Seuil, 1954 and 1955 respectively.

229

underpinnings would be found in Bachelard, Jean Wahl, and Sartre—a grouping that, in the case of every one of these, requires reservations and qualifications. Implicitly, they are also opposed to the historical and philological scholarship of the universities, from traditional *explication de texte* to the writings of Etiemble, as well as to other current trends: Jean Paulhan's work, Marxist criticism, history of ideas, etc. All of these trends—and there are others—are mutually incompatible.

In the United States, the state of criticism appears more stable. It is well known that since roughly 1935, alongside traditional approaches to criticism such as the historical and the sociological or the biographical and psychological, there has arisen a trend that without constituting a school or even a homogeneous group, nevertheless shares certain premises. These are the authors generally known under the term "New Critics" (even though, once again, this term does not designate a well-defined group) and they can generally be subsumed under the denomination of "formalist" criticism—a term we will seek to make more explicit later on. This movement has come to wield considerable influence, in journals and in books, and especially in university teaching; to such an extent that one could legitimately speak of a certain formalist orthodoxy. In some cases, an entire generation has been trained in this approach to literature without awareness of any other.

It is true, though, that at the very moment when it comes into its own, this generation is apt to turn against the training of which it is the product. Recently there have been attacks upon the methods of the prevalent criticism and calls for a clean sweeping away, a new start. It is hard to tell if these are portents of a more general reaction or merely individual and isolated occurrences. But even if it were on the point of being overtaken, formalist criticism would still have made a considerable contribution: on the positive side, by fostering the refinement of analytical and didactic techniques that have often led to remarkable exegeses; on the negative side, by highlighting the inadequacies of the historical approach as it was practiced in the United States. But it is also interesting from the perspective of theory: its internal evolution leads it to put into question the conception of the literary work upon which it was implicitly founded. Its development may well have a premonitory value for the new French criticism just as the latter, especially in the case of Roland Barthes, appears to be moving in the direction of a formalism that, appearances notwithstanding, is not that different from New Criticism. In addition, it also has a certain demonstrative value for ontological criticism, for it proceeds in particularly clear fashion from a theory based upon more or less hidden or unconscious philosophical presuppositions. In its own inadequacy, it brings them out to the surface, and thus leads to authentic ontological questions.

It has been said that all of American formalist criticism originates in the works of the English linguist and psychologist I. A. Richards.[3] As a historical statement such an assertion is questionable, for the mutual relations of American and English criticism are rendered more complex by the existence of purely native strands on both sides; but it is certainly true that Richards's theories have found fertile terrain in the United States, and that all American works of formalist criticism accord him a special status.

For Richards, the task of criticism consists in correctly apprehending the signifying value, or meaning, of the work; an exact correspondence between the author's originary experience and its communicated expression. For the author, the labor of formal elaboration consists in constructing a linguistic structure that will correspond as closely as possible to the initial experience. Once it is granted that such a correspondence is established by the author, it will exist for the reader as well, and what is called communication can then occur.

The initial experience may be anything at all and need not have anything specifically "aesthetic" about it. Art is justified as the preservation of moments in "the lives of exceptional people, when their control and command of experience is at its highest degree . . ."[4] The critic's task consists in retracing the author's journey backward: he will proceed from a careful and precise study of the signifying form toward the experience that produced this form. Correct critical understanding is achieved when it reaches the cluster of experiences elicited through reading, insofar as they remain sufficiently close to

3. Stanley Hyman, *The Armed Vision* (New York: A. A. Knopf, 1948), p. 7.
4. I. A. Richards, *Principles of Literary Criticism* (London: Kegan Paul, Trench, Trubner and Co., 1926), p. 32. Richards's reasons for attaching such an importance to the knowledge of what he calls "experiences" are of a moral order. As a disciple of Bentham's utilitarianism, moral order consists for him in a correctly hierarchised organization of human needs, and these needs can be evaluated through the study of the "experiences" of consciousness.

the experience or experiences the author started out with. It becomes possible then to define a poem, for example, as the series of experiences comprised within such a cluster. Since there are numerous possibilities of error in the carrying out of these analytical tasks, it is Richards's intention to elaborate techniques for avoiding them; but there never is the slightest doubt that in every case a correct procedure can be arrived at.

This theory, which appears to be governed by common sense, implies, in fact, some highly questionable ontological presuppositions, the most basic of which is, no doubt, the notion that language, poetic or otherwise, can *say* any experience, of whatever kind, even a simple perception. Neither the statement "I see a cat" nor, for that matter, Baudelaire's poem *"Le Chat"* contains wholly the experience of this perception. It can be said that there is a perceptual consciousness of the object and an experience of this consciousness, but the working out of a *logos* of this experience or, in the case of art, of a *form* of this experience, encounters considerable difficulties. Almost immediately the existential status of the experience seems to be in question, and we conclude by considering as constructed that which at first appeared to be given: instead of containing or reflecting experience, language constitutes it. And a theory of constituting form is altogether different from a theory of signifying form. Language is no longer a mediation between two subjectivities but between a being and a non-being. And the problem of criticism is no longer to discover to what experience the form refers, but how it can constitute a world, a totality of beings without which there would be no experience. It is no longer a question of imitation but one of creation; no longer communication but participation. And when this form becomes the object of consideration of a third person who seeks to state the experience of his perception, the least that can be said is that this latest venture into language will be quite distant from the original experience. Between the originary cat and a critic's commentary on Baudelaire's poem, quite a few things have occurred.

Nonetheless, Richards postulates a perfect continuity between the sign and the thing signified.[5] Through repeated association, the sign comes to take the place of the thing signified; and consciousness is consciousness *of* "the missing part of the sign, or, more strictly, 'of'

5. This theory is outlined in *Principles of Literary Criticism*, pp. 127ff.

anything which would complete the sign as cause."[6] The cat is the cause of the consciousness that perceives the cat; when we read the word "cat," we are conscious of the sign "cat" inasmuch as it refers back to the cause of this sign. Richards adds immediately that, for such a consciousness to be specific as experience perforce is, language must achieve a spatial and temporal determination, implying, for example, "this cat here and now." But what do the words "here" and "now" refer to—not to mention the words "to be" that are always implied—if not to a general space and time that permit *this* here and this now? Thus the "cause" of the perception of the sign becomes, at the least, the object plus time and space, with, in addition, a specific causal relation between the object and space and time. When we read the word "cat," we are forced to construct an entire universe in order to understand it, whereas direct experience makes no such requirements. We are driven back to the problem of constitution, which does not appear to have arisen for Richards.[7]

Richards insists continually on the fact that criticism does not deal with any given material object but with a consciousness (or an experience) of this object, and he quotes Hume to this effect: "Beauty is no quality in things themselves; it exists merely in the mind which contemplates them."[8] Form, as the object of the critic's reflection, is not a thing then but stands as the equivalent of the experience. An object described or painted or sculpted is the object initially given; it is the sign of the experience of a consciousness of that object. However, since form is the imitation of a mental experience in a substance (language, pigment, or marble), it is legitimate for an observer to treat it as a signifying object that refers to a prior mental experience. In this sense, one can speak of a form-object in Richards. And one can also understand his insistent claim that poetic language is purely affective and, therefore, can never lead to cognition, since it has no verifiable referential value in reference to an external object. But for the critic who seeks to apprehend correctly the experience that is con-

6. *Ibid.*, p. 127.
7. In reference to this problem, one can draw a useful comparison between Richards's analysis and that of the phenomenologist and student of Husserl, Roman Ingarden, in *Das Literarische Kunstwerk* (Halle, 1931; 3rd ed., Tübingen: Max Niemeyer, 1965); trans. George G. Grabowicz, *The Literary Work of Art* (Evanston, Ill.: Northwestern University Press, 1973).
8. Quoted by Richards in *Principles of Literary Criticism*, p. 186.

veyed to him, the work itself is an object of cognition insofar as he respects its affective tenor exclusively.

The route may be different, but the starting point is the same for Roland Barthes. He, too, defines writing, or form, as the faithful reflection of the writer's free and signifying experience. It is true, though, that for him this form is not necessarily an object; when human actions are historically free, form is transparent. It is an object but not an object of reflection. But the moment this freedom is curtailed, the artist's endeavor and his choice of form become problematic; any restriction in the free choice of experience requires a justification of the form selected, an operation whose net effect is the genuine objectification of form. Richards's form-object resulted from the postulate of a perfect continuity of consciousness with its linguistic correlates; Barthes, on the other hand, proceeds from a historical situation. But, from the point of view of criticism, the result is the same, since, in both instances, criticism begins and ends with the study of form. There is, to be sure, a parting of the ways ultimately: for Richards, the next stage would be the working out of a utilitarian morality, while for Barthes it would more likely be revolutionary action. But, for the time being, we are concerned with issues of critical methodology; and it turns out that in the examples that he provides (the uses of the past tense in the novel, of the third person pronoun in Balzac, or of the "realistic" style of Garaudy—I am leaving aside his *Michelet*) Barthes's analyses are quite close to Richards's and those of his disciples. He could well profit, in fact, from the storehouse of techniques contained in their works in the preparation of his announced History of Writing.

As befits its origins in the pedagogical research Richards conducted at Cambridge University,[9] his method derives much of its influence from its undeniable didactic power. His conception of form permits, at once, the development of a critical vocabulary of an almost scientific power and the elaboration of easily taught analytic techniques possessing the virtues of *explication de texte*, yet not thwarting the freedom of formal imagination. In its suggestion of a balanced and stable moral climate, it is also reassuring criticism. By bringing down poetic language to the level of the language of communication, and in its steadfast refusal to grant aesthetic experience any difference from

9. A very instructive narrative of this research appears in the volume published after *Principles of Literary Criticism* entitled *Practical Criticism* (Edinburgh: Edinburgh Press, 1929).

other human experiences, it is opposed to any attempt to confer upon poetry an excessively exalted function, while still preserving for it the freshness and originality of invention.

But what happens when one studies poetry a little closer following these instructions? A surprising answer is to be found in the work of William Empson, a brilliant student of Richards.[10] Empson, a poet in his own right, and, moreover, a reader of great acuity, applied Richards's principles faithfully to a set of texts drawn mainly, though not exclusively, from Shakespeare and the metaphysical poets of the seventeenth century. From the very first example studied in *Seven Types of Ambiguity*, the results are troubling. It is a line from one of Shakespeare's sonnets. To evoke old age, the poet thinks of winter, more precisely a forest in winter, which, he says, is like:

Bare ruined choirs, where late the sweet birds sang.[11]

The thought is stated in a metaphor whose perfection is immediately felt. But if it is asked what is the common experience awakened by the forest and the ruined choir, one does not discover just one but an indefinite number. Empson lists a dozen of them and there are many others; it would be impossible to tell which was dominant in the poet's mind or at which we should stop. What the metaphor does is actually the opposite: instead of setting up an adequation between two experiences, and thereby fixing the mind on the repose of an established equation, it deploys the initial experience into an infinity of associated experiences that spring from it. In the manner of a vibration spreading in infinitude from its center, metaphor is endowed with the capacity to situate the experience at the heart of a universe that it generates. It provides the ground rather than the frame, a limitless anteriority that permits the limiting of a specific entity. Experience sheds its uniqueness and leads instead to a dizziness of the mind. Far from referring back to an object that would be its cause, the poetic sign sets in motion an imaging activity that refers to no object in particular. The "meaning" of the metaphor is that it does not "mean" in any definite manner.

10. I will deal with two of William Empson's works: *Seven Types of Ambiguity* (London: Chatto and Windus, 1930; 2nd revised edition, 1947) and *Some Versions of Pastoral* (London: Chatto and Windus, 1935). A third, and somewhat more technical, work is outside the scope of our study.
11. William Shakespeare, *Sonnets* #73.

This is obviously problematic. For if a simple metaphor suffices to suggest an infinity of initial experiences and, therefore, an infinity of valid readings, how can we live up to Richards's injunction to bring the reader's experience in line with the typical experience ascribed to the author? Can we still speak of communication here, when the text's effect is to transform a perfectly well-defined unity into a multiplicity whose actual number must remain undetermined? Empson's argument, as it proceeds from simple to increasingly complex examples, becomes apparent: a fundamental ambiguity is constitutive of all poetry. The correspondence between the initial experience and the reader's own remains forever problematic because poetry sets particular beings in a world yet to be constituted, as a task to fulfill.

Not all ambiguities are of this basic type. Some are pure signifying forms, condensed means of evoking real adequation, of stating rapidly a perfectly determined mental structure. In such cases, and whatever the degree of complexity of the text, exegesis is primarily a matter of concentration and intelligence, and it is in search of a precise signification. It ends up either with a single reading concealed in the apparent multiplicity, or in a controlled, even when antithetical, superposition of significations to be uncovered. The latter type of ambiguity would be like the proffered "explication" of Mallarmé's hermetic sonnets as purely erotic or scatological poems—a perfectly legitimate and possible reading in many instances, provided one adds immediately that they are something else and that Mallarmé was striving to achieve precisely this layered presence of different significations. This type of form occurs most frequently in Elizabethan and metaphysical poetry, as indeed in any precious or baroque poetry, and lends itself particularly well to a deciphering along I. A. Richards's line. Some of the more notable achievements of formalist criticism are to be found in this area.

Although Empson does not draw this basic distinction himself, it is clear that five of his seven types of ambiguity fall within this category of controlled pseudo-ambiguity, and that only the first and the last relate to a more fundamental property of poetic language. Any poetic sentence, even one devoid of artifice or baroque subtlety, must, by virtue of being poetic, constitute an infinite plurality of significations all melded into a single linguistic unit: that is the first type. But as Empson's inquiry proceeds, there occurs a visible increase in what he calls the logical disorder of his examples until, in the seventh and last type of ambiguity, the form blows up under our very eyes. This occurs when the text implies not merely distinct significations but significations that, against the will of their author, are mutually exclusive. And here Empson's advance beyond the teachings of his master becomes apparent. For under the outward appearance of a simple list classifying random examples, chapter seven develops a thought Richards never wanted to consider: true poetic ambiguity proceeds from the deep division of Being itself, and poetry does no more than state and repeat this division. Richards did recognize the existence of conflicts, but he invoked Coleridge, not without some simplification, to appeal to the reassuring notion of art as the reconciliation of opposites.[12] Empson's less serene mind is not content with this formula. In a note added to the text, he writes: "It may be said that the contradiction must somehow form a larger unity if the final effect is to be satisfying. But the onus of reconciliation can be laid very heavily on the receiving end,"[13] that is, on the reader, for the reconciliation does not occur in the text. The text does not resolve the conflict, it *names* it. And there is no doubt as to the nature of the conflict. Empson has already prepared us by saying that it is "at once an indecision and a structure, like the symbol of the Cross,"[14] and he ends his book on George Herbert's extraordinary poem entitled "The Sacrifice," a monologue uttered by Christ upon the cross, whose refrain is drawn from the "Laments of Jeremiah" (1, 12). "Is it nothing to you, all ye that pass by? Behold, and see if there be any sorrow like unto my sorrow, which is done unto me, wherewith the Lord hath afflicted me in the day of his fierce anger."

This conflict can be resolved only by the supreme sacrifice: there is no stronger way of stating the impossibility of an incarnate and happy truth. The ambiguity poetry speaks of is the fundamental one that prevails between the world of the spirit and the world of sentient substance: to ground itself, the spirit must turn itself into sentient substance, but the latter is knowable only in its dissolution into non-being. The spirit cannot coincide with its object and this separation is infinitely sorrowful.

Empson sheds light upon this dialectic, which is that of the unhappy consciousness, through some very well-chosen examples. He begins

12. *Principles of Literary Criticism*, pp. 251ff.
13. *Seven Types of Ambiguity*, note on p. 193.
14. *Ibid.*, p. 192.

with Keats's "Ode to Melancholy;" a very good selection, for Keats lived this tension especially acutely and lived it in its very substance. The growth of his consciousness results most often in a reversal that takes him from a happy and immediate sense impression to a painful knowledge. His sorrow is that of the man who can know substance only as he loses it; for whom any love immediately brings about the death of what is being loved. Empson illustrates this problematic by adducing mystical texts of the seventeenth century which show that spiritual happiness is conceivable only in terms of sensations, of the very substantial joys whose tragic fragility Keats knew so well. Man stands in utter distress before a God whom he risks destroying by wanting to know Him; he feels envy for the natural creature that is the direct emanation of Being. A sonnet by the Jesuit poet Gerard Manley Hopkins states the torture of this indecision. To be sure, George Herbert's serene tone does seem to convey a kind of peaceableness, for he managed in his poem to bring these contradictions and paradoxes side-by-side without occulting their outrageousness; but we must bear in mind that the protagonist here is not man but the Son of God, and that the display of error and human misery has been relegated to the background. We have traveled far from Richards's universe where there never is any error, only misunderstanding. Empson's inquiry, drawn by the very weight of his cogitations to problems that can no longer be ignored, has led him to broader questions. Instead of concentrating on details of poetic form, he will have to reflect henceforth upon the poetic phenomenon as such; a phenomenon that does seem to deserve this kind of attention since it leads, willy-nilly, to unsuspected perspectives upon human complexity.

These broader questions are not addressed in the rather pedestrian last chapter of *Seven Types of Ambiguity*, but they are raised in the book Empson published a few years later. The tone of the exposition, as well as the selection of works commented upon in *Some Versions of Pastoral*, could lead to the supposition that he had undertaken the study of one literary form among others, and that this study could be followed by others in a similar vein, upon the epic tradition, let us say, or the tragic. Nothing could be further from the truth, as a consideration of the central theme of the book, to be found in the commentary of Andrew Marvell's famous "The Garden" (Chapter IV), makes abundantly clear. The central strophe of the poem happens to name the

very problem upon which Empson's previous work ended: the contradictory relations between natural being and the being of consciousness:

> The Mind, that Ocean where each kind
> Does straight its own resemblance find;
> Yet it creates, transcending these,
> Far other worlds, and other Seas,
> Annihilating all that's made
> To a green thought in a green shade.

The dialectical armature of this strophe defines what Empson calls
the pastoral convention. It is the movement of consciousness as it contemplates the natural entity and finds itself integrally reflected down
to the most peculiar aspects of *phusis*. But a reflection is not an identification, and the simple correspondence of the mind with the natural,
far from being appeasing, turns troublesome. The mind recovers its
balance only in domination over that which is its complete other. Thus
the essentially negative activity of all thought takes place, and poetic
thought in particular: "Annihilating all that's made." One would be
hard pressed to state it any more strongly. However, the recourse to
the modifier "green" to qualify what is then created by thought, reintroduces the pastoral world of innocence, of "humble, permanent,
undeveloped nature which sustains everything, and to which everything
must return."[15] And it is reintroduced at the very moment that this
world has been annihilated. It is the freshness, the greenness of bud-
ding thought that can evoke itself only through the memory of what
it destroys on its way.

What is the pastoral convention, then, if not the eternal separation
between the mind that distinguishes, negates, legislates, and the
originary simplicity of the natural? A separation that may be lived,
as in Homer's epic poetry (evoked by Empson as an example of the
universality of its definition), or it may be thought in full consciousness
of itself as in Marvell's poem. There is no doubt that the pastoral theme
is, in fact, the only poetic theme, that it is poetry itself. Under the deceitful title of a genre study, Empson has actually written an ontology of
the poetic, but wrapped it, as is his wont, in some extraneous matter
that may well conceal the essential.

In light of this, what is the link between these considerations and

15. *Some Versions of Pastoral*, p. 128.

the first chapter of the book, entitled "Proletarian Literature," which concludes, paradoxically enough, that Marxist thought is pastoral thought disguised. Marxism draws its attractiveness from the reconciliation it promises, in all sincerity to be sure, but with a naive prematurity. "I do not mean to say," writes Empson, "that the [Marxist] philosophy is wrong; for that matter pastoral is worked from the same philosophical ideas as proletarian literature—the difference is that it brings in the absolute less prematurely."[16] The pastoral problematic, which turns out to be the problematic of Being itself, is lived in our day by Marxist thought, as by any genuine thought. In motivation, if not in its claims, Marxism is, ultimately, a poetic thought that lacks the patience to pursue its own conclusions to their end; this explains why Empson's book, which is all about separation and alienation, places itself at the outset under the aegis of Marxism; a convergence confirmed by the apparent contradiction of the attraction exerted upon our generation by the problematic of poetry and the solution of Marxism.[17]

Having started from the premises of the strictest aesthetical formalism, Empson winds up facing the ontological question. And it is by virtue of this question that he stands as a warning against certain Marxist illusions. The problem of separation inheres in Being, which means that social forms of separation derive from ontological and meta-social attitudes. For poetry, the divide exists forever. "To produce pure proletarian art the artist must be at one with the worker; this is impossible, not for political reasons, but because the artist never is at one with any public."[18] This conclusion is grounded in a very thorough study and it is especially difficult to take issue with since it originated in the opposite conviction. It stands as an irrefutable critique by anticipation of Roland Barthes's position, for whom the separation is a

16. *Ibid.*, p. 23.
17. A remark by Heidegger confirms and sheds light on this encounter: "The fate of the world announces itself in poetry, without already appearing nonetheless as a history of Being. . . . Alienation has become fated on a world-scale. Which is why this destiny must be thought at the outset of the history of Being. What Marx recognized, basing himself upon Hegel, as essentially and significantly the alienation of man, takes root in the fundamentally exiled character of modern man. . . . It is because he had a real experience of this alienation that Marx has attained a profound dimension of history. That is why the Marxist conception of history by far surpasses all of the forms of contemporary historicism." *Platons Lehre von der Wahrheit; mit einem Brief über den 'Humanismus'* (Bern: A. Francke, 1947), p. 87.
18. *Pastoral*, p. 15.

phenomenon that admits of precise dating. "It is because there is no reconciliation in society that language, at once necessary and necessarily oriented, institutes a torn condition for the writer,"[19] writes Barthes, and he has tried, in his *Michelet* and elsewhere, to show the socially imposed abyss that confines the modern writer to an interiority he hates. Such a writer exists in a sort of historical transition, whose boundaries Barthes sets by inventing the myth of a genuinely univocal form in Classicism—but an Empsonian study of Racine would quickly dispose of this illusion—and the future myth of a "new Adamic world where language would no longer be alienated."[20] This is a good instance of falling all at once into all the traps of impatient "pastoral" thought: formalism, false historicism, and utopianism.

The promise held out in Richards's work, of a convergence between logical positivism and literary criticism, has failed to materialize. After the writings of an Empson, little is left of the scientific claims of formalist criticism. All of its basic assumptions have been put into question: the notions of communication, form, signifying experience, and objective precision. And Empson is but an example among others.[21] Their routes may at times have differed, but numerous critics have come to recognize within poetic language the same pluralism and the disorders signaling ontological complexities. Terms such as paradox, tension, and ambiguity abound in American criticism to the point of nearly losing all meaning.

A conception of poetic consciousness as an essentially divided, sorrowful, and tragic consciousness (or as representing, in stoical or ironical guises, attempts to transcend this pain without eliminating it) forces some choices upon critical reflection. The impression of crisis and uncertainty that one gathers from reading contemporary criticism derives from these hesitations. Without simplifying excessively, we may distinguish three possible avenues for reflection: historical poetics, salvational poetics, and naïve poetics.

Historical poetics can be spoken of only in the conditional, for it

19. *Degré Zéro de l'Ecriture*, p. 119; in English, p. 83.
20. *Ibid.*, p. 126; in English, p. 88.
21. The French reader unfamiliar with Empson's work should be warned that this has been an interpretation and not an exposition, and that it is, therefore, subject to discussion. I suppose that the author especially, who has always proclaimed his agreement with Richards, would have some difficulty endorsing it.

exists but in scattered form. Strictly speaking, Marxist criticism is not historical for it is bound to the necessity of a reconciliation scheduled to occur at the end of a linear temporal development, and its dialectical movement does not include time itself as one of its terms. A truly historical poetics would attempt to think the divide in truly temporal dimensions instead of imposing upon it cyclical or eternalist schemata of a spatial nature. Poetic consciousness, which emerges from the separation, *constitutes* a certain time as the noematic correlate of its action. Such a poetics promises nothing except the fact that poetic thought will keep on becoming, will continue to ground itself in a space beyond its failure. Although it is true that a poetics of this kind has not found expression in an established critical language, it has, nevertheless, presided over certain great poetic works, at times even consciously.

Salvational criticism, on the other hand, has taken on considerable proportions in the United States. "The ground-base of poetic truth is the truth, contextual but real, of man's possible redemption through the fullest imaginative response":[22] this sentence from a recent and representative work is typical of a trend in which formalist techniques are overlaid with intentions of a mythical and religious order. Since the sorrow of separation is most acutely felt at the level of historical reality in the emptiness and impoverishment of the times, salvational thought turns eagerly to primordial origins, hence its mythico-poetic concerns: "The true nature of mythic perspective reveals itself in its concern for origins; the Holy, in mythic perspective, finds its ulterior reference in an original act of creation."[23] Originary beginnings take on the appearance of privileged moments beyond time, and their remembrance serves as the promise of a new fruitfulness. This is a way of conquering history: redemption is conceived of as an event residing *in potentia* in arid reality, and whose prior occurrences are guarantees of permanent presence. Although it remains caught in time when it is practiced as a discipline of thought, the return to origins is, nonetheless, an attempt to reconquer the timeless. It aspires to an

22. Philip Wheelwright, *The Burning Fountain* (Bloomington: Indiana University Press, 1954), p. 302.
23. Ernst Cassirer, *Die Philosophie der symbolischen Formen*, cited by Wheelwright, p. 164. These approaches have found a rich source of information in the works of the anthropologists and British classicists known as the Cambridge school: Gilbert Murray, James Frazer, and their students, I. E. Harrison, F. M. Cornford, Jessie Weston, etc.

ultimate reconciliation on a cosmic scale, or, in any case, to a new beginning, cut off from the memories of the past and fresh with the innocence
of new dawns. But the intellectual atmosphere specific to this criticism
unites a barely veiled nostalgia for immediate revelation with a very
conscious expressivity, which wants to sacrifice nothing of the lucidity
and the prudence of mediate distinctions. More than any other, the
work of T. S. Eliot sums this up best, and it is not at all surprising
to find Wheelwright make reference to the poet who wrote:

> Only through time is time conquered

and for whom divine incarnation is described in purely cerebral terms,
muffled by the reservations of a consciousness incapable of sustaining
itself, but constituting, nonetheless, the sole means of access to the
eternal:

> The hint half-guessed, the gift half understood
> is Incarnation

The same hesitancy at the prospect of surrendering to the faith of
salvation is to be found in Wheelwright, together with a presentation
of poetry as a presage of redemption. Under the guise of a critique
of the scientific claims of I. A. Richards's positivism, where he has
little to add to what had been established by Empson, Wheelright's
book introduces an eternalist and religious conception of poetry: "the
language . . . of poetry . . . speak[s] in a way that truly 'mounts to the
dwelling-place of the gods,' and testifies to the reality of that dwelling."[24]
But these declarations of faith alternate with more prudent and less
embracing statements, such as: "The dual role, the in-and-out movement of the mind seeking to penetrate its object, frames every experience
with the irony of its own finitude;"[25] or even a definition of expressive
thought as: "Some such vitalizing tension between the beholder's intuition of oneness with an object and his intuition of the object's
otherness."[26] For Empson such paradoxes constituted the very essence
of the poetic, insofar as they had to remain unresolved. How are they
to be reconciled with a belief in the poetic as a salvational act capable
of deciding these dilemmas?

24. Wheelwright, p. 7.
25. *Ibid.*, p. 13.
26. *Ibid.*, p. 187.

In its own way, this type of criticism attempts also to reconcile the need for a substantial incarnation with the need for knowledge; it is the tension from which springs all thought, poetic as well as philosophical. But, if it is to have validity, it must have such an intense experience of both of these necessities that it can never name the one without having the other integrally present. Therein lies the difference between genuine ontological ambiguity and contradiction; in the latter, the two mutually exclusive poles are simply overlaid or successively present instead of establishing themselves, as in Marvell's poem, in an unsoluble co-presence. Instead of saying that Wheelwright's thought, or, for that matter, T. S. Eliot's to whom it is so close, sacrifices consciousness to faith, it is better to say that it alternates moments of faith without consciousness with moments of consciousness without faith. This is possible only if negation and affirmation are both wielded carelessly.

It remains for us to define the attitude we called naïve, which rests on the belief that poetry is capable of effecting reconciliation because it provides an immediate contact with substance through its own sensible form. In a famous letter, Keats had already cried out: "O for a life of sensation not of thought," but he had sense enough to speak of sensation as something one desires but cannot have. A contemporary American poet is far less prudent when he writes: "[the poet] searches for meanings in terms of the senses. The intelligence of art is a sensory intelligence, the meaning of art is a sensory meaning. . . . There is no such thing as a good work of art which is not immediately apprehensible in the senses."[27] There is no doubt that there is a sensory dimension, as intention, in all poetry, but to assert its exclusive and immediate presence is to ignore the origin of all creative and imaging consciousness. The distinction, so often formulated, that the experience of the object is not the experience of the consciousness of the object, remains basic and valid. In a way, if it were not for the fact that substance is problematic and absent, there would not be art.

It is apparent, then, that the *criticism of sensation* reappropriates and extends the illusion that had already occurred in a different form in I. A. Richards and according to which there is a continuity between experience and language. To go further, the practitioners of this criticism seem to believe in an adequation of the object itself with the language that names it. They assert that some texts establish such an

27. Karl Shapiro, *Beyond Criticism* (Lincoln: University of Nebraska Press, 1953), pp. 43, 45.

adequation and they are willing to erect it into a critical norm: "Great literature [constitutes] . . . the preferred domain of the happy relation," writes Jean-Pierre Richard; and, in his introduction to Richards's two books, Georges Poulet opposes the criticism of sensation to the criticism of consciousness by writing: "[Criticism] must reach the act through which the mind, coming to terms with its own body and that of others, joined with the object in order to invent itself as subject."[28] It is a little fast going to assign to criticism the task of installing itself at a point where no work in the world, however inspired, has ever been able to install itself. To justify such a claim, Husserl is eagerly invoked: all consciousness is consciousness of something. Must it be recalled that for Husserl this statement is the point of departure for a transcendental idealism most decidedly at a far remove from any naïve sensualism? And without wanting to enter into the intricacies of the topic, one can also add that Bachelard, who is also eagerly invoked by this criticism, is more likely closer to Husserl than to any of the authors who claim him for their own.

Whether it be in France or in the United States, the foremost characteristic of contemporary criticism is the tendency to expect a reconciliation from poetry; to see it in a possibility of filling the gap that cleaves Being. It is a hope shared, in very different forms, by different critical approaches: the positivist formalist, the Marxist, the salvational, and the criticism of substance.[29] But if the latter appears furthest removed in the ability to faithfully account for the texts, it is closest to the naming of the center of the problem. For it reveals, in the impatience of which it is the symptom, the desire that haunts modern thought: "to communicate substantially with what is substantial in things."[30] One is far from the truth when, with Jean-Pierre Richard, one describes Baudelaire as a happy poet whose word is capable of "filling the depth by substituting for the emptiness of the abyss the warm plenitude of substance."[31] But one is also quite close to it, in the sense that for Baudelaire it is this possibility that constitutes the supreme wager; however, since it must remain wager, it is substance itself that is the abyss. As long as that remains the case, there is left but the sorrowful time of patience, i.e., history.

28. Jean-Pierre Richard, *Poésie et Profondeur* (Paris: Seuil, 1955), p. 10.
29. I omit mention of Maurice Blanchot, whose work does not fall in the trends mentioned here.
30. Jean Wahl, *Traité de Métaphysique* (Paris: Payot, 1953), p. 73.
31. *Poésie et Profondeur*, p. 161.

XII

Heidegger's
Exegeses of Hölderlin

Heidegger's exegeses of Hölderlin are sufficiently important to have elicited two studies of some size.[1] Owing to the unusual influence of the commentator as much as to the exceptional difficulty of the poet commented upon, these readings give rise to several problems. One need ask what is Heidegger's contribution to the sum total of Hölderlin studies; one need ask as well what is the place of these exegeses in Heidegger's own philosophical work and to what extent have they influenced its development; finally, Heidegger's own exegetical method requires attention.

The three questions are related, but, undeniably, the third one is the link between the first two. Heidegger's exegetical method flows directly from the premises of his philosophy; it is inseparable from it

1. Else Buddeberg, "Heidegger und die Dichtung: Hölderlin," *Deutsche Vierteljahrschrift für Literaturwissenschaft und Geistesgeschichte*, 26, no. 3 (1952), pp. 293-330; Beda Alleman, *Hölderlin und Heidegger* (Zurich: Atlantis Verlag, 1954). There are four essays by Heidegger dealing with specific poems by Hölderlin: the commentaries to "Heimkunft" (1943), "Wie wenn am Feiertage . . ." (1939), "Andenken" (1943) published in *Erläuterungen zu Hölderlins Dichtung* (Frankfurt, 1950), and to ". . . dichterisch wohnet der Mensch . . ." (1951) published in *Vorträge und Aufsätze* (Pfüllingen, 1954). In addition there are two broader essays on the poetic work directly inspired by Hölderlin: "Hölderlin und das Wesen der Dichtung" (1936), also in *Erläuterungen*; and "Der Ursprung des Kunstwerkes" (1935-36), in *Holzwege* (Frankfurt, 1950). There are frequent allusions to Hölderlin in several other essays of the same periods.

to the point that one cannot speak here of "method" in the formal sense of the term, but rather of Heidegger's very thought in relation to the poetic. The value of his contribution to Hölderlin scholarship will be determined by the validity of this thought, which, strictly speaking, is an ontology and not of aesthetics. The study of the method is a necessary introduction, then, to the other questions; their scope exceeds the capacity of a single article.

To understand the literary scholars' reception of Heidegger's essays, we must bear in mind the special circumstances of the editing and elucidation of Hölderlin's works. Almost entirely forgotten throughout the nineteenth century (with some rare exceptions, Nietzsche among them), a renewal of interest occurred late in the century with Dilthey playing a leading role. Once attention was awakened, it did not take long for the extraordinary work conceived between 1800 and 1803 and mostly left unpublished, to be discovered. Norbert von Hellingrath undertook the preparation of the first critical edition, which was completed after his death in 1906 by Seebass and von Pigenot. For a long time it has been authoritative, and it is the one Heidegger uses in his commentaries.

The considerable influence exercised by Hölderlin following these discoveries, first in Germany, then in France and England, is well-known; today he is taken not only as the most important figure of German romanticism but as one of the great poets of the West, and even more as a poet whose thought is so close to our most immediate concerns that his vision takes on the aspect of a premonition. Heidegger is right in applying to the poet himself this mysterious, and perhaps spurious, line:

> Der König Oedipus hat ein
> Auge zuviel vielleicht (Hellingrath VI, 26)
> [King Oedipus has one eye too many perhaps]

But we are far from knowing this great poet, for he presents the major difficulty of being precise above all. The abundance and the beauty of the images, the richness and the diversity of the rhymes entrance us, but this ebullience is always accompanied by a thought and an expression that are always in search of the extreme rigor and meticulousness. Through erasures, drafts, reworked fragments, Hölderlin seeks an ever truer and more correct expression.

More so than for everyone else, the reliability of his text is all important. But the Hellingrath edition soon turned out to be inadequate. New discoveries and a more extensive knowledge of the works established the need for a new critical edition. This is a task now partially completed: under the direction of Friedrich Beissner, three parts of the so-called great Stuttgart edition have been published: all of the poetry, the letters, and the translations. It is one of the great achievements of modern scientific philology. By drawing upon the most proven methods (detailed study of the sources and of historical and biographical references, internal comparative references, syntactic explanations, study of formal metrics, etc.) as well as upon some modern technical processes (study of paper and writing with the aid, I am told, of slides of enlargements of the manuscript) Beissner has produced the irreproachable critical edition, something that, in the case of Hölderlin, was at once necessary and most difficult to achieve.

The editor insists upon his objectivity; he has decided not to write a preface, and his commentaries are of a purely informational nature; his work is intended solely to provide the materials for a future interpretation at last well grounded. The virtues of such an asceticism are obvious, but there is a drawback to this very virtue; prudent philological modesty, which bars itself any interpretation as long as the objective dimensions of the work have not been established, is forced to leave unresolved a number of issues, including some at the level of the text establishment. In the case of Hölderlin, this margin of indeterminacy is especially large, for the material condition of the manuscripts is frequently such that it is often impossible to choose between two possible lessons in the very places where explication is most necessary. The editor finds himself obliged to rely upon the principle that he follows; as a result, scientific philology attempts to find objective and quantitative criteria, while Heidegger decides in the name of the internal logic of his own commentary.

Here is an example among others. Beda Alleman (pp. 8ff.) cites the case of line 39 in the hymn "Wie wenn am Feiertage..." Beissner reads:

Wenn es [das Lied] der Sonne des Tags und warmer Erd/Entwächst...
[When the song grows out from the sun of the day and the warm earth...]

But it appears that for *Entwächst,* Hölderlin had written *entwacht* [awakens], which results in a stranger meaning, but happens to work perfectly well with Heidegger's general interpretation of this poem; against both Hellingrath and Beissner, he preserves the lesson *entwacht,* whereas Beissner refers to seven other instances in the complete works where Hölderlin wrote *entwacht* for *entwächst,* and decides from this quantitative evidence in favor of *entwächst.* A rational decision between these two criteria is obviously difficult. The quantitative method does have in its favor a certain positive probability, but its final choice remains nonetheless arbitrary for it is most unlikely that Hölderlin chose his term on the basis of statistical distribution. Philology knows this well and proceeds in the honest and sensible way: in a note, the editor draws attention to the problem and leaves the question open. But it cannot be denied that the exegete capable of providing a coherent and responsible interpretation has the right, indeed the obligation, to decide according to the conclusions of his interpretation; that is, after all, one of the goals of all exegesis. Everything rests, then, on the intrinsic value of the interpretation.

The matter becomes even more complicated insofar as Heidegger's interpretation is based in turn upon a notion of the poetic that seeks to assert the fundamental impossibility of applying objective discourse to a work of art. Heidegger reduces philology to a subordinate position, although he does not hesitate to call upon it when his cause requires it; and he declares himself free of the restrictions it has imposed upon itself. Such violence has been found shocking, and rightly so, but it must be seen that it derives directly from Heidegger's conception of the poetic, which he claims to have deduced from Hölderlin's thought. To accept this poetics is to accept its consequences. Unlike Else Buddeberg, one cannot follow Heidegger in his philosophical statements and then disavow him in the name of a methodology that these very statements claim to transcend. The strictly philological objections that she raises against him are without merit, for it is manifestly by design that Heidegger goes against the established canons of literary scholarship. He relies upon a text whose unreliability must have been known to him, and engages in detailed analyses, referring to manuscript corrections, marginal notes, and the like, without verifying for accuracy, or at least without doing so enough. He comments upon the poems independently of one another and draws analogies only in support of his own thesis. When a passage is at odds with his interpretation—we shall see an example of this—he simply sets it aside. He ignores the context, isolates lines or words to give them an absolute value, without any regard for their specific function in the poem from which he plucks them. He bases an entire, and fundamental, study (". . . dichterisch wohnet der Mensch [poetically man dwells] . . ."), upon a text, probably apocryphal, included by Beissner under the heading: "of dubious authenticity." In the very same study, he quotes without qualms, and in the same manner as the other works, a poem from Hölderlin's madness, a poem that Hölderlin signed and dated: "Very humbly yours, Scardanelli. 24 May 1748." He ignores altogether all matters of poetic technique that had certainly been of great import to Hölderlin; a number of anomalies and obscurities in these poems cannot be explained without reference to them. And one could go on listing Heidegger's heresies against the most elementary rules of text analysis. However, these heresies are not arbitrary because of a lack of rigor but because they rely upon a poetics that permits, or even requires, arbitrariness. It is incumbent upon us, then, to examine briefly this poetics.

For Heidegger, Hölderlin is the greatest of poets ("the poet of poets") because he states the essence (*Wesen*) of poetry. The essence of poetry consists in stating the parousia, the absolute presence of Being. In this, Hölderlin differs from the metaphysicians Heidegger dismisses: all, at least in some degree, are in error; Hölderlin is the only one whom Heidegger cites as a believer cites Holy Writ. It is not merely a matter of a critique, in the epistemological sense of the term. Just like Hölderlin, every great thinker is in the parousia, for it is of the essence of the parousia that no one may escape it. There is, however, an essential difference: Hölderlin states the presence of Being, his word is Being present, and he knows that this is the case; the metaphysicians, on the other hand, state their desire for the presence of Being, but, since it is Being's essence to reveal itself by hiding in that which it is not, they can never name it. They are the dupes of Being's subterfuge; they are naïve even though they claim to be hyperconscious, for that which they name as the essential is nothing more than Being disguised, and that which they dismiss as the negation of the essential is, in fact, the authentic face of the very same Being. They say the truth but without knowing it, and this truth is apparent only to the meta-metaphysician (Heidegger), who finds himself in a position akin to that of the "philosopher" who already possesses the Absolute Spirit in Hegel's *Phenomenology of Mind:* just as the latter had penetrated the movement of consciousness and was able to denounce the naïve certainty of natural consciousness in the name of the absolute truth of the consciousness-of-the-self, Heidegger has penetrated the movement of Being and can unmask the will to presence of Being as it manifests itself in being (*étant*), in the name of the parousia of Being. This thought is most clearly and generally advanced in the commentary added to *Was ist Metaphysik?*, where it is said that what metaphysics conceives of as non-being is in fact forgotten Being (p. 21).

Hölderlin, on the other hand, knows this movement of Being. He describes it in the elegy "Heimkunft," especially in two passages:

> Was du suchest, es ist nahe, begegnet dir schon
> [What you seek, it is near, it meets you already]

a line that states the parousia and the paradoxical necessity that what gives itself immediately must be sought. This line is completed and explained by the following:

> Aber das Beste, der Fund, die unter des heiligen Friedens
> Bogen lieget, er ist Jungen und Alten gespart
> [But the best, the find, which lies under the arch of sacred peace,
> is preserved for young and old]

Read Heidegger's way, this line states the movement of Being as it absconds. The poet who has seen and thought this, has seen and thought more than any metaphysician, for he has seen Being as it truly is. He finds himself in the absolute presence of Being, he has been struck by the Heraclitean bolt of lightning of truth, henceforth he will no longer name the deceitful mask that Being presents to the metaphysician, but its authentic face.

> Jetzt aber tagts! Ich harrt und sah es kommen
> Und was ich sah, das Heilige sei mein Wort.
> [But now day breaks! I waited and I saw it coming
> And what I saw, the Holy be my word.]

The commentary to the elegy "Heimkunft" states the ambiguous character of Being, in which we ought to recognize the particular wavering, the ecstatic character of human *Dasein* in *Being and Time*.[2] The commentary to the hymn "Wie wenn am Feiertage . . .", from which the lines quoted above are taken, states the destiny that results from this revelation: the proximate end of the night of error by a cyclical return to the original illumination of truth, the temporal ecstasis that reopens upon a historical future conceived of in the form of an eschatology, and a closer adequation of destiny to Being. In a somewhat different idiom, a portent of Heidegger's latest manner, the commentary to "Andenken" reworks and brings together the two previous commentaries in the final line:

> Was bleibet aber stiften die Dichter
> [But what remains, is founded by the poets]

which Heidegger takes to mean: the poet founds the immediate presence of Being by naming it.

One question arises above all: why does Heidegger need to refer to Hölderlin? It has been said and repeated that these commentaries do no more than formulate his own thought and use Hölderlin as a pretext, or merely as a prestigious reference that would give more authority to his assertion. But Heidegger is the thinker who has shoved aside all available authorities (in ambiguous fashion, to be sure, and much could be said about his treatment of Kant and Hegel); why would he spare Hölderlin in particular? It is not because Hölderlin is a poet, for we know from the Rilke study that poets are just as capable of "error" as metaphysicians: to Else Buddeberg's outrage, Heidegger equates the angel of the Elegies to Nietzsche's Zarathustra. And yet Rilke seems to be the poet closest to Heidegger, the one who shares the same concerns. This anomaly may set us on the track of an explanation.

As one reads the last commentary on Hölderlin (". . . dichterisch wohnet der Mensch [poetically man dwells] . . ."), one understands why Heidegger is in need of a witness, of someone of whom he can say that he has named the immediate presence of Being. The witness is Heidegger's solution to the problem that had tormented equally poets and thinkers, and even mystics: how to preserve the moment of truth. All Western metaphysicians, from Anaximander to Nietzsche, have forgotten the truth, according to Heidegger, by forgetting Being. Of Eastern

2. On this, see Heidegger's own note in *Über den Humanismus* (Frankfurt: Vittorio Klostermann, 1949), p. 25.

philosophies no more is known than what Hölderlin said in the mysterious poem "Der Ister." How are we to shore up our remembrance of authentic Being so that we can find our way back to it? This *Fund,* this find, it must be somewhere; if it had never revealed itself, how could we speak of its presence? But here is someone—Hölderlin— who tells us that he has seen it, and that, moreover, he can speak of it, name it, and describe it; he has visited Being, and Being has told him some things that he has collected and that he is bringing back to mankind. With respect to himself, Heidegger is not so sure that he has seen Being and, in any case, he knows that he has nothing to say about it beyond the fact that it conceals itself. Yet he does not intend to give up discourse since it is still his intention to collect and found Being by means of language. And he intends to remain a thinker and not turn to mysticism. The experience of Being must be sayable; in fact, it is in language that it is preserved. There must be someone, then, of unquestionable purity, who can say that he has traveled this route and seen the flash of illumination. One such person is enough, but there must be one. For then, the truth, which is the presence of the present, has entered the work that is language. Language— Hölderlin's language—is the immediate presence of Being. And the task that we, who, like Heidegger, cannot speak of Being, inherit, is to preserve this language, to preserve Being.

The preservation of Being is the commentary, the "thinking-of" (*an-denken*) Hölderlin. That is the method. Hölderlin knows Being immediately and he says it immediately; the commentator need only know how to listen. The work is there, itself a parousia. Being speaks through Hölderlin's mouth as God did through the mouth of the seer Calchas in the *Iliad* (cf. M. Heidegger "Der Spruch Anaximanders," *Holzwege,* pp. 318 ff.). To preserve the work is simply to listen to it, in all passivity, knowing that it is uniquely and absolutely true. Borrowing an image from Hölderlin, Heidegger compares the work to a bell; the commentator causes it to resound (*Erläuterung:* interpretation, commentary contains *lauten,* to sound, peal); he makes us hear what it holds wholly by itself, as when snow falls on the bell. It is not a case of a freedom grasping another freedom that, like it, attempts to clear a way to the truth: that would be interpreting and critiquing, and there simply can be no question of interpreting Being; all that can be done is to receive it and preserve it. Interpretation is applicable only to metaphysicians, and then it takes the form of an onto-analysis, a purification that can be carried out by one who has been able to listen to the voice of Being. With Hölderlin, there never is any critical dialogue.[3] There is nothing in his work, not an erasure, no obscurity, no ambiguity, that is not absolutely and totally willed by Being itself. Only one who has truly grasped this can become the "editor" of Being and impose commas that spring forth "from the very necessity of thought." We are far from scientific philology.

In its apparent excesses, such a position invites parody, but from within Heideggerian thought it is necessary, for the ambition of this thought is not to merely say the truth, but to install itself in parousia, to dwell in it, to inhabit it. Commentary, which is the preservation of Being, is also, in the final analysis, the manner in which we can dwell in real Being instead of dwelling as we do in its reverse. The immediate unity of the three entities: Being, the poet, and human *Dasein*, which listens, found a construction in which we can proceed to install ourselves. In Heidegger's most recent texts, the supreme promise that concealed itself behind the slaughter of traditional metaphysics proclaims itself more and more openly. Since Being has founded itself in language in the work of the poet (Hölderlin), by "thinking-of" (*an-denken*) this work as we do in the commentary, we ready ourselves to live in the presence of Being, to "dwell poetically on earth."

Heidegger's need for a witness is understandable, then, but why must it be Hölderlin? There are, to be sure, secondary reasons, of a sentimental and national nature, in his favor. Heidegger's commentaries were thought out just before and during World War II, and are directly linked to an anguished meditation upon the historical destiny of Germany, a meditation that finds an echo in the "national" poems of Hölderlin. But that is a side issue that would take us away from our topic. There is, however, another and much deeper reason that justifies this choice: *it is the fact that Hölderlin says exactly the op-*

3. It is possible to perhaps detect a slight hesitancy in Heidegger's attitude on this point. On very rare occasions, even Hölderlin appears to be placed within the metaphysical tradition. On this score, Beda Alleman's remarks (pp. 150-55) are valid, though they shift the emphasis overly toward the active notion of a dialogue against the more passive one of audition. It is in the commentary to "Andenken" at most that one may find, and not without applying some force, the traces of a dialogue. In all of the other commentaries, dialogue is out of the question, and Heidegger's attitude differs fundamentally from the one he adopts toward all metaphysicians, the Pre-Socratics included. This difference is confirmed and solidified in the last commentary, the one on "... dichterisch wohnet der Mensch...."

posite of what Heidegger makes him say. Such an assertion is paradoxical only in appearance. At this level of thought it is difficult to
distinguish between a proposition and that which constitutes its opposite. In fact, to state the opposite is still to talk of the same thing
though in an opposite sense, and it is already a major achievement
to have, in a dialogue of this sort, the two interlocutors manage to speak
of the same thing. It can indeed be said that Heidegger and Hölderlin
speak of the same thing; whatever one may otherwise reproach in
Heidegger's commentaries, their great merit remains to have brought
out precisely the central "concern" of Hölderlin's work; and in this,
they surpass other studies. Nonetheless, they reverse his thought.

A demonstration of this proposition would require an extensive study
of Hölderlin's work. We must limit ourselves to sketching out some
of the elements of such a demonstration, basing ourselves upon the
central commentary, that of the hymn "Wie wenn am Feiertage. . . ."
Before we begin, though, we must stress the importance of this question for all of Heidegger's philosophy. With Hölderlin, Heidegger cannot
take refuge in the ambiguity that constitutes at once his positive contribution and his defense strategy: he cannot say, as in the case of the
metaphysicians, that they proclaim both the true and the false, that
they are the greater the more they are in error, that the closer they
are to Being, the more they are possessed by its absconding movement.
For the promise of Heidegger's ontology to be realized, Hölderlin must
be Icarus returned from his flight: he must state directly and positively the presence of Being as well as the possibility of maintaining it
in time. Heidegger has staked his entire "system" on the possibility
of this experience. This may explain why, obeying a tactic perhaps not
fully conscious, he feels the need to base himself upon the work which
proclaims that it is this experience, among all others, that is totally
forbidden to man.

The unfinished and untitled hymn that begins with the line "Wie
wenn am Feiertage das Feld zu sehen" [Just as on a feast day, to see
his field] (1800) is one of Hölderlin's most famous poems. It has moved
poets deeply, Stefan George and Rilke in particular, because it deals
with the specific tension from which the poetic act is born and, more
than any poem, expresses its essence.

Heidegger's commentary begins by establishing that the hymn names

the poet as the one who is in the presence of Being, and that the word
"Nature" must make us think not of even the Pre-Socratic's *phusis,*
for it is a term corrupted by the metaphysical tradition, but of Being
as Hölderlin thinks it and as it truly is. This definition of the word
"Nature" is established in the following passage:

> Denn sie, sie selbst, die älter denn die Zeiten
> Und über die Götter des Abends und Orients ist,
> Die Natur . . .
> [For she, she herself, who is older than the ages
> and above the gods of the Occident and the Orient,
> Nature . . .]

a definition completed by adjectives that characterize nature and its
action, and especially the term *wunderbar allegegenwärtig* [wondrous-
ly all-present]. The identification posited by Heidegger between Being and nature is therefore justified by the description: it is clear that
this is no longer nature in the pastoral sense, not even in the sense
of nonconsciousness that the term possesses in the philosophical
fragments of the Homburg period; it is rather the immediate apprehen-
sion (presence) of that which serves as a support to all beings, that
which precedes and makes possible their re-presentation to consciousness. It is indeed that which in Heidegger's own terminology is
generally called the presence of the presents, the common *Wesen* of
all individual presents that makes for the all-presence of things. It is
the immediate givenness of Being that, for Hegel, is *"just* being" (*nur
Sein*) as long as it has not been re-presented to consciousness. From
a Hegelian perspective, it is legitimate to refer to it as *"just* being"
because, of itself, it has neither the possibility nor the necessity to constitute itself into logos. Its all-presence is a matter of indifference, then,
for there is no need for the philosopher to linger on in the nostalgia
of originary immediacy, a state about which there is, after all, nothing
to say. But for Hölderlin, the poet, this all-presence is "wondrous,"
for it is the immediate revelation of what appears most desirable to
him. For the poet the anguishing question—and it is indeed the subject of the poem—is: how can one not only speak *of* Being, but say
Being itself. Poetry is the experience of this question.

Heidegger is right, then, to see in the poem a statement of the relation of poet to Being; this is a good example of the fundamental wor-
thiness of his commentaries. But he begins to distort the meaning when

he continues by showing the poet as naming the presence of the present. His demonstration rests on these two passages:

> So stehn sie unter günstiger Witterung
> Sie die kein Meister allein, die wunderbar
> Allgegenwärtig erziehet in leichtem Umfangen
> Die Mächtige, die göttlichschöne Natur.
> [literally: Thus they stand under balmy skies
> Those whom no master alone, whom wonderously
> All-present educates in a light embrace
> The powerful, the divinely beautiful nature][4]

and

> Jetzt aber tagts! Ich harrt und sah es kommen
> Und was ich sah, das Heilige sei mein Wort.

Does the first passage tell us that poets stand under propitious skies because they dwell in the presence of Being? Does it say that poets belong to Being (*zugehören und entsprechen*), as Heidegger claims (p. 52)? The text says that Being (nature) educates (*erzieht*) the poet: nature is for him an example of a state he wishes to attain and imitate. This imitation is not the Aristotelian *mimesis* but rather the Romantic *Bildung:* initiation through the conscious experience of Being. It is perfectly legitimate and indeed necessary to refer to *Hyperion*, the novel of Hölderlin's youth, where the notion of *Bildung*, synonymous with *Erziehung*, is defined as the eccentric road man travels toward the primeval unity of the immediate. The poet is one who accepts nature

---

4. The literal translation does not reveal the meaning of the second line. A possible reading of it would put *allein* in opposition to *Natur:*

> Those whom no master educates, save, wondrously
> All-present, in a light embrace
> The powerful, the divinely beautiful nature.

Heidegger reads: "Those who, unable to be masters themselves . . . , are educated by nature"—undeniably a richer reading; the ambiguity is not essential to the commentary. French translators generally take *allein* as an adjective modifying *Meister*, but the necessity of insisting on "a single master" is not clear, unless one sees here the unique God of Christianity. This may be going too far in the direction of a pantheistic interpretation. Grammatically, all three versions are justifiable.

These syntactical difficulties, better revealed by literal translation than any reading, give an idea of the difficulty of interpreting Hölderlin. Next to him, Mallarmé is easy, because there at least, we know that the ambiguities occur by design.

(the immediate unity of Being) as his guide instead of submitting to some institution that accepts and perpetuates the separation between man and Being. One may think of Rousseau, taking care to avoid a pantheistic interpretation: to accept someone as one's master, far from signifying that one identifies with him and that one belongs to him, means rather that there is, and continues to be, an unbridgeable gap. In any case, the passage in Hölderlin does not say that the poet dwells in the parousia, but only that it is the principle of his becoming, in the same way as the absolute is the moving principle of the becoming of consciousness in Hegel's *Phenomenology.*

Now, to the second passage: "And what I saw, the Holy be my word." Hölderlin says that, guided by Nature, he has seen the Holy. He does not say that he has seen God, but indeed the essence of the divine, the Holy, which transcends the gods as Being transcends beings. We may well grant Heidegger that we are indeed dealing with what he calls Being. The poet, faithful disciple of Being, is privileged because he is called upon to see it in its wondrous all-presence. He is struck by the bolt of this truth insofar as he knows the supreme value of this vision that, locked up as it is for ordinary mortals in false partial consciousness, does not appear in the full force of its positivity. But Hölderlin knows as well that to see Being is not enough, that, in fact, the difficulty arises immediately *after* this moment. Before Being produces itself, one lives in expectation; the mind stands vigil (*ahnen*) and is brought closer to the moment as concentration increases, in thought and in prayer. It produces itself then in the lightning of the *Jetzt,* in absolute temporal present. If one could say it, it would be founded because the word has durability and founds the moment in a spatial presence where one could dwell. That is the supreme goal, the ultimate desire of the poet, which is why Hölderlin adopts the tone of prayer:

> Und was ich sah, das Heilige sei mein Wort.

He does not say: das Heilige *ist* mein Wort. The subjunctive is here really an optative; it indicates prayer, it marks desire, and these lines state the eternal poetic intention, but immediately state also that it can be no more than intention. It is not because he has seen Being that the poet is, therefore, capable of naming it; his word prays for the parousia, it does not establish it.

It cannot establish it for as soon as the word is uttered, it destroys
the immediate and discovers that instead of stating Being, it can only
state mediation. For man the presence of Being is always in becoming, and Being necessarily appears under a non-simple form. In its moment of highest achievement, language manages to mediate between
the two dimensions we distinguish in Being. It does it by attempting
to name them and by seeking to grasp and arbitrate their difference
and their opposition. But it cannot reunite them. Their unity is ineffable and cannot be said, because it is language itself that introduces
the distinction. Propelled by the appeal of parousia, it seeks to establish
the absolute presence of immediate Being, but can do no more than
pray or struggle, never found. Heidegger contests this, relying on the
following:

> Und hoch vom Aether bis zum Abgrund nieder
> Nach vestem Geseze, wie einst, aus heiligem Chaos gezeugt,
> Fühlt neu die Begeisterung sich,
> Die Allerschaffende wieder.

A literal translation, which follows Heidegger's profound interpretation, reads

> And high from ether to the netherdepths below
> Following stable law, as one, from holy chaos drawn
> Being manifests itself anew
> The all-creator again.

"The essence (*Wesen*) of what is named (Being) is revealed in the
word," writes Heidegger. "By naming Being's essence, the word
separates the essential from the non-essential (or the absolute from the
contingent: *das Wesen vom Unwesen*). And because it separates
(*scheidet*), it decides (*entscheidet*) their struggle" (*Erläuterungen*, p.
57). The separation does occur; however, from the point of view of immediate Being, all the inessential is on the word's side, since it is the
word that separates the ineffable from the named and destroys it. The
spirit (Being) does not manifest itself (*erscheint*, p. 59) but feels itself
anew ("*fühlt sich neu*"); it acts once more as the goal of becoming,
but more than ever it appears in the form of struggle. The play on the
the words *scheiden-entscheiden* is a misprision, because it is by virtue
of the separation that it causes that the word prevents the struggle

reaching conclusion. It transfers the struggle within itself, which is why it is ever-renewed mediation. Heidegger seems on the verge of granting it: "Nature must preserve this opening where mortals and immortals can meet. The opening intercedes to create relations between all real beings. The real is constituted only through this intercession, and is, therefore, a mediated thing. What is thus mediated is nothing but the power of mediation. But the opening itself, which permits the existence of all relations of appurtenance and simultaneity, does not come from a mediation (an intercession: *Vermittlung*). The opening itself is the immediate. No mediate thing, be it god or man, can attain the immediate immediately." The necessity of mediation is clearly stated. This passage is a faithful commentary of one of Hölderlin's philosophical fragments, which Heidegger quotes ("Das Höchste," Hellingrath V 2, p. 276). He continues: "That which was ever present in all things gathers all isolated presents in a single presence and intercedes to allow each thing to manifest itself. Immediate all-presence is the power that intercedes for all that must be manifested through intercession, that is for all mediate things. But the immediate, it can never be mediated; rigorously speaking, the immediate is the intercession, that is the mediate character of the mediate (*Mittelbarkeit des Mittelbaren*), because it permits mediation in its being. 'Nature' is the mediation which mediates all things, it is the 'Law'" (*ibid.*, p. 60).

This passage, which is the turning point of the demonstration, is contradictory.[5] It states that mediation is possible thanks to the very immediate that is its agent; indeed, in this movement, it is the immediate that appears as the positive and moving element. It does not follow, though, that the immediate, as the sole agent of action, must be identifiable to mediation itself, which defines the multiple structure of the action. If the word mediation has any meaning, it is that what mediation ends up with is never identical to one of the two elements in presence to the exclusion of the other; it is a third entity that contains them both. To say that the immediate contains the possibility of the mediation of the mediate because it permits it in its being, is correct, but it is not correct to go on to the conclusion that the immediate *is*, therefore, itself the mediating intercession.

Heidegger's thesis can be considered as demonstrated if the follow-

5. This passage has its counterpart in the commentary to "Andenken," *op. cit.* p. 103.

ing identification is granted: the intercession, which is language, is also the immediate itself; the law, the language that differentiates, is the intercession, the immediate or Being itself: everything is united at the plane of Being. By saying the law, the poet says the sacred; it appears as chaos (*heiliges Chaos*) because of our forgetfulness of Being. However, nothing, in this poem or in any of Hölderlin's writings, authorizes such a conclusion. The poet may have varied in his way of naming the two dimensions of Being, which he has designed by several pairs of terms: nature and art; chaotic and organic; divine and human; heaven and earth; but at no point has he wavered with respect to his knowledge of its necessarily antithetical structure. The line

> Nach vestem Geseze, wie einst, aus heiligem Chaos gezeugt

contains a direct allusion to the creation as that which institutes, by means of the Word taken in a quasi-juridical sense (*Gesez, zeugen*), the distinction between the sacred (chaotic because it does not differentiate) and the mediate, which has come forth (*aus . . . gezeugt*) from the sacred, and, therefore, is no longer in it. When he states the law, the poet does not say Being, then, but, rather, the impossibility of naming anything but an order that, in its essence, is distinct from immediate Being.

Heidegger's proposed identification of language and the sacred fails, in any case, to account for the remainder of the hymn; he keeps on running into the very question he thought he had resolved, but which, for Hölderlin, must remain without answer: if the poet has seen Being immediately, how is he to put it into language? For the same reason, Heidegger is forced to suppress half a strophe (the myth of Semele's death and the birth of Dionysios offered in illustration by Hölderlin, in the manner of Pindar), and he does so without offering any justification, treating it as if it were a fugal countersubject arbitrarily interpolated. By contrast, if it is admitted that the hymn expressed the impossibility of the desired identification between language and the sacred, then its development and the difficulties of its conclusion become apparent. The awakening of nature, caused by the poet, is not the immediate manifestation of Being, but the awakening of history that resumes its progress. The poet cannot say Being, but he can awaken its indirect action, because he has advanced in the experience of his mediate relation to the sacred. He assumes the superhuman task of ensuring, through his own person, the mediation between Being and the consciousness of Being, its law founded in the Word. This supreme act is also a supreme sacrifice, for the restoration of Being to consciousness is effected at the cost of necessarily denying its ineffable all-presence and the no less necessary acquisition of the finite and alienated character of *Dasein*. The poet knows this necessity, but to those who have not reached this stage of consciousness, it appears in the guise of sorrow. By interiorizing the sorrow, the poet assumes it (the prose project of this hymn states: *mitleidend die Leiden des Lebens* [share-suffering the sorrows of life] Beissner, II. 2, p. 670) and through his total sacrifice, which goes beyond death, gives it the value of an example and a warning: *Dasz ich . . . das warnend ängstige Lied/den Unerfahren singe* [that I may sing the warning anguished song/to the inexperienced] (*ibid.*). It is impossible not to be reminded of the drama *Empedokles,* written shortly before this poem, which defines the theme that will be dominant in the national and historical poems.

Hölderlin begins to perceive, however, the traces of a new tension. The internal death (it is the "death" of a natural consciousness superseded by a superior consciousness, in Hegel's sense of the term "death" in the introduction to the *Phenomenology*) is at first thought of as human sorrow. However, the interior experience (*Erinnerung*) of this sorrow no longer suffices. In the later version of the poem instead of "suffering the sorrows of life" we have "suffering the sorrows of a God" and "the sorrow of a mightier one." Human suffering is transposed to a higher plane, which means that this sorrow transcends the mortal and, as Heidegger did not fail to see, that mediation is also, although in a form barely conceivable to us, law for divine being with respect to its essence, which is the sacred. For us, however, the sorrow of mediation lies in finitude, and we are able to conceive of it only under the form of death. As long as we remain within the human sphere, which is also the sphere of poetic word, we can think of divine sorrow only in the form of God's death. The poet's task is then to interiorize this death, to "think-of" God's death. But this is much too vast a matter for this particular hymn, whose critical orientation was historical rather than religious, and it remains only sketched out to become, later, the central theme of the Christian hymns. "Wie wenn am Feiertage . . ." is a transition piece marking the new period. The very possibility of the transition shows that there is no essential transformation in the structure of the act, and that, for Hölderlin, religious experience is also a mediation.[6]

In conclusion, this hymn suggests a conception of the poetic as an essentially open and free act, a pure intention, a mediated and conscious prayer that achieves self-consciousness in its failure; in short, a conception diametrically opposed to Heidegger's. As long as Hölderlin's poetic concentration lasts, this aspect of wager and challenge asserts itself, if nowhere else in the nearly insuperable formal and metrical tasks he imposes upon himself, which he resolves only to seek even more complex ones. In the works of his madness, the complexity gives way to a childlike simplicity, coupled, one suspects, with a terrifyingly lucid irony. Who will dare say whether this madness was a collapse of the mind or Hölderlin's way of experiencing totally, absolute skepticism? And would it not require even greater daring to give this madness an exemplary force and to cite, as Heidegger does, Hölderlin's last poem as the final promise of dwelling in the parousia of Being?

A commentary on Hölderlin's poetry must essentially be critical, if it wishes to be faithful to its author's definition of poetry, just as this poetry is critical of its own certitudes, their illusory character unveiled. Such a critique could achieve the status of the dialogue Heidegger wished so often for among thinkers, but denies to Hölderlin. This is the more regrettable because Heidegger's meditation upon the poetic is, in fact, a meditation on the ineffable, and as such it follows a way diametrically opposite to Hölderlin's. Yet the encounter between these two possible attitudes could constitute the center of a valid poetics.

Any exegetical method will ultimately have to come to grips with the same problem: how to elaborate a language capable of dealing with the tension between the ineffable and the mediate. The ineffable demands the direct adherence and the blind and violent passion with which Heidegger treats his texts. Mediation, on the other hand, implies a reflection that tends toward a critical language as systematic and rigorous as possible, but not overly eager to make claims of certitude that it can substantiate only in the long run. As a control

6. This transition is quite close to the dialectics of the unhappy consciousness, as well as to its counterpart in the second half of Hegel's *Phenomenology*, which leads to religion from the spiritual work of art, with some notable differences (such as the absence, in Hölderlin, of the stage of comedy at this point) having to do with the essence of the distinction between poetical thought and philosophical thought. The problem of the relation between Hegel and Hölderlin is inexhaustible.

discipline, equally scornful of arbitrariness and pseudo-science, philology represents a store of established knowledge; to seek to supersede it, and it is far from obvious that that is possible, is without merit. When it is negated by equally excessive mysticism or scientism, it gains in increased self-awareness and provokes the development of methodological movements within the discipline itself, which ultimately reinforce it.

Beda Alleman's study of the same questions we have covered represents a viewpoint exactly opposed to ours, since he argues for a parallelism and a homogeneity between Heidegger's and Hölderlin's thought. Alleman defends this perspective with an intelligence capable of introducing original dimensions in the interpretation of Hölderlin, and of raising fruitful questions concerning the philosophical fragments of the Homburg period, the commentaries to the translations, and the last hymns. And although the author follows Heidegger's thought, he never does so in slavish or automatic fashion, but rather evinces an intellectual passion that reveals a personal and independent partaking in the procedures of Heideggerian ontology.

Without entering into exegetical polemics that would need be very detailed, there is reason to oppose Beda Alleman's theses, not so much in their general conclusion as for their philosophical implications. The claimed homogeneity between Hölderlin and Heidegger rests upon the movement of "reversal" (*Kehre*) that occurs in both thoughts, and whose structure and intention are supposed to be analogous. Hölderlin's reversal manifests itself in a radical turnabout that takes him away from a philosophy of reconciliation toward a philosophy of necessary separation. Heidegger's reversal is the ambiguous movement of Being itself, although Alleman sees it rather, and quite correctly, in the historical perspective that derives from this movement: a backtracking to the far side of traditional metaphysics in order to go beyond this very metaphysics.

If it is true that there is a reversal in Heidegger, it is not the case that it occurs in the same way in Hölderlin. Alleman's case rests upon an unacceptable interpretation of Empedocles' death, which he sees in conventional terms as a return to undifferentiated *pan*—an absolute reconciliation. Quite the opposite, Empedocles' death is "death" in the Hegelian sense. The reversal is the reversal of consciousness in the *Phenomenology* (Introduction, § 14), the transition, through mediation, to a higher level of consciousness, which in Empedocles' case is historical consciousness. There is not to be found in Hölderlin a singular ontological reversal, but a lived philosophy of repeated reversal, that is nothing more than the notion of becoming. Since there is always reversal, there is never any effective reconciliation, not even in the early works. The reversal makes a last appearance in the form of the extraordinary effort to think it within the divine. The description of the last period as the mediation of the divine is therefore correct, but not the account of its genesis. As a result, the movement of *Kehre* is transformed into an absolute phenomenon and Hölderlin's situation within what is called Idealist philosophy is presented in a false light. By emphasizing the idea of reconciliation as a basic feature of all idealism, Alleman writes of Hölderlin and Hegel as if he were dealing with the young Schelling. The body of Hegel's works, in its most essential intention, gives the lie to such a description; the critique it has been subjected to, from Kierkegaard to our day, confirms this fact. If there ever was a philosophy of necessary separation, it is Hegel's; to assimilate the notion of Absolute Spirit with idealist reconciliation is to simplify all the way into misprision. Hegel's and Hölderlin's thoughts are remarkably parallel on this point; their difference lies deeper since it requires so dissimilar a tone and a vocation in spite of the relative similarity of thought. If one wanted to make use of this nearly miraculous happenstance to really shed light on the relations of philosophy and the poetic, it would be better not to start with the setting-up of non-existent differences when the analogies are so much more fruitful.

Hölderlin and Hegel's critique of Schelling's teachings applies equally to Beda Alleman who discovers ultimately the impossibility of preserving the immediate. But in this, he moves away from Heidegger's thought, whose most recent efforts have consisted in a return to a more originary unicity. From this perspective, it is regrettable that Alleman has written his study at this early a juncture when it appears that Heidegger's thought is about to undergo a reversal and does not lend itself to any definitive study. It seems quite clear that the notion of "dwelling" (*wohnen*), as it begins to emerge from the texts of the *Vorträge*, is totally opposite to the torn and struggling thought that Beda Alleman discovers in the last Hölderlin. It is true that Heidegger goes beyond this point and includes the work from the madness period and sees it as containing the promise of the desired peaceableness. Alleman stops short at the fragments immediately preceding the madness; these are texts rendered hallucinatory and obsessive by the mental torture they evoke, most certainly among the least peaceable. Actually, Beda Alleman's Hölderlin is much closer to Hegel than to Heidegger. Alleman has fallen victim to an error that Heidegger's influence may indeed induce: to preserve the historical perspective which requires that Hegel remain short of the superseding of Western metaphysics while Hölderlin is already on the far side of it, he has deformed the issue at hand which he refuses to seek in the very place where it is most explicitly formulated.

Appendix A
Review of Harold Bloom's
Anxiety of Influence

Like most good books, Harold Bloom's latest essay is by no means what it pretends to be. It calls itself, in subtitle, "a theory of poetry" and claims to be corrective in at least three ways: by debunking the humanistic view of literary influence as the productive integration of individual talent within tradition; by contributing, through a refinement of the techniques of reading, to a more rigorous practical criticism; and by enriching the taken-for-granted patterns on which academic literary history is based. Under the aegis of a general theory, this large order brings together ideological, textual, and historical criticism, in a combination that is no longer unusual in recent influential essays on literature. The "corrective" aspect is not new with Bloom, who has never been inhibited by the orthodoxies that dominate the field and has always shown himself willing to go his own way. He has been corrective in the best sense of the term, not out of a vain desire to assert his originality, still less because he wants to set up his own orthodoxy as a center of influence, but because he has always tended to be more attuned to the language of the poets than to the reigning academic trends. Even with regard to the critics to whom he is indebted—Northrop Frye, Meyer Abrams, Walter Jackson Bate—he has never been paralyzed by undue anxiety. He can be called, in his own terms, a "strong" critic and it does not come as a surprise to hear him assert his intention to change rather than just to expand the course of literary studies.

Yet, if read in the light of this intention, one will fail to do justice to this book. Corrective work supposes at least some emphasis on the techniques, the know-how, of criticism and assumes directives which, without necessarily being "scientific," still lay claim to didactic effectiveness. It raises expectations of exemplary displays of interpretive skill and historical erudition. But *The Anxiety of Influence,* in contrast to some of Bloom's earlier books, contains very few detailed readings, and Bloom's considerable erudition is not especially in evidence. There is an abundance of poetic quotation and, in the case of Milton, Blake, Stevens, Emerson, and others, implicit interpretation on an advanced level, but always embedded within the argument and without clarifying comment, as if the inferred meaning of difficult and ambiguous passages could be taken for granted. One senses Bloom's legitimate impatience with detail in a book that has much wider ambitions. Not even on the avowed major theme, on the question of influence or, more specifically, on the manner in which the new conception of influence is to be integrated within the reading process, is the essay very explicit. For the most part, the examples are *a priori* assertions of influence based on verbal and thematic echoes and stated as if they spoke for themselves. Bloom has no time to waste on technical refinements. In fact, he cares little for the corrective consequences of his argument; his interest in the methodological debates that agitate American and European criticism is peripheral.

The book is inspired by less specialized concerns. Despite the subtitle, it is not really a *theory* of poetry, or only to the extent that it conforms literally to the quotation from Wallace Stevens which serves as a motto: "that the theory / Of poetry is the theory of life, / As it is . . ." "Life as it is" is by no means a manageable notion and thus the motto points to the highly problematical nature of poetry. In this essay, literature is not the well-defined subject matter of a traditional discipline. It is a volatile term, in the midst of undergoing dramatic changes of content and of value. Within the context of Bloom's own work, the presuppositions about literature that supported his previous writings now begin to be put in question. As a result, the book may be somewhat hard to follow unless one is familiar with Bloom's earlier work. The precursor who worries him perhaps most of all is not Frye, or Bate, or contemporary rivals, but Bloom himself. In the case of a self-centered critic, such a self-confrontation would be trivial and self-indulgent, but because Bloom's concerns were always dominated by the un-centered otherness we call literature, the essay is anything but trivial or solipsistic. It is not every day, after all, that one has a chance to watch literature fight itself over its own claims.

In his previous books, these claims were almost extravagantly all-encompassing. They were rooted in the high evaluation of English romanticism, boldly and accurately interpreted as asserting the absolute power of the imagination to set the norms for aesthetic, ethical, and epistemological judgment. Though Bloom could sound turgid and overemphatic at times, the originality of his reading of English romanticism cannot be sufficiently stressed. He may well have felt that he had to raise his voice to be heard, for in his understanding of the catch-all term "imagination" he was philosophically shrewder and, in some respects, better informed than all the other historians and theoreticians of English romanticism, including Frye, Abrams, Wasserman, and others. Ever since his book on Shelley, Bloom has always implicitly understood that, all appearances to the contrary, the romantic imagination is *not* to be understood in dialectical interplay with the presumably antithetical category of "nature." This inside-outside, subject-object dichotomy has driven a fatal wedge between the accepted interpretation of the romantic poets and their actual statement, a statement that is certainly difficult and ambiguous, but not in the manner in which it is usually rendered. Increased misgivings about the validity of this model led to a shift in valorization: whereas romanticism often used to be described as a cult of nature, or as a reconciliation between mind and nature, the positive emphasis on nature (and on the kind of poetic diction that is assumed to reflect this emphasis), was reversed and replaced by its opposite. Terms such as "interiorization," "mind," "consciousness," and "self," gained currency as the worthy counterpart of "nature." Geoffrey Hartman's important essay on the *Via naturaliter negativa,* the core of his book on Wordsworth, is a fine example of this reversal, but it also shows clearly that, as long as the polar structure is not itself questioned, a reversal of valorization is in

fact immaterial. The story of the reversals, however intricate, complicated, or suspenseful it might be, is bound to end up in the reconciliation of opposites, in the effacement of differences that were only
the superficial manifestations of a deeper identity.

Bloom has contributed his share to this necessary first step, as when
he tells us, in an essay dating from 1968, that "the poems of symbolic
voyaging that move in a continuous tradition from Shelley's *Alastor*
to Yeats's *The Wanderings of Oisin,* tend to see the context of nature
as a trap for the mature imagination" and adds, in some despair at
the blindness of his fellow critics: "This point requires much laboring, as the influence of older views of Romanticism is very hard to
slough off" (*The Ringers in the Tower,* Chicago: University of Chicago
Press, 1971, p. 20). But, unlike others, Bloom does not stop at this stage.
Beyond the mind-nature dialectic, he gropes for a description of what
he still has to call the romantic imagination, but now sees as an
autonomous power that develops according to its own laws into areas
where the category of nature no longer operates, whether positively
or negatively. It is extremely difficult to describe this power, for the
impact of the tradition on post-romantic poetry and criticism is so over-
riding that it has once and for all determined the rhetoric and the terminology available to us, thus making it necessary to assert the inadequacy of a conceptual language by means of the very langauge that
is being rejected.

In this difficult philosophical predicament, Bloom's perhaps unconscious strategy has been to reach out for a new definition of the
imagination by means of near-extravagant overstatement. Since the
imagination is unimaginable, it can only be stated by hyperbole. Poetry,
the product of this hyperbolic imagination, can do anything. It reaches
well beyond Shelley's claim, in the *Defense,* that "the greatest instrument of moral good is the imagination." There is no longer anything
natural about its supernaturalism: "The program of Romanticism, and
not just in Blake, demands something more than a natural man to carry
it through. Enlarged and more numerous senses are necessary, an enormous virtue of Romantic poetry clearly being that it not only demands
such expansion but begins to make it possible, or at least attempts
to so do" (*ibid.* p. 21). "A poet shall leave his Great Original . . . and
nature—according to the precepts of Poetic Genius—and cleave to his
Muse or Imagination; then are the generous and solitary halves united."

This union is no synthesis but the ultimate triumph of poetry over the discontinuity of existence: "The . . . dream (of the strong poet) is not merely a phantasmagoria of endless gratification, but is the greatest of all human illusions, the vision of immortality" (*The Anxiety of Influence,* p. 9). "Wordsworth's Tharmas, besides being the shepherd image of human divinity, is present in the poem himself as a desperate need for continuity in the self, a desperation that at its worst sacrifices the living moment, but at its best produces a saving urgency that protects the imagination from the strong enchantments of nature" (*The Ringers in the Tower,* p. 27).

One sees how the very acumen of Bloom's insight, which sets him apart and above other interpreters of English romanticism, forces him into making untenable claims for poetry. These claims are still being stated in the very language they attempt to supersede: a naturalistic language of desire, possession, and power. Throughout the various essays in *The Ringers in the Tower,* the hyperbolic claim is unwaveringly sustained. One the other hand, the failure of the stance is also being stated, although in terms that are historical rather than theoretical. Romanticism begins to split into a new, temporal polarity that distinguishes between early and late romanticism. Bloom historicizes the imagination into a tension between its early, original manifestations and its later, derivative ones. Thus the failure to name the imagination for what it is becomes a temporal predicament in which the latecomer is forever overshadowed by his precursor. A theory of influence replaces a still unformulated theory of the imagination. The phrase "anxiety of influence," which appears tangentially in the essays of *The Ringers in the Tower* becomes the title of the subsequent book.

In some respects this is a step backward. Just when we were about to free poetic language from the constraints of natural reference, we return to a scheme which, for all its generality, is still clearly a relapse into a psychological naturalism. Bloom refines the concept of influence well beyond any naively empirical event: he makes it clear, for example, that it has nothing to do with source studies, that the influence can emanate from texts a poet has never read or, even more surrealistically, that it can be chronologically reversed, with the late poet "influencing," by retrospective anticipation, the early one. Nevertheless, he becomes more dependent than before on a pathos which is more literal than hyperbolic. From a relationship between words and things, or words and words, we return to a relationship between subjects. Hence the agonistic language of anxiety, power, rivalry, and bad faith. The regression can be traced in various ways. It is apparent, for example, in the way Freud is used in the earlier as compared to the later essay. Bloom, who at that time seems to have held a rather conventional view of Freud as a rationalistic humanist, respectfully dismisses him in *The Ringers in the Tower*, as the prisoner of a reality principle the romantics had left behind. In *The Anxiety of Influence* Bloom's reading of Freud has gained in complexity, yet he is still, in principle, discarded as "not severe enough," his wisdom outranked by "the wisdom of the strong poets" (p. 9). Still, the argument is stated in oedipal terms and the story of influence told in the naturalistic language of desire. Frustrated by the difficulty of stating his insight into the nonreferential quality of the imagination, Bloom has become the subject of his own desire for clarification. His theoretical concerns are now displaced into a symbolic narrative recentered in a subject. But no theory of poetry is possible without a truly epistemological moment when the literary text is considered from the perspective of its truth or falsehood rather than from a love-hate point of view. The presence of such a moment offers no guarantee of truth but it serves to alert our understanding to distortions brought about by desire. It may reveal in their stead patterns of error that are perhaps more disturbing, but rooted in language rather than in the self.

The return of psychologism dramatically changes the value attributed to literature. From being able to do anything, it becomes an absurd, lowly comical gesture, since no poet can conquer a Muse that has not already betrayed him with his precursor. Like all valorizations based on unreflected affectivity, the mood and the meaning can be reversed at will. By founding literature in a literal, genetic priority Bloom becomes the prisoner of a linear scheme that engenders a highly familiar set of historical fallacies. The best known is that of a prelapsarian age that preceded the age of anxiety, a "great age before the Flood" (p. 122) predating the time when "the shadow fell" (p. 77). Romanticism becomes once more the solipsism of an alienated self, an "enormous curtailment" which we "can recognize as the diminished thing it is" (p. 122). It would take only one small step, without having to change the premise, to make the same statement in a jovial rather than a saturnine mood, and to replace the anxiety by a serene, pre-Johnsonian theory of decorous imitation.

Or rather, it would do so if one took Bloom at his word and considered his theory of influence as the central statement it appears to be. Since Bloom is a forceful and convincing writer, this is bound to happen and to produce critical protest as well as laudatory imitation, both equally beside the point. Behind the arbitrariness of the psychological plot, one feels that the book deals with something else, that it is an oblique version of something much closer to literary problems, much closer to this poetic "imagination" than Bloom tried in vain to define in a vaguely existential terminology. In his description of influence as a cunning, malicious distortion of tradition Bloom gives a displaced version of a very genuine problem. It begins to shine through, for example, in the cavalier way in which the trust in the authority of the literary statement is undermined. Within the avowed thesis of the book, this attitude of suspicion is contradictory. It is not the weakness of the present, but the strength attributed to the past that is mystifying. The description of the powerful ancestors, especially Milton, is ambivalent, and literature remains quartered between shortcoming and excess. The true difference between this essay and Bloom's previous books is that whereas the strength remains a mere assertion without evidence to make it convincing, the weakness is, for the first time, systematically documented. We can forget about the temporal scheme and about the pathos of the oedipal son; underneath, the book deals with the difficulty or, rather, the impossibility of reading and, by inference, with the indeterminacy of literary meaning. If we are willing to set aside the trappings of psychology, Bloom's essay has much to say on the encounter between latecomer and precursor as a displaced version of the paradigmatic encounter between reader and text.

The first insight provided by Bloom is that the encounter *must* take place and that it takes precedence over any other events, biographical or historical, in the poet's experience. This means that texts originate in contact with other texts rather than in contact with the events or the agents of life (unless, of course, these agents or events are themselves treated as texts). To say that literature is based on influence is to say that it is intratextual. And intratextual relationships necessarily contain a moment that is interpretive. In order to be literally productive the encounter implies a reading, however sketchy and superficial this reading may be (though it can, of course, also be very thorough). The main insight of *The Anxiety of Influence* is the categorical assertion that this reading be a misreading or, as Bloom calls it, a "misprision."

The intentional schemes by means of which Bloom dramatizes the "causes" of the misreading can be ignored; one should focus instead on the structural pattern of the misprisions. Such a reading doesn't go entirely against the grain of Bloom's text. He has not, after all, organized his book as an epic battle, but as a taxonomy of recurrent patterns of error in the act of reading; and he attracts attention to the categorical, Aristotelian aspect of his exposition by means of an eye-catching, flamboyant terminology. The actual description of the six categories or "revisionary ratios" (clinamen, tessera, kenosis, daemonization, askesis, and apophrades) is again heavily emotional, to the point that it is not easy to distinguish between the various structures that are described. But underneath all the drama stands a pretty tight linguistic model that could be described in a very different tone and terminology.

The substantial emphasis, in the description of the six ratios, falls on temporal priority: a polarity of strength and weakness (Bloom consistently speaks of "strong" and "weak" poets) is correlated with a temporal polarity that pits early against late. The effort of the late poet's revisionary reading is to achieve a reversal in which lateness will become associated with strength instead of with weakness. This aim is achieved by means of a play of substitutions. "We can redirect our needs by substitution or sublimation" says Bloom (p. 9); the reference is to Wordsworth, but the sentence summarizes the underlying structure that all the revisionary ratios have in common. If the substantial emphasis is temporal, the structural stress entirely falls on substitution as a key concept. And from the moment we begin to deal with substitutive systems, we are governed by linguistic rather than by natural or psychological models: one can always substitute one word for another but one cannot, by a mere act of the will, substitute night for day or bliss for gloom. However, the very ease with which the linguistic substitution, or trope, can be carried out hides the fact that it is epistemologically unreliable. It remains something of a mystery how rhetorical figures have been so minutely described and classified over the centuries with relatively little attention paid to their mischievous powers over the truth and falsehood of statements. Bloom truly rejoins Freud and Nietzsche, as well as the poets themselves, in his categorical assertion that the substitution is always, by necessity, a falsification, if only because it assumes that the meaning from which it deviates could itself be considered to be definite and authoritative.

It would be a somewhat trivial exercise to transpose Bloom's six ratios back to the paradigmatic rhetorical structures in which they are rooted. *Clinamen* is the most general description of the trope as misreading; the dramatic narrative, derived from Satan's Fall in *Paradise Lost,* symbolizes the universality of the substitutive pattern. The five other ratios describe more specific types of rhetorical substitution: *tessera* defines the potentially misleading totalization from part to whole of synecdoche; *apophrades* rightly figures in the climactic last place as the sixth ratio, because it destroys the principle on which the system itself is patterned: it substitutes early for late in a metaleptic reversal. *Askesis* returns to the set of problems that were prominent in the earlier essay "The Internalization of Quest Romance," the key text in the previous book on the romantic tradition. This is not surprising, since the substitutive play on an inside-outside polarity that is characteristic of askesis also describes the type of metaphor that figures prominently in romantic diction. *Daemonization* is particularly interesting for this is the very place where Bloom fights the shadow of his former self. The substitution here uses another set of spatial antinomies: not inside and outside as in askesis (metaphor) but high and low, as in hyperbole (sublimation); and hyperbole is precisely the rhetorical mode, the type of misreading, favored by Bloom in his own works. *Kenosis* is a more complex case, because it is the only class in which a figure is used to undo systematically the substantial claim implied in the use of another figure; it is the figure of a figure, in which the one de-constructs the universe produced by the other. As opposed to tessera, kenosis breaks up a totality into discontinuous fragments: it substitutes a contiguity (in temporal terms, a repetition) for an analogy or resemblance (in temporal terms, a genesis) and thus rediscovers, in its turn, the familiar metaphor-metonymy opposition, though with an epistemological twist that was lacking in Jakobson's version.

There would be ample opportunity to expand and to refine on each of these descriptions, for Bloom's text contains a wealth of allusive material, both literary and philosophical, that invites endless discussion. One could sum up the results by stating that one would generally find him to be wrong in precisely the way his own theory of error anticipates—the highest compliment one can pay to a theorist of misprision. I use proper restraint in refraining from showing how this is the case with regard to such choice examples as, for instance, Wordsworth and Nietzsche.

What is achieved by thus translating back from a subject-centered vocabulary of intent and desire to a more linguistic terminology? If we admit that the term "influence" is itself a metaphor that dramatizes a linguistic structure into a diachronic narrative, then it follows that Bloom's categories of misreading not only operate between authors, but also between the various texts of a single author or, within a given text, between the different parts, down to each particular chapter, paragraph, sentence, and, finally, down to the interplay between literal and figurative meaning within a single word or grammatical sign. Whether this form of semantic tension can still on this level be called "influence" is far from certain, though it remains a suggestive line of thought. A further implication is even more important. The passage through rhetoric reveals that the traditional scheme, still much in evidence in *The Anxiety of Influence,* according to which language is a tool manipulated by extralinguistic impulses rooted in a subject, can be dislodged by the equally reasonable alternative that the affective appeal of text could just as well be the result of a linguistic structure as its cause. By showing that such a reversal of the priority of meaning over sign is conceivable, the causal scheme is not simply reversed and meaning shown to be centered in a linguistic property instead of centered in a subject. The very scheme of things based on such terms as cause, effect, center, and meaning is put in question. By raising such a question, Bloom's book may be even more subversive with regard to tradition than it claims to be.

I do not wish to suggest that Bloom's criticism would benefit from the use of a linguistic rather than a psychological vocabulary. This would be a great loss all around. The rhetorical terminology de-constructs thematic modes of discourse but it has no assertive power of its own. This assertive power (if it can still be called that) resides in the interplay between the various modes of error that constitute a literary text. Similarly, the main interest of *The Anxiety of Influence* is not the literal theory of influence it contains but the structural interplay between the six types of misreading, the six "intricate evasions" that govern the relationships between texts. The thread of his particular discourse has taken Bloom far along in his own labyrinth. It will probably turn out that, in his understanding of the patterns of misreading, as in his understanding of romanticism, Harold Bloom has been ahead of everybody else all along.

Appendix B

Literature and Language:
A Commentary

Whenever questions about the language *of* literature, about the distinctiveness of literary language, are being asked, some predictable difficulties occur. It is quite possible to describe a certain type of literary language with more than adequate precision, as Cyril Birch does in his article on Chinese literature or, to some extent, Isaac Rabinowitz in his study on the language of the Old Testament—although, in the latter case, ominous questions are very close to making their appearance over the horizon of the text. But this works only as long as one describes the species without getting too close to the genus: taking for granted there is such a thing as "literary language," one can describe a particular subset of the class, but as soon as one confronts the question of defining the specificity of literary language as such, complications arise. The more theoretical among the studies on literature and language published in this and in recent issues of *New Literary History* should allow us to speculate on the systematization of this difficulty.

The juxtaposition of these essays[1] reveals a recurrent narrative pattern that may well be more than a mere result of chance or a commonplace of academic exposition: all of the essays suggest that the study of literary language could progress if only we could rid ourselves of misconceptions that have hampered it persistently in the past. The tone is one of impatience with recurrent errors of definition: "It is evident," writes Seymour Chatman, "that stylistics, like linguistics before it, must rid itself of normative preoccupations *if it is ever to get around* to the task of describing its object"[2] (my italics). Michael Riffaterre can see no other obstacle to the natural cooperation between literary history and textual analysis (a cooperation which, he says, "has remained largely unexplored") than the reluctance of the historians to realize that "texts are made up of words, not things or ideas."[3] Stanley Fish is eager to get under way with a method of which he claims that "it works,"[4] but he first has to clear the decks of a number of obstacles such as Wimsatt, Beardsley, Richards, Empson, and, as it happens, Riffaterre. The stance is dramatized most intensely in the prose of George Steiner. He has few doubts about the specificity of literary language; no dialectical complexities mar his assertion that in reading literature "we are implicated in a matrix of inexhaustible specificity."[5] If he seems perhaps slightly less sanguine than the others about the prospects of a science of literature, this is only because the literary work stands glorified in a semidivine status of inaccessible perfection. Provided only we can get rid of universalist aberrations that pretend to see connections between literary and ordinary language, linguists, critics, and social scientists can unite in a joint effort that may elevate us towards the exalted level of the world's literary masterpieces.

1. The commentary is based on most of the articles published in *New Literary History* 4, no. 1 (1972) and on the following earlier essays: Michael Riffaterre, "The Stylistic Approach to Literary History"; Stanley Fish, "Literature in the Reader: Affective Stylistics" (both in *NLH*, 2 [1970]); Seymour Chatman, "On Defining 'Form'" (*NLH*, 2 [1971]). The articles in this issue (*The Language of Literature*) are so diverse that no inclusive commentary could possibly do them justice. I have preferred therefore to narrow down the choice of illustrative material to the smallest number of articles possible, at the risk of leaving out outstanding contributions. Their inclusion would have extended the commentary beyond reasonable proportions.
2. Chatman, p. 220.
3. Riffaterre, p. 39.
4. Fish, p. 161.
5. George Steiner, "Whorf, Chomsky and the Student of Literature," *NLH* 4 (1972), pp. 15-34.

The same basic story underlies all of these essays. None of the authors speak as if they merely had to perform a straightforward, unhampered task of description or understanding. All have to set out against an erroneous conception of literature that stands in their way. This is certainly not because they happen to be a particularly aggressive or self-satisfied group of people: all are eminently fair and respectful of their predecessors. It seems to be in the nature of the question that it has to be asked *against* previous answers that first have to be shown to be aberrant before the proper definition of literary language can be stated.

The nature of this obstacle varies to the point of diametrical opposition, but in a manner that defies easy systematization. For Riffaterre (at least in this article), literature is static and monumental: "the text . . . is unchanging"[6]; "the more of a monument it is . . . the more literary"[7]; and it is the task of stylistics to rescue this monumentality from the shifting changes of successive interpretations. But for Stanley Fish, there can be no greater aberration than thus to reduce a text to the monumental objectivity of a static entity: "The objectivity of the text," he writes, "is an illusion, and moreover, a dangerous illusion, because it is so physically convincing. The illusion is one of self-sufficiency and completeness. . . ."[8] His entire effort is directed towards substituting the dynamics of reading, conceived as a successive act in time, to the immobilism of mere description.[9] For Steiner, the major obstacle to literary studies stems from whatever puts into question the ineffable specificity of a work that is totally self-sufficient and self-identical in the radical difference that separates it from anything that is not itself; whereas Seymour Chatman and Josephine Miles are looking instead for "classes of elements which under their surface differences can provide patterns of sustaining likeness."[10] The question of the linguistic specificity of literature is equally divided: universalists like Riffaterre insist on the uniqueness of literature as opposed to or-

6. Riffaterre, p. 39.
7. *Ibid.*, p. 47.
8. Fish, p. 140.
9. In his discussion of Riffaterre, Stanley Fish's characterization of the latter's dynamics of reading (see Fish, pp. 156-57), based on "Criteria for Style Analysis" (*Word*, 15 [1959]), is actually a great deal subtler than the categorical assertion of monumentality in Riffaterre's article published in the same issue of *NLH*.
10. Josephine Miles, "Forest and Trees," *NLH* 4 (1972): 35-45.

dinary language in hierarchical terms to which a particularist like Steiner could subscribe, whereas Miles and Chatman tend to erase the borderlines between literature and ordinary speech, a position also vigorously defended by Fish (against Riffaterre) who, on the other hand, has little sympathy for the intrinsic formalism of stylistic or structuralist methods. The spatial metaphor of intrinsic/extrinsic (inside/outside) literary methods is not more consistent: Riffaterre's traditional historical philologism, based on erudition and factual information, is extrinsic, whereas for Fish, the act of reading is an intratextual event between two successive moments in the temporal constitution of an understanding. Steiner's organic totalizations allow for no inconsistencies or intrusions coming from the outside—he lines up with Fish on this point— whereas Chatman's insistence on content and on message gives his work an undeniably extrinsic flavor. Isolating only these eight relatively simple (and, of course, not unrelated) polarities—static/dynamic, universal/particular, privileged/ordinary, inside/outside—we find no consistency: the polarities are distributed in what seems to be a random pattern, suggesting that none of these antithetical pairs possess a decisive authority. The actual content of the antinomies seems to be less important than the formal necessity of their existence. The texts draw their energy from tensions that can be substituted almost at will, but they could not come into being without an opposite against which they offer their own definitions and alternatives. They imply a fundamental misreading of literature which is always, systematically, a misreading performed by others.[11]

If one accepts this complication as a purely formal pattern, without going into the specific merits and demerits of each individual position, it would follow that the specificity of literary language resides in the possibility of misreading and misinterpretation. We realize this all the more strongly when passing from the critical parts of the articles—with which it is, in general, quite easy to agree—to the parts in which the authors propose their own corrected readings. As soon as this happens, we feel inclined to find them in error together with the writers they have been censoring. One experiences little difficulty following Fish in his criticism of Richards, Riffaterre in his assault on literal-minded historians, Chatman in his strictures on Barthes, or

11. Lest this be misconstrued as a criticism, let me hasten to point out that the same observation also applies to this brief commentary.

Steiner in his admonitions to Chomsky. But as soon as they offer their own readings, our own critical sense reawakens. The *critiqués* deserve the treatment they get at the hands of the *critiquants,* but the latter turn at once into *critiqués* in their own right without in the least redeeming their original targets. We are entirely willing to accept what has by now grown into a double pattern of juxtaposed aberration.

When Riffaterre, for example (singled out for no other reason than that the example he uses happens to be in a field with which I am familiar), in his reading of Baudelaire's poem "Bohémiens en voyage,"[12] denies any relevance to the Callot etchings which served as a model for the poem, the temptation to disagree with him is irresistible. How can he claim that the Callot work is merely an "exercise in the picturesque" when, for Baudelaire, Callot, the inspirer of E. T. A. Hoffmann, rates with Goya, Breughel, Constantin Guys, and other revered names as a representative of the highest "philosophical art" and a practitioner of an aesthetics of absolute irony?[13] How can he fail to see the impact that Callot's background-presence in the poem is bound to have on the concluding lines, which, according to Riffaterre, the reader is "free to interpret as Death or cosmic mystery"?[14] How can he find an opposition between Callot and the Quest theme, when it is Callot himself who introduced the prophetic, future-oriented dimension from the start?[15] How can he so peremptorily separate the source's genetic from its allusive function in a case when the transposition from one medium (painting) into another (poetry), always a crucial event in Baudelaire, makes the juxtaposition particularly delicate and complex? My point is not to disagree with Michael Riffaterre on the exegesis of a specific Baudelaire text; I merely want to demonstrate how his remarks, by their very pertinence, allow for the immediate eclosion of a critical counterdiscourse which (if I had been uncautious enough

12. Riffaterre, pp. 41-42.
13. The main references to Callot in Baudelaire are in the well-known essays "De L'essence du rire" and "L'art philosophique."
14. Riffaterre, p. 42. The last lines of the poem speak of ". . . ces voyageurs, pour lesquels est ouvert/ L'empire familier des ténèbres futures."
15. Interestingly enough in two lines of verse inscribed on the etching: "Ces pauvres gueux pleins de bonadventures / Ne portent rien que des choses futures." Obviously, Callot does not account for all the details in the poem, which combines various allusive strands. But the semantic impact of these allusive configurations is distorted if Callot is excluded from consideration. The Callot source of the poem was pointed out as early as 1919 by Antoine Adam.

to develop it fully) it would not be difficult to subject, in its turn, to a similar inquisition, to another turn of the critical screw.[16]

Similar observations could be made about each of the essays. They leave us confronted with a self-defeating situation. How are literary studies ever to get started when every proposed method seems based on a misreading and a misconceived preconception about the nature of literary language? The next step, obviously, will have to reflect on the nature and status of these misreadings. But, on this point, our authors are curiously uninformative: they argue vigorously and effectively against the specific substantial issue they reject, but have little to say about the reasons that have so persistently misled the *other* critics. Why have historians been, for centuries, so dull-witted that they failed to realize the obvious fact that poems are made of words? Why do writers on literature keep so stubbornly returning to irrelevant value judgments? Riffaterre and Chatman have nothing to tell us on this point. It seems obvious to them that once the proper methodological assumptions have been made, a correct reading, or a controlled set of readings, will ensue. The difficulty of reading, for nearly all of these authors (with the possible exception of Stanley Fish), when it is mentioned at all, exists at most as a contingent, never as a constitutive obstacle to literary understanding.

In this particular respect, the articles are by no means atypical of literary studies as they are practiced today. The systematic avoidance of the problem of reading, of the interpretive or hermeneutic moment, is a general symptom shared by all methods of literary analysis, whether they be structural or thematic, formalist or referential, American or European, apolitical or socially committed. It is as if an organized conspiracy made it anathema to raise the question, perhaps because the vested interests in literary studies as a respectable intellectual discipline are at stake or perhaps for more ominous reasons. As for the critics who are interested in the theory of interpretation, their main task seems to be to reassure at all costs their more pragmatically or more for-

---

16. This countercriticism undermines the methodological foundations of the reading it attacks. We can hardly believe in Riffaterre's assertion that the literary work consists of an "immutable code" bound to elicit a definite response in the reader if we can legitimately put in question all the readings he suggests and if he himself, when confronted with a crucial line in which the two readings differ literally as life differs from death, is forced to leave the reader "free to interpret" as he pleases.

malistically oriented colleagues about the self-evident possibility of achieving correct readings.

This is hardly the place to offer alternatives or to speculate on the origin of difficulties that are implicitly recognized but not openly stated in these articles. I would instead like to follow up the argument of the papers that come closest to entering into the orbit of the question that is being systematically avoided. There is some interest in isolating the moment when the writers recoil before the evidence they have produced. What would happen beyond this moment, if they had chosen to continue their course, is another story, with a scenario that would have to differ somewhat from the recurrent plot shared by all of them. It would at any rate have to include as a visible articulation this moment of recoil that now unwittingly gets written into some of the essays.

I can take space for two examples only. Starting out from German philosophical traditions and from Slavic studies of linguistic form, Henryk Markiewicz[17] offers a succinct but precise set of properties whose existence is a necessary condition for "literariness." These properties are (1) fictionality (the possible absence, in literary discourse, of an empirical referent), (2) figurality (the presence of representational or nonrepresentational tropes), and (3) what Markiewicz, with reference to Jakobson, calls "superimposed ordering," i.e., principles of linguistic choice guided by considerations that are not purely referential, as when a word is preferred to a synonym for phonetic rather than semantic reasons. The obvious advantage of this terminology over traditionally expressive or aesthetic characterizations of literature resides in a precision that gives at least an illusion of objectivity, of responsible reference to identifiable linguistic facts. But is this really the case? Markiewicz's primarily historical argument tries to show that the presence of a single one of these "properties" suffices to confer a degree of literariness on any discourse and that it is not necessary to have all three of them simultaneously present; he is clearly treating his three categories as distinct properties of language, as distinct from each other as red is distinct from green, or acidity from sweetness. But if we translate the three terms back into the rhetorical modes of which they are the conceptualization, a less clear-cut model is revealed. Fictionality, as discussed by Markiewicz, is clearly another term for mimesis; figurality is directly, and with a helpful reference to Hegel, identified as metaphor.

17. Henryk Markiewicz, "The Limits of Literature," *NLH* 4 (1972): 5-14.

As for "superimposed ordering," the mention of Jakobson labels it as paranomasis, the pairing or combining of words on a phonetic basis (as in rhyme, assonance, or alliteration). Mimesis, metaphor, and paranomasis all are, of course, rhetorical figures; when Markiewicz therefore, near the end of his essay, asks whether "it is indeed possible to find a common denominator for the three characterizations of 'literariness' . . . ," then a first and obvious answer to this question would be that rhetoric considered as a property of language, or "rhetoricity," constitutes this common denominator. But can rhetoricity be called a definite property that, in Markiewicz's words, would "justify . . . an objective relationship between words described as literary, and indirectly justify also a relative unity of the subject matter of literary studies"? As anyone who has ever consulted a treatise of rhetoric will testify, it is notoriously difficult, logically as well as historically, to keep the various tropes and figures rigorously apart, to establish precisely when catachresis becomes metaphor and when metaphor turns into metonymy; to quote an apt water-metaphor to which an expert in the field has to resort precisely in his discussion of metaphor: "the transition (of one figure to another, in this case, from metaphor to metonymy) is fluid."[18] And the three figures picked by Markiewicz are particularly redoubtable: paranomasis can be considered as one special, sound-based case of metaphor in which the phonic resemblance at least intimates the possibility of a substitution on the level of substance. And metaphor can be considered as an imitation (which is how Markiewicz, perhaps mistakenly, understands mimesis) in which the tenor imitates the vehicle or, to use another terminology, the literal meaning imitates the figural meaning on the basis of a common resemblance to a third term of comparison. One could and should pursue this discussion at length, but enough has perhaps been said to suggest that the three terms overlap to such an extent that it makes little sense to speak of any of them being present at the exclusion of the other. More important still, each of the terms is highly ambiguous in its own right. Each has the possibility of misreading built into its own constitution; they can indeed be said to be the conceptual denomination of this possibility. To start with imitation, Markiewicz denies that

18. Heinrich Lausberg "Der Übergang von der Metonymis zur Metapher ist fliessend . . . ," *Handbuch der literarischen Rhetorik* (Munich, 1960), § 571, p. 295.

fictionality can be called a universal characteristic of literature by invoking the case of memoirs and letters as opposed to novels: are we to infer from this that everything stated in memoirs or in letters is true and that novels are made up exclusively of lies? Mimesis can be said to imply a referential verification as well as to dodge it; the only thing that can be stated with certainty is that it allows for the confusion between the two choices. As for metaphor, the mischief wrecked by this wiliest of Pandora's boxes defies the challenge of trying to evoke it in a few words; the one example mentioned by Markiewicz, Hegel's distinction between *"eigentliche Verbildlichung"* and *"uneigentliche Verbildlichung"* (literal and figural representation) leads directly into the infinitely deceiving epistemology of representation and into the innumerable ways in which it is possible to confuse images and things. The dangerously seductive powers of paranomasis are easier to convey. We only have to remind ourselves that Jakobson based his discussion of the figure on the phonetic analysis of the slogan "I like Ike"; euphony is probably the most insidious of all sources of error. By merely following up Markiewicz's own categories, we reach the conclusion that the determining characteristic of literary language is indeed figurality, in the somewhat wider sense of rhetoricity, but that, far from constituting an objective basis for literary study, rhetoric implies the persistent threat of misreading. Whether it also implies the impossibility of truthful reading could hardly be decided in the space of a few sentences. Markiewicz's brief but suggestive essay provides categories and a terminology by means of which this investigation could proceed, but concludes in the illusion of a false precision at the very moment when it has in fact revealed the inevitability of confusion.

Of all the essays considered in this commentary, the one closest to treating reading explicitly as a problem is Stanley Fish's "Literature in the Reader: Affective Stylistics." For Fish, the utterance of meaning cannot be separated from the process by means of which this meaning is reached or, stated more radically, meaning can only be the narrative of this temporal process and cannot be reduced to statement. "An observation about the [literary] sentence as an utterance—its refusal to yield a declarative statement—has been transformed into an account of its experience (not being able to get a fact out of it). It is no longer an object, a thing-in-itself, but an *event*, something that *happens* to, and with the participation of, the reader. And it is this event, this happening . . . that is, I would argue, the *meaning* of the sentence."[19] The merits of the position are clearly in evidence in the examples discussed in the article: we are freed at last from the tedious business of paraphrase and from the less tedious but mystified practice of thematic reconstruction and rearrangement. What we are offered instead is certainly much closer to the actual event of literary understanding.

The question must arise, however, what the truth value of such a narrative can be and whether one can afford to be as unworried about this as Fish seems to be. His reading-stories unquestionably contain many episodes of aberration and deceit: "what the sentence does is give the reader something and then take it away, drawing him on with the unredeemed promise of its return"; "the two negatives combine . . . to prevent the reader from making the simple (declarative) sense which would be the goal of a logical analysis"; "that construction . . . pressures the reader to perform exactly those mental operations whose propriety the statement of the sentence—what it is saying—is challenging,"[20] etc. The relationship between author and reader is a highly dramatic one, but it tells a rather sordid story in which the reader is manipulated and exploited by a callous author who, in the course of a few random quotations, appears as an evil counselor, a temptor who fails to deliver the goods, and, above all, as a falsifier of truth.

The reason why this sorry situation is allowed to develop is not because the category of meaning has been undermined but because it has been displaced: the author himself, rather than the referent of the statement, now seems to be the sole depository of meaning. He can play with the reader as a cat plays with a mouse because, being in full control of his own meaning, he can conceal and reveal it at his discretion. We are told, for example, that Pater's sentence "deliberately frustrates the reader's natural desire to organize the particulars it offers" and the dynamics of reading are persistently referred to as a "strategy" or as an "effect."[21] The same self-confidence is present in the felicitous formulation of Fish's own critical procedure. The reading-stories he

19. Fish, p. 125.
20. *Ibid.*, pp. 125, 126, 133.
21. ". . . what makes problematical sense as a statement makes perfect sense as a strategy, as an action made upon a reader" (Fish, p. 124); "In my account of reading . . . the temporary adoption of these inappropriate strategies is itself a response to the strategy of an author: and the resulting mistakes are part of the experience provided by that author's language and therefore part of the meaning" (p. 144), etc.

tells are true because they are *given* to us by an author in full control of his language. By tracing back the meandering thread of the writer's strategies, we recover the totality of the literary experience which was only temporarily hidden from us. "Analysis in terms of doings and happenings is . . . truly objective because it recognizes the fluidity, 'the movingness,' of the meaning experience and because it directs us to where the action is—the active and activating consciousness of the reader." Reading is no real problem because it coincides with the successive unfolding of its own process. It traces the trajectory of its own truth; "the developing responses of the reader to the words as they succeed one another on the page" or "the temporal left to right reception of the verbal string." Like Riffaterre, Fish can promise that, by following this "verbal string" into the labyrinth of the text, "I am able to chart and project *the* developing response" (Fish's own italics). The critic shares the same fundamental self-assurance with the author— who perhaps borrowed it from him in the first place.

I may have overstated Fish's assurance, for his text has its share of reservations and ambivalences with regard to its own doctrine. It is, for example, never clear whether the concealment and complication of meaning emanates from the author, considered as a conscious subject, or from the (his?) text. Fish carefully states that Pater's "*sentence* deliberately frustrates . . ." or that errors are forced upon the reader by the "author's *language*" (my italics), which is presumably not quite the same as Pater or the author doing these things themselves. On the other hand, his commitment to the dramatics of action compels him to make these ambivalent subjects (centaurs that are half-man, half-text) into the grammatical subjects of transitive verbs that perform highly anthropomorphic gestures. It is impossible to speak of a text as performing strategically without projecting into it the metaphor of an intentional consciousness or subject. No trace in Fish's text suggests that the possibility of such an unwarranted metaphorization is ever being considered, let alone dominated. Yet it dominates his own discourse throughout, as is apparent, among other things, from his choice of examples.

The first two examples, which set the tone,[22] deal with lines from Thomas Browne and Milton centered on Judas and on Satan, and each

22. The examples are amplified rather than contradicted by the other examples from Pater and Plato.

of these lines, as Fish convincingly demonstrates, casts doubt on whether the evildoers perceived the gravity of their own plight. There is only one other character in the essay whose behavior bears a close resemblance to these Satanic models: if the authors are indeed as deliberate and responsible as Fish makes them out to be, they can be charged with the gravest sins in Hell, including the betrayal of their benefactors, the readers. But the passages that have been selected assert the impossibility of passing judgment because the evidence of guilt, either by Scriptural authority or by the inner voice of conscience, cannot be ascertained. Within the inner logic of Fish's argument, the examples thus reveal the utter bewilderment of the author before his own text: did he, or did he not know what he was saying? No one can tell, neither reader nor author. The author is ahead of the reader only in the knowledge of his impossibility, but, by his very utterance, he reduces the reader to the same condition of ignorance. It is doubtful whether the conveyance of this negative insight could still be called an act, let alone a process. And it is equally doubtful whether this no-act can be represented by a geometrical line ("verbal string") or by a narrative that lays claim to mimetic veracity. Neither reading nor writing resemble action; both tend to fuse in their common deviation from referential models, whether they be things, acts, or feelings. The ideal reader is the author himself, because he does not share the illusions of the naive reader—in this case Stanley Fish—about the writer's authority. Fish's own text infers this, although it reduces his methodological claims to nought. To place Plato's *Phaedrus* at the center of an essay on the rhetoric of reading, to read it correctly as a radical deconstruction of the truth of all literary texts, and then to go on to claim of one's own critical discourse that it will "chart and project *the* developing response" in a "truly objective way" is making things almost too easy for the critical commentator.

Or is it perhaps a not-so-naive gesture of self-defense? Stanley Fish has more than glimpsed the implications of the *Phaedrus,* of the poetic texts he quotes, and of his own critique of thematic and structural semanticism. Reflecting apologetically on the one-sidedness of his examples, he remarks that "perhaps literature is what disturbs our sense of self-sufficiency, personal and linguistic," a formulation that, in the final analysis, spells the end of criticism as a scientific mode of discourse. But he immediately retreats from such implications: "the result [of thus defining literature] would probably be more a reflection of personal psychological need than of a universally true aesthetic."[23] The only need that can be at play here is that of *not* seeing the universal negativity of what then can no longer be called an aesthetics of literature, and this need is neither personal nor psychological. Later in the article, the same unavoidable threat of semantic nihilism is again perceived: "Nothing is [the meaning]. Perhaps, then, the word meaning should also be discarded. . . ."[24] But this speculative moment is also at once repressed by substituting a regressive notion of unmediated "experience" for meaning and by a curiously primitivistic statement about experience being "immediately compromised the moment you say anything about it," a pseudoelegiac theme which, despite its assumed hostility towards language, has generated even more words than the wars of Troy.

The systematic avoidance of reading is not a time- or place-bound phenomenon characteristic of American formalist criticism in the early seventies. The double movement of revelation and recoil will always be inherent in the nature of a genuine critical discourse; its presence in these essays bears witness to their vitality. It can appear in infinitely varied versions and this diversity creates the possibility of a history of critical trends and movements. In the case of most of these articles, the particular obstacle that interferes with reading stems from a wishful confusion between the analytical rigor of the exegetic procedure and the epistemological authority of the ensuing results.

23. Fish, p. 147.
24. *Ibid.*, p. 160.

Index

Index by Terry Cochràn.

Booth, Wayne, 53
Bostetter, E. E., 198n
Bowles, William Lisle, 193
Browne, Thomas, 287
Brueghel, Pieter, the Elder, 281; and *folie*, 216
Buddeberg, Else, 249, 252
Bunyan, John, 204
Butor, Michel, 79
Byron, George Gordon Byron, 205

Callot, Jacques, 218, 281
Camus, Albert, 60
Cancellation, of the immediate, xxiv-xxv
Cassirer, Ernst, 242n
Catachresis, 284
Celan, Paul, 185-86
Center: as locus of temporal articulation, 86; as structural principle, 82. *See also* Origin
Chant des Sirènes, Le, 79
Char, René, 71
Chartreuse de Parme, as combining allegory and irony, 227-28
"Chat, Le," 232
Chateaubriand, François René, 203
Chatman, Seymour, 278-80 *passim*, 282
Chomsky, Noam, 281
Clinamen, 274-75
Cogito, 106; based on original plenitude, 34; as *moment de passage*, 91; relation of, to ontology, 49-50; as subjective experience of time, 87
Cognition: and literature, xvii; and poetic language, 233. *See also* Knowledge
Cohn, Robert G., 71n
Coleridge, Samuel Taylor, 194-99 *passim*, 237; importance of, for New Criticism, 28; influence of, 193-94; symbol characterization of, 191-93.
"Coleridge, Baudelaire and Modernist Poetics," 173
Comique absolu, Le. See Irony
Condillac, Etienne Bonnot de, 134, 140, 199
Confessions, 116
Consciousness: and absolute irony, 216; ac-

cess of, to the intemporal, 92-93; attack on literary privileging of, 9; of author vs. interpreter, 36; becoming of, 258, 265; of Being, 262; beings' representation to, 256; circularity of, 75-77; and *dédoublement*, 212-13; discontinuity of, 89, 91; dissolution of, 73; Hegelian reversal of, 264-65; as historical, 37-38; and historical poetics, 242; and intentionality, 23-24, 54-55; joined with sensation, 87-88; and literature as demystifying, 13-14; and Mallarméan conception of language, 69-72; vs. natural object, 200; nature-reflection of, 239; and non-linear time, 58; and novel, 53, 56; and originary movement, 86-87; of poetic personality, 45, 47-48; and presence, 134; as presence of nothingness, 18; and progressive-retrogressive movement, 120; and resistance in reading, 63; and reversal of knowledge, 238; of self, 251, 263; and self-reflection, 15-16; vs. sensation, 244-45; of sign, 232-33; in time, vs. in being, 72; and Wimsatt's notion of poetic unity, 24-25. *See also* Knowledge; Self
Constant, Benjamin, 88; radical reversal of, 91-92
Constitution: and being, 232-33; of literary text, 276; of time, 242
Content: as the existent, xxiv. *See also* Meaning; Truth
Contrat social, Le, 141
Cornford, F. M., 242n
Creuzer, Georg Friedrich, 190
Crise de vers, 6, 16
Crisis: and blindness, 18; in criticism, 3-19; epistemological structure of statement of, 14-17; response of American criticism to, 5-6; and self-reflexive writing, 7-8
Crisis of the European Sciences and Transcendental Phenomenology, The, 14
Criticism: continental trend in, 8-9; crisis in, 3-19; and literary language, viii, 31-32; as metaphor for reading, 107; in

Paul de Man is Sterling Professor of the Humanities at Yale University, where he has taught comparative literature since 1970. He has taught at Harvard, Cornell, and Johns Hopkins, and has held a chair in comparative literature at the University of Zürich. De Man is the author of *Allegories of Reading: Figural Language in Rousseau, Nietzsche, Rilke, and Proust.*

Wlad Godzich is associate professor and director of the comparative literature program at the University of Minnesota. He is co-editor, with Jochen Schulte-Sasse, of the series Theory and History of Literature.